The Fabulous Dark Cloister

The Fabulous Dark Cloister

Romance in England after the Reformation

TIFFANY JO WERTH

The Johns Hopkins University Press

Baltimore

© 2011 The Johns Hopkins University Press
All rights reserved. Published 2011
Printed in the United States of America on acid-free paper

2   4   6   8   9   7   5   3   1

The Johns Hopkins University Press
2715 North Charles Street
Baltimore, Maryland 21218-4363
www.press.jhu.edu

Library of Congress Cataloging-in-Publication Data

Werth, Tiffany Jo.
The fabulous dark cloister : romance in England after the Reformation /
Tiffany Jo Werth.
p.   cm.
Includes bibliographical references and index.
ISBN-13: 978-1-4214-0301-4 (hardcover : alk. paper)
ISBN-10: 1-4214-0301-3 (hardcover : alk. paper)
1. Romances, English—History and criticism.   2. Sidney, Philip, Sir,
1554–1586. Arcadia.   3. Spenser, Edmund, 1552?–1599. Faerie
queene.   4. Shakespeare, William, 1564–1616. Pericles.   5. Wroth,
Mary, Lady, ca. 1586–ca. 1640. Countesse of Mountgomeries
Urania.   6. Reformation—England.   7. Protestantism and
literature—History—16th century.   8. Romanticism—England—
History—16th century.   9. Religion and literature—England—
History—16th century.   I. Title.   II. Title: Romance in
England after the Reformation.
PR428.R65W47 2011
820.9'003—dc22   2011011225

A catalog record for this book is available from the British Library.

*Special discounts are available for bulk purchases of this book. For more
information, please contact Special Sales at 410-516-6936 or
specialsales@press.jhu.edu.*

The Johns Hopkins University Press uses environmentally friendly book
materials, including recycled text paper that is composed of at least
30 percent post-consumer waste, whenever possible.

Contents

Acknowledgments

Romance notoriously resists closure and courts error. I escaped a deferred ending and an unfinished manuscript only through the generous interventions of the many voices I name below. As for the errors that crept in, those I acknowledge as mine.

Once upon a time, this book took root as a dissertation at Columbia University. First thanks belong to Rich McCoy, who supported my crossover, and to David Scott Kastan for setting me on the path. Anne Lake Prescott offered sage advice and jogged my memory with forgotten emblems whenever I asked; I can only aspire to her wit and knowledge of Renaissance arcana. I also benefited from conversations with Peter Platt, who fostered my fascination with wonder and never hesitated to loan precious books. I read many stanzas with Erik Gray, who was a lively Palmer. Instrumental too were the clarifying ministrations offered during the Renaissance dissertation seminars at Columbia University by Daniel Swift, Alan Farmer, Adam Zucker, András Kiséry, Matt Zarnowiecki, and William Weaver. Marie Rutkoski and Andrew Tumminia also deserve praise. Finally, a shout out to Molly Murray, my intervening Arthur, who saved me from Despair by reminding me to think on Daft Punk: harder, faster, leaner.

The trinity of my final committee deserves special dispensation for their long-suffering enthusiasm. Alan Stewart read repeatedly and proffered spot-on line-by-line emendations. Beyond this, his humor and willingness to share a pint sparked surprising illuminations. Julie Crawford is all and more than legend says. Simultaneously rigorous and enthusiastic, she encouraged me to dig deeper into the archive and brought me up for air when I was faint. To Jean Howard, my intellectual fealty. Her championing of me and of this project overgoes duty. Her fierce eye and unflagging confidence saw it through valley and fen. Her magnanimity and commitment set a gold standard of exceptional academic mentoring.

The contours of early modern romance came into focus for me through several conference encounters. Sarah Wall Randall has been a delightful conspirator, fellow panelist, and seminarian at the Renaissance Society of America and Shakespeare Association of America conferences. Joyce Boro too provided cheer and continental corrections. Especially helpful too were the sharp interlocutors Alex Davis, Mary Ellen Lamb, and Arthur Kinney, who were present at the Romance conference in honor of Victor Skretkowicz in Dundee, Scotland.

For their encouragement, astute reading, and advice, but most of all their friendship: Sarah Rivett, Sharon Oster, Heidi Brayman Hackel, Rebecca Lemon, and Peter Mancall (who remains the king of titles).

Vin Nardizzi is a mighty oak. His pit-saw wit, verdant imagination, and felling criticism shaped many a branch of thought. He read, with patience and verve, more than anyone. To him I owe many Happy Hours.

This book came into being through the generous support of institutions and foundations as well as people. A Marjorie Hope Nicolson Fellowship at Columbia University funded its inception, and its final stages as a dissertation were underwritten by the Whiting Foundation and a Michael J. Connell Foundation fellowship at the Huntington Library. Thanks to time spent as a Francis Bacon Foundation Fellow at the Huntington Library and the aid of a Simon Fraser University Presidential Research Grant, Simon Fraser University Endowed Grant, and a Simon Fraser University Publications Rapid Response Fund grant, I was able to complete the manuscript.

Many seasons were passed in the Ahmanson Reading Room of the Huntington Library, and to its expert and ever-clever wardens I owe my sanity—and many felicitous word choices. Special thanks go to Juan Gomez, Kadin Henningsen, Meredith Berbée, Catherine Wehrey, Laura Stalker, the once and future Claire Kennedy and, of course, Phil Brontosaurus, who kept close watch.

Versions of this work were first published in other venues. Earlier versions of portions of chapters 1 and 2 appeared as "The Reformation of Romance in Sir Philip Sidney's *New Arcadia*," *English Literary Renaissance* (Winter 2010): 33–55, and "Great Miracle or Lying Wonder? Janus-Faced Romance in *Pericles*," *Shakespeare International Yearbook*, (August 2008): 183–203. This material is being reused by the kind permission of Arthur Kinney, editor in chief, and John Wiley and Sons for *English Literary Renaissance* and by permission of the publishers for *The Shakespearean International Yearbook*, volume 8: special section, European Shakespeares, edited by Graham Bradshaw, Tom Bishop, Ton Hoenselaars, and Clara Calvo (Farnham, UK: Ashgate, © 2008). I thank the Huntington Library for permission to reproduce images from their collection.

I feel fortunate to have been under the care of a superb editor at the Johns

Hopkins University Press, Matt McAdam, who has modeled professionalism, timeliness, and integrity as he shepherded this project through the review boards and to press. In addition, the copy editor, George Roupe, and the managing editor, Julie McCarthy, lent keen, attentive eyes at the final stage. I am also indebted to the anonymous press reader of the typescript, whose insightful reading provided the necessary stimulus to fortify the argument and to achieve balance in between.

To my peerless friends from New York who punctuated writing time with many a pleasant diversion, I am grateful to Alexis Soloski, Joanna Cheetham, Jennifer White, Cóilín Parsons, Marilee Scott, Charles Donohoe, and Ramona Thomasius Mosse. Jared Weinstein too was always there. Fortune blessed me with savvy colleagues in Vancouver—Ronda Arab, Susan Brook, Genevieve Fuji Johnson, Roxanne Panchasi, and Peter Dickinson—who kept me in a mischievous tango and far from boredom. Annette Stenning staved off Titivillus with considerable ingenuity. To my Los Angeles angels who never let me get lost: word to Mariko McKittrick, who gave me a room of my own; and to Jeff Davis, who promised to read it all; a heavenly guerdon to Janelle Miau, who caught the palimpsest, as well as the misplaced commas, of the typescript. In Portland, Herman Asarnow deserves a deep bow for his endless mentoring that began many years ago in a junior Shakespeare seminar; Grace Dillon gets credit for urging me to brave the Spenserian bower. I also am grateful for the friendship of Kirk Hamlin Perry, a master of words.

My debt to Bertrand W., who brought more than glamour into my life, goes beyond language. A wise friend once said, "Every woman deserves a man who is not afraid to be French." His *amour* made everything possible.

My aunt Jo Well has been my kindred spirit and family ally. My parents, Willard and Lenora, have never abandoned me, despite all my wandering paths. This book is dedicated to them and their vision at the Black Hills Health and Education Center. Finally, the presence, devotion, and interruptions of my tiger-striped muse filled the solitary hours. Buck found me at the beginning and stayed until I was contracted. He will always be a prince of canines.

The Fabulous Dark Cloister

Introduction

In Shakespeare's sonnet 73, the speaker evokes a landscape haunted by echoes of a season past. A few yellow leaves cling yet to their boughs, "which shake against the cold" and are now but "bare ruined choirs, where late the sweet birds sang."[1] The imagery of "bare ruined choirs" offers an architectural, visual reference to English history, calling to mind the state of the priories after Henry VIII's dissolution of almost half a century earlier: among them, the abbeys of Egglestone, Rievaulx, and Fountains in Yorkshire; Bury Saint Edmunds, Suffolk, Tintern Abbey in Monmouthshire; and, perhaps most famously, Glastonbury in Somerset.[2] The language of ruin made golden or "yellow" provides poignant "sweet" testimony to the early waves of reform in England when certain "popish" attributes formerly revered in the churches of England were destroyed, suppressed, or appropriated.[3] The "ruined choirs," all the more memorable for what they erase, express in concrete form the disruptive continuity between English Protestantism and its older Catholic heritage. The sonnet's imagery captures the riddled contradiction of post-Reformation England: the mutilated remains stir memory even as they suppress the not-so-distant past.

By the time James I came to the throne, many artifacts—material and textual—witnessed various stages of religious reform. Church rood screens at Saint Mary's Priory at Binham in Norfolk, for instance, starkly recall the Josiah-like vigor of reform under the young king Edward in the mid-1500s. Rood screens, once vivid with images of medieval Catholic piety, were cut down, whitewashed, and painted over with texts from Tyndale's translation of the New Testament and eventually incorporated into choir stalls.[4] Below the black-letter text taken from the newly vernacular Bible, the shadowy outline of the original figures might still be spied as ghostly watchers over the new words. Mutilated stained glass on the chancel for the parish church in Great Massingham, Norfolk, shows the outlines of defaced saints and the Lamb of God, their heads "blotted," highlighted by the additional light streaming in where their faces once were.[5] Other erasures memorialize Elizabethan reform. Saint Margaret's Church in Tivetshall, Norfolk, for example, portrays the arms of Elizabeth replacing the tympanum Doom painting. Similar redecorating of rood screens occurred in various chapels, altering the traditional images of the crucified Christ with Mary and John on either side to a gigantic version of the royal arms.[6] These material traces, like the metaphor of sonnet 73, recall conscious acts of destructive appropriation.[7] The impulses of iconoclastic reform remain etched in physical and cultural memory even after the particular historical urgency and fervor faded.[8] In retrospect, they provide mute evidence to the protracted, recursive nature of English church reform.

These acts of erasure, with their unintended effect of memorialization, happened not only to churches but also to books and to the narratives they contained. The palimpsestic remnants of England's religious past dot story as well as history. In the "ruined" metaphor of Shakespeare's lyric poetry, we glimpse in short form a memory that will silhouette one of the most common, and contested, literary forms after the Reformation. This book will examine the implications of the long Reformation on an avidly popular "kind" of story: the romance. In particular, it focuses on how romances, both old and new, came to be flash points in the Protestant polemic as tools of an alleged papist subversion. In the words of one Protestant preacher, Edward Dering, romances were carriers of "the superstition of the elder world," connecting, often uncomfortably, early modern readers to their Catholic past.[9] This monograph focuses on how a literary form, reviled by polemists as a repository of "superstition," nonetheless bridges the ostensible sectarian division between Protestant and Catholic culture. In its continuity, it vividly enshrines the instability of the period's religious and literary identity.

The argument of this book positions the romance as a perfect register of the hybridity that spans Catholicism and Protestantism in sixteenth- and early seventeenth-century England. By "hybrid" I refer to the word's original meaning as a biological term: a thing composed of mixed parts. I draw on Homi Bhabha's development of hybridity theory in *The Location of Culture*, which analyzes cultural anxiety with respect to cultural imperialism.[10] His argument that the hybrid represents both fusion and disjunction, a conjoining of difference that cannot simply harmonize, points the way for extending this biological metaphor into a dialogue about cultural forms. For my work, it provides a useful touchstone for my discussion of literary form, history, and religious identity.

Reformation polemicists stressed the separation, the difference, of the new from the old, and their rhetoric deliberately obscured any middle ground. Writers solidified the borders of new cultural and confessional identities by demonizing what had come before. Yet, upon peeling the veneer over the middle ground, layers of interpenetrating, conflicting loyalties can be glimpsed. These vexed allegiances have become the focus for a new generation of "post-Revisionist" historians who have taught us to see England's Reformation as long and complicated.[11] Yet even as historians have mapped this confessional confusion with greater subtlety, the place of imaginative literature as both reflection and constituent of a hybrid or in-between religious climate has only intermittently come into scholarly focus.[12] Because of the ways that the formal attributes of romance are interleaved with English religious identity, this book argues it is a literary genre that provides a singular portal into the contested, tempestuous intermediacies that undermine these newly formed, and forming, communities. They are the "ruined choirs" in the changing landscape of post-Reformation English literature.

Romance was both dangerous and pedagogically beneficial, seductive in pejorative ways but also capable of mobilizing a vast readership; for these reasons, my approach to romance provides new ways of looking at the study of religion in the early modern period. Rather than presenting a study of doctrine per se, I will focus on the popular imaginative structures through which religious thoughts and feeling were expressed, romance being one of the most important and hotly contested. The formal continuity, despite revisions to its content, between medieval and early modern romance, compounded by romance's troubling kinship to hagiography, testifies to an unfinished Reformation. It shows how religious struggle not only engaged theology and questions of practice but also shook the imaginative core of sixteenth-century culture in one of its most popularly acclaimed genres. In this regard, I seek to make a contribution to what has been termed, by Stephen Cohen and others, the new historical formalism.[13] Fredric Jameson has argued that genre emerges from historical circumstances.[14] I argue that those generic forms themselves become the bearers of historical meaning, encoding within themselves the congealed history of particular modes of representation and belief. Studying the history of literary forms, therefore, is key to the historical study of literature. Genre and history are in my reading mutually constitutive.

Historically, early modern English romance was a cultural reservoir. What made romance a source of conflict also made it popular. The stories I examine throughout the following pages all testify to a telling paradox: romances, despite their dubious lineage, were among the most popular genres in sixteenth- and seventeenth-century culture among Protestant as well as Catholic readers. In fact, the popularity of Spanish, medieval, and "Catholic" romances made them hot imports, while other genres, traditionally seen as of "higher literary" value (vernacular dramatic works, lyrical poetry, epic) were not translated so frequently. William Copland's reprints of old medieval classics like *The Four Sons of Aymon* (1554), Thomas East's *Morte Darthur* (1585), Margaret Tyler and Anthony Munday's translations of continental favorites such as the *Mirrour of Knighthood* (1578) and *Amadis de Gaule* (1590–1619) as well as a crop of newly minted vernacular romances by writers like Richard Johnson, Christopher Middleton, Robert Greene, and Emanuel Ford glutted the English book market, whetting readers' taste for what Edmund Spenser called the "antique history" of heroes such as Arthur, Saint George, Bevis, and Rosicleer.[15]

As these examples suggest, although reformers such as Edward Dering fulminated against romance, putting up obstructions to cultural and intellectual exchange with the "superstitious" narratives of Catholic culture, continental, Spanish, medieval, and other "Catholic" romances were widely available and selling briskly to English readers, a fact that only fueled the polemical ire.[16] Romances were regularly abused as frivolous, trivial, and a danger to moral and religious piety, yet they were never officially censored or banned.[17] They were not seen by authorities as an overwhelming threat to the religious order in the way that, for example, the writings of Francisco Suarez, Robert Parsons, or other Jesuits were perceived to be, and thus were published abroad and smuggled into England.[18]

The Fabulous Dark Cloister is a book about how, within this hybrid context of historical continuity and lack of explicit governmental censorship, sectarian anxiety mounted around the ways that romances seemed to be modeled after Catholic narratives, especially the lives of saints. It addresses the confluence of religious history with literary form to argue that the fascination with romance lay precisely in its contested use of successful motifs drawn from a discredited Catholic heritage. While there was nothing inherently Catholic about the romance, its supernaturalism, its affective force over readers—especially those deemed most vulnerable—and ultimately the entire aspect of the "marvelous" that comprises such an important part of the form came to be identified, post-Reformation, as part of the Catholicity that carried with it Dering's feared "superstition" into an age justified by acts of "faith."[19]

As my argument reveals, English romance is deeply embedded and engaged in the cultural milieu of the Reformation. The Reformation was self-consciously a return to the book, and reformers embraced written language as a vehicle of Christian, godly truth. Under the banner of *"sola scriptura,"* texts became especially fraught catalysts for—or against—faith. Within this context of a complex and contentious struggle over books, the act of reading necessarily came under new scrutiny. My exploration of the ways that ostensibly secular texts were imagined to be efficacious agents for confessional allegiance in Reformation England thus draws me into a larger conversation about habits of reading.[20] I attend to how some writers addressed the post-Reformation problem of affective reading, epitomized in the figure of the erring "superstitious" female romance reader. The transformative effect renders reading and interpretive sagacity an urgent cultural concern. And the implied or imagined readership of romance, whether accurately or fictitiously presented, exerts a profound influence meant to appeal to a burgeoning audience composed of women as well as men, non-elite as well as elite readers.[21] The function of romance could be variously amorous, seditious, heretical, or ethical and educative—its reading dependent, in part, upon the hermeneutical savvy of a new generation of readers.

This book takes as its subject romances that address these cultural, religious tensions and take it upon themselves to reform an old, perennially favored mode of storytelling and habit of reading.[22] Notable for their departure from a popular canon of stories, the romances of Sir Philip Sidney, Edmund Spenser, William Shakespeare, and Lady Mary Wroth engage, with eyes wide open, the form's controversial motifs in a bid to justify and render it, as Spenser claims, matter fit for "just memory."[23] I analyze a handful of texts within the flourishing field of romance, but if the story I tell is partial, I believe that it is also suggestive. These texts speak to a broader crisis of identity and bring us to some of the core concerns of Tudor and Stuart England.[24] The authors at the center of this book write texts that take seriously the Protestant indictments against an imaginative genre and by so doing reveal how profoundly religious attacks affected the ways these authors thought about romance, provoking a battle over its recuperation as well as its interpretation.

Although books do not provide direct access to the beliefs and motivations of those who wrote, published, or read them, their material and textual legacy do tell a unique story of early modern England, one in which genre functions as a kind of repository for religious exchange across the ostensible Protestant/ Catholic divide. The romances I discuss, moreover, do not simply combine a "residual" Catholic belief system with an emergent Protestant one; rather they appropriate the old for new religious ends in ways that are as violent, and often as contradictory, even haphazard, as were the reformations to the physical church. Directed toward an audience still surrounded by the remnants of the old religion, these stories that relied heavily on the marvelous and the breaching of the material by the divine came to be appropriated in the service of Protestant reform as had the old Catholic rood screens that now bore the monarch's arms painted over their familiar shapes. Like these material objects, while the post-Reformation adoption of old stories initially appears as a triumph of literary reform, their most enduring legacy lies in their ambiguous, mixed success at casting out, or even reinterpreting, the long shadow of the elder world. Theirs is a story of conflictual convergence.

The "revised" or "new" *Countesse of Pembrokes Arcadia*, *The Faerie Queene*, *Urania*, and the late dramatic romance of *Pericles*, I will argue in the following chapters, share a cultural, religious, and literary hybridity reflective of a partial transformation, an ongoing, incomplete reformation.[25] Throughout their diverse narratives, each of these four texts invokes a variety of traditions and poetic and aesthetic codes that owe much to the particular ways that each responds to and considers the unsettling subject of religious change. I will follow some of the implications of this hybridity, exploring the ways that these early modern romances actively transform the terms of conflict, challenging as they do so the definitive claims of polemicists, whether Catholic or Protestant. Spanning what is perhaps the greatest period of simultaneous anxiety and popularity of English romance, from the early stirrings of Protestant, Henrician reform to the complex religious negotiations under King James I in the first quarter of the seventeenth century, these texts set forth the literary implications of religious and cultural reform. Considered together, they form, over the course of a half-century, a literary counterpart to the monumental effort of John Foxe, who labored to distinguish a Protestant martyrology from Catholic hagiography. And, as the authors themselves uneasily recognize, their "antique histories," like Foxe's martyrs, become defined as much by their framing of difference as by difference itself. Such, then, is the broad trajectory of this book, to account for how romances continue to flourish, in spite, or perhaps because of, their crisis of self-definition.

In the rest of this introduction, I offer a preliminary explanation of why early modern English romance is such a confusing, vexed, elusive, and often critically slighted genre. My goal is not to demystify what the early modern romance really was, but rather to identify its function as a hybrid genre, expressing the complex, overlapping, and intersecting history of forms and formal representations that were never fully reducible to simple binaries. These texts consistently trouble such categorization, whether literary (such as "epic" or "romance," prose or poetry, dramatic or nondramatic), religious ("Protestant" or "Catholic"), or even historical periodization (medieval, early modern, or "Renaissance"). Romance's quality of being in-between—both in its formal attributes and in its historical development—disrupts a familiar narrative whereby the medieval and Catholic give way to the early modern and the Protestant.[26] Its unsettling hybridity may explain why it came to play such a major role, as a site of both cultural conflict and commemoration, within English culture.

INDEXING ROMANCE

How did post-Reformation English readers and writers understand romance? It is a question whose answer takes us to debates over religious belief as much as to debates over literary form. Factors explored in the pages that follow show that, in England, what the romance was understood to be can be found in the arguments over its disruption of Protestant belief. As this book's title, *The Fabulous Dark Cloister*, implies, romance was understood to span these two contexts of imaginative and spiritual writing. In Ben Jonson's play *The New Inn* (1631), the character Lovel praises the library of his mentor, Lord Beaufort, as "right" because "He had no Arthurs, nor no *Rosicleers*, / no *Knights o'the Sun*, nor *Amadis de Gaules / Primaleons*, and *Pantagruels*, publick Nothings; / Abortives of the Fabulus dark Cloyster," books that were "sent out to poison Courts, and infest Manners."[27] Lovel's critique of the excluded books targets a secular effect of romance: poisoned courts and infested manners. The terms of abuse, however, draw directly from the inflammatory, religiously zealous rhetoric of the Catholic Juan Luis Vives, who influentially compared reading romance to taking poison. Lovel adapts Vives's cant, charging it with a sectarian slur. Aborted from not "a" but "the" "Fabulus dark Cloyster," these romances spring from a place tagged by its connotations of religious chapels and monastic life; "Cloyster" invokes the remnants of Catholic worship, for "friers and nunnes," the elder Giles Fletcher knowingly writes in his survey of the ecclesiastical system in Russia, reveal "the hypocrisie and uncleannesse of that cloysterbroode" bred in Rome.[28] The adjectives "fabulus" and "dark," furthermore, gesture at what constitutes a defining—and problematic—characteristic of post-Reformation romance, the presence of nonmimetic and usually marvelous motifs—motifs tinged by "dark" and potentially superstitious, if not downright devilish, forces.[29]

Lovel's judgment points toward two interrelated and enduring problems with romance for a good Protestant Englishman as well as an astute man of taste. The first concerns romance's unique historical development in England as a genre that hybridized with religious narratives born of the "cloister." The second grows out of the first and has to do with literary matters and genre motifs that appear sympathetic to a "fabulous" and "superstitious" Catholic habit of storytelling. Built into these concerns, moreover, is a misogynist language that feminizes both romance and papists by means of quasi-uterine imagery of "abortive" nothings and "dark" cloisters. The cumulative force of a dialogue of antipopery, with its concomitant fear of anything that looked "superstitious," and a latent misogyny form a powerful rhetorical triumvirate. Ben Jonson, first and foremost a literary man whose religious loyalties were far from obdurate, voices a literary objection to romance, but one, nonetheless, colored by the terms of religious bias.[30] His language engages the persistent concerns surrounding the questions of books and devotional allegiance, showing that polemical accounts bled into literary ones.

This book's title thus sketches its argument for a homologous reading that shows history and genre to be in tandem. Unlike Fredric Jameson, who sees genre as emerging out of, in response to, historical change, I argue that in the romance we witness a parallel process in which formal modes of representation coalesce with historical particulars.[31] As my opening reading of the palimpsestic material remainders of religious change proposes, Protestant whitewash provided only a cover over the architecture and forms of a Catholic past. Within this context of religious flux, we can better understand why romance might be such a vexed, "dark," and elusive genre by understanding how the formal representations of Protestant/Catholic were themselves contradictory and frequently subtle. Indeed, to trace the discourse of romance in sixteenth-century England can be a protracted and confusing process, for its identity was malleable, being reworked and reformed alongside the discourse of confessional allegiance.

Identifying post-Reformation English romance, in fact, requires deductive sleuthing, for no sixteenth-century definition exists.[32] Medieval English writers could, with some clarity, distinguish a *romaunce* from a *geste*, *tragedie*, or *fabliau* while still identifying it within a generic network.[33] On the Continent, particularly in Italy, Renaissance authors vigorously debated the *romanzi*'s merit as compared to epic.[34] Yet in post-Reformation England, "romance" as a designation of generic kind slipped from critical use, not to reemerge until the mid-seventeenth century.[35] No title page declares itself a romance; no catalog of kinds includes romance as a dramatic category. It did not exist. Tellingly, Polonius's expansive list of the best actors in the world for "tragedy, comedy, history, pastoral, pastorical-comical, historical-pastoral, tragical-historical, tragical-comical-historical-pastoral" does not include "romance."[36] George Puttenham uses the term "romances" dismissively to refer to medieval tales usually told in taverns, and Fulke Greville once refers to Sidney's *Arcadia* as his "Romanties," but these two references stand alone amid a growing interest in other literary kinds, especially epic.[37] To assume, though, that the kind of stories once known to medieval audiences as "romances" disappear ignores the forest of black-letter editions of reprinted medieval stories, freshly translated Greek romance, imported continental romance, and newly written vernacular tales that fell from the presses (as Louis B. Wright memorably puts it) "like the leaves of autumn."[38] The consequent heterogeneity coupled with the lack of vernacular description makes these leaves into a forest difficult to parse with precision, thus rendering the romance a confusing, elusive genre.[39]

Among the consequences of this confusion is a scholarly proliferation of adjectival qualifiers: chivalric romance, Heliodoran or erotic romance, pastoral romance, epic romance, popular romance, sentimental romance, elite romance, and so forth. As these modifiers suggest, because it omnivorously poaches from other literary modes (lyric, epic, pastoral, comic, among others), romance's chaotic proliferation of texts complicates decisive definitions. Its expansiveness cultivates hybridity that spans other more established genres just as it bridges disparate geographical landscapes and merges temporalities, mixing pre-Reformation tales with what Gower will call "latter times" in *Pericles*.[40] Yet in spite of the composite nature of this literary form, post-Reformation writers and readers implicitly recognized the "romance" forest even if they did not call it by name. The negotiation and juxtaposition of incompatible material was a formal, and familiar, motif.

The contours of the romance forest sharpen into focus most vividly through the voices of its opposition: the strikingly consistent lists of popular, translated, and vernacular tales repeatedly censured by religious polemicists. Although romances were seldom identified by name, they frequently appeared, cataloged together, in blacklists (serial titles of undesirable books). The resulting "negative canon," or what I will call the "index," provides the best insight into the particular formal qualities of romance—its tropes, its effects, and its distinctive style of signifying—that are used to confront the unsettling process of religious change.[41] These indexes, in turn, survey a genre.[42] While not an exact generic definition, these lists suggest a sympathy of kind or, what in his reader's address to Heliodorus's *Aethiopian Historie* the translator Thomas Underdowne calls books "of like argument."[43] To use modern critical terminology, the index names books of similar "narrative strategies" (Barbara Fuchs) or "memes" (Helen Cooper), believed to foster a dangerously seductive, and persistent, kind of story.[44]

What was at stake in these condemnations, and thus what constituted romance, can be found in the paradigmatic attack made by the Protestant divine Edward Dering. When preachers on the ground in early modern England sought to rally a public to their faith, they often did so by defining themselves against the older, rival beliefs, as had, for instance, Paul's followers in Ephesus. Setting up the one true Christian God, the book of Acts records, necessitated destroying the images of the pagan Diana and burning the local books containing sorcerous and curious arts.[45] A similar desideratum to discredit an older, rival religious belief stands behind the various lines of Protestant polemic hostile to romance. Some reformers prayed for a bonfire that might, like the Ephesian purge, open the way for new kinds of faith, cleared of "curious artes" and superstitious, cloister-like beliefs.

We can see a parody of religious figures' desire to destroy books of romance for their sorcerous potential in Cervantes's *Don Quixote*. After the titular hero's failed first sally forth as an aspiring knight errant, his niece, his housekeeper, the curate, and the barber launch an inquisition into his library, whose books, they believe, represent "the onley authors of his harme."[46] Rifling through the shelves, these eager judges defenestrate volumes that are shortly burned, some with vitiation but many without. The book-burning episode parodies the overly zealous passions of reformers both abroad and at home who condemned, wholesale, tales of knights and *amour*. In England, at least one zealous preacher had already had such fantasies. Revising the unpublished work of John More, Edward Dering saw to print *A Briefe and Necessarie Catachisme or Instrucion, Verie Needefull to Bee Knowne of All Householders* (1575), a popular manual of religious instruction.[47] In it, amid his sage advice for the moral improvement of households, he calls for a great bonfire of books, torching by name many popular romances. His hit list, "bookes of so great vanity," is a familiar index of romance titles, books he believes guilty of kindling within their readers "the idolatrous supersticion of the elder worlde." They pose greater harm to readers than even Quixote's delusions:

> O that there were among us some zealous Ephesians, that bookes of so great vanity might be burned up. The spirite of God wrought in them so mightily, that they contemned the price of so great iniquitie, in one Citie, and at one fire they

brought together the books valued to twoo thousand markes, and burnt them at once. O happy light & clearer as the Sun beames, if we might see the lyke in London, that the chiefe streete might be sanctified with so holy sacrifice. The place it self doth crave it, and holdeth up so gorgeous Idoll, a fyt stake for so good a fire.[48]

This episode centers on a crisis of identity. Rhetorically conflating sorcerous books burned by the Ephesians after hearing Paul's sermons with romances and their perpetuation of an elder superstition, in this case Catholicism, Dering does not imagine a Reformation, or even appropriation; he fantasizes an auto-da-fé on the London streets, fueled by a "fyt stake" of books. In action not unlike Quixote's housekeeper, who takes a "holy water pot and a sprinkler in her hand" lest some "inchanter" contained in the books be released, Dering wastes no time for a curatorial sifting of sheep from goat.[49] He as swiftly condemns romances as the niece of Quixote who condemns his library, which "deserved the fire" lest its books "minister occasion againe to such as may reade them."[50] Dering's urgency speaks for many Protestant reformers fearful of romance's effect on its readership. Readers, it seems, were likely to be, as was Don Quixote, infected by the seductions of knight errantry with all its trappings of an "idolatrous supersticion" from an "elder worlde." Even though the Catholic priest in *Don-Quixote* found many of the books worthy of being saved from the flames, Dering condemns the lot because all are tainted by a "superstitious" past. Thus he, in his bonfire fantasies, erects a confessional identity built from the ashes of condemned books. Just as the Ephesians' willingness to burn their pagan books signaled their turn to Christianity, so, Dering hopes, will the immolation of "bookes of so great vanity" mark a turn away from Catholicism. By repudiating the romance, Dering and others hope, Protestants may synecdochically repudiate the superstitious and idolatrous tendencies of the Catholic faith, just as the acts of iconoclasm in Ephesus marked a turn away from idolatry.

Dering's fiery attack illustrates what was at stake for imaginative literature and its effects in the formation of a new religious identity. Such suspicion came from a fraught point of genuine religious difference that goes straight to romance's distinctive style of signifying and its evocative deployment of a cloistral "fabulous." Scholars since Baxter Hathaway have pointed to the "fabulous" and "marvelous" dimension as a central romance trope; this book, while indebted to these studies, offers a broader synthesis for how and why these concerns raised such clamorous attention.[51] For none have parsed its ramifications for oppositional reading practices of Catholic and Protestant. Reformers, with all their eagerness for a clean break from the "elder worlde," ignore a very old dilemma posed by earlier Catholic preachers. The books of "so great vanity," tales of Arthur and others of like argument, that Dering wishes burned, were in fact tested, powerful tools to rouse and to move an audience. The "fabulous" motifs were compellingly memorable and affectively penetrating. Romance's effects on readers were held to be, by many accounts, as transformational as Quixote's. They were subtle conduits toward religious conversion.

By making categorical, sweeping claims for their respective position and claims to conclusive truth, the polemical accounts of romance noisily reiterated each decade can be read as efforts to underscore the differences between Catholic and Protestant texts and their readers. But if we look at the antiromance polemic in terms of its indexes and argumentative strategies, as opposed to the alleged doctrinal allegiance, they can appear surprisingly similar. To make matters more confusing, Protestants borrowed heavily from a Catholic legacy of antiromance writings. In other words, the indexes, like the genre they survey, were hybrid composites. Old rhetoric was repurposed for a new context. The Catholic Juan Luis Vives set the template for later indexes in his *Instruction of a Christen Woman* (1529). *Amadis de Gaule, Lancelot du Lake, Arthur, Guy of Warwick*, and *Bevis of Hampton* represent some of the most popularly reprinted and circulated titles on Vives's index. Mobilizing a language of contagion, Vives compares romance reading to a "deedly sickenes" that, like a "poysen," addicts readers to various forms of vice.[52] His metaphors of addiction, damnation, and hyperstimulated passions, especially in respect to women, were taken up by later Protestant polemicists in debates over "right" reading and salvation, which Dering's concerns reflect. Reformed accounts of various stripes continued to adapt the index and even the rhetoric of their Catholic counterpart: the humanist educator Roger Ascham (1545, 1570), the hotter sort of Protestant preacher Edward Dering (1575), the Calvinist translator Nathaniel Baxter (1578), the university wit Thomas Nashe (1589), the writer and translator Francis Meres (1598), the Puritan Henry Crosse (1603), the clergyman and religious writer Arthur Dent (1605), and the author and king's army captain Mathias Prideaux (1650), among others, draw on the same intellectual inheritance. Scholars have read such schematic accounts drawn from a variety of constituencies as illustrative of a "tendentious strategy of insult."[53] By contrast, I contend the fierce argumentative posturing reveals what both sides fear: the papist and the Protestant antagonists become harder to distinguish the more furiously they rail at each other. What their debates reveal is not tendentiousness but rather a confusing continuum that refuses the simple binary opposition upon which they construct their identity.

The troubled progress of the English Reformation and the specific ways that romance harbored seemingly orthodox forms of piety made it an ongoing touchstone of religious controversy. Of course romance texts had always been open to the accusation that they were painted forgeries, a collection of "antique" lies; just as opposition to fiction has Platonic antecedents, antiromance polemic too has a long history, sparking debates in Catholic strongholds like Spain as well as in Protestant countries across Europe. The Italian debates over Ariosto's work, Tasso's anxiety regarding Counter-Reformation authorities for his *Gerusalemme liberata* (1573), as well as the decree in Spain issued by Charles V that prohibited the export of romances to the Indies (despite his own enjoyment of them) illustrate how continental attacks on romance comprise a hearty catalog of resentment.[54] Catholics had worked, as Tobias Gregory shows, to distinguish their tales from pagan sources when they reconciled a pantheon of romance gods and their magic with the monotheistic belief in one God and miracle.[55] Protestants had a further turn to make, cleansing romance not only of its pagan but also its Catholic heritages. Thus although criticism simmered elsewhere, England's religious climate magnified the problems of continuity; they had to think harder and manipulate their material with greater ingenuity. As the official religious creed swung back and forth between Catholic- and Protestant-sympathetic monarchs during the sixteenth century, polemicists scrambled harder to accentuate the difference between Protestant and Catholic. The confusing shifts and turns of government religious policy served, as Peter Marshall argues, to have a "profoundly catechizing effect," encouraging people to think more intensely about religious meanings than they had done previously.[56]

Thus while it might make sense to speak of an "early modern Christianity" vis-à-vis the romance and its detractors, the assertion of confessional difference was precisely the point.[57] "As communities divided," Marshall continues, "the presence of 'others'—'heretics,' often labeled as 'papists'—invariably sharpened in a dialectical way a self-awareness of religious belonging" as polemicists spoke of a "Reformation" and an "ejection of Popery."[58] Romance becomes mobilized as part of this assertion of difference, mitigating the complex, overlapping, and intersecting history of forms and formal representations that, to make matters more confusing, in the end are never fully reducible to "popery" or Protestantism except within the oppositional realm of polemics. The underlying structure of my argument explores this tension between the history of polemical genres and a continuum of religious and literary history.[59] After the Reformation, the English index of romance, although it appears definitive, in fact obscures a more complex story of indictment.

REFORMING ROMANCE

The tensions raised by romance's cloistered heritage, its delight in the fabulous, its consequent affective force over readers, and its seduction of those allegedly most vulnerable are constituent aspects of the romance form that engage, from a variety of perspectives, Sidney's *Arcadia*, Spenser's *Faerie Queene*, Shakespeare's *Pericles*, and Lady Mary Wroth's *Urania*. Three of these four authors, Philip Sidney, Edmund Spenser, and Lady Mary Wroth, all held degrees of investment in the Protestant cause. Yet while cognizant of the biases of those who shared their faith, each also denied the inferno advocated by polemical controversialists such as Edward Dering. Their religious positions thus illustrate a more fluid and flexible reality of religious conviction. They acknowledge what many religious apologists sought to deny: that reformation was a mottled and complex undertaking. Additionally, all three held interconnected personal as well as literary relationships. And, most importantly, all produced acutely self-reflexive, self-conscious texts that worked within and against a vernacular romance tradition, addressing the religious tensions in individually complex ways. William Shakespeare, who may or may not have been Catholic (but who is seldom accused of being Protestant), and who worked within a dramatic context, may seem the odd man out.[60] His keen interest, however, in experimenting with romance narratives for the stage provides a test case for how the concerns of more Protestant-invested authors translate for an equally self-conscious writer whose religious convictions remain opaque. Of all the dramatic romances in which Shakespeare had a hand, *Pericles* most betrays the struggle to repurpose a fabulous tale for a new audience. In brief, all four authors share what we might call a "hybrid" faith that both confirms and denies the stability of any religious identity. My focus throughout will be on how the formal characteristics and argumentative strategies of the texts themselves take on Roman and Protestant practice as opposed to concentrating on mercurial authorial belief.

The texts, and their authors, appear across chapters and sections as I examine related controversies involving competing religious arguments in literary contexts. The readings throughout this book seek to answer these questions: what does the Reformation of romance look like, and how might we trace its effects? Each chapter will consider how literary texts engage from a variety of perspectives with disruptive facets of reform. Because they engage multiple aspects of reform, the works of Sidney and Spenser appear in more than one chapter and more than one context. Resisting the strident credos of polemic, each seeks to tack between positions, making virtuosic use as they do so of the formal capacities of the romance form. My argument also illustrates that these self-determined efforts of reform frequently shattered the host into textual shards, a further aspect that unites the four texts at this book's center. Each reveals how the struggle to contain a hybrid form destabilized the narrative integrity. The romances of Sidney, Spenser, Shakespeare, and Wroth all express a troubling doubt that romance could ever be entirely stripped of its so-called lying wonders and yet maintain its seductive appeal.[61] For underneath the patina of reform, the skeletal architecture of romance, like the "choirs" of Shakespeare's sonnet 73, would always be a reminder of its older heritage.

The logic at work behind the Protestant index indicted both romance texts and its readers—finding both to tend toward the "superstitious." Following this polemical logic, this book divides into two parts. The first part, "Fabulous Texts," takes up the problem of the genre itself, specifically illustrating why, from a post-Reformation perspective, the form was condemned for its "cloistered" heritage; and how conscientious English authors mined it for new forms of piety, modifying the fabulous as they did so. Chapters 1 and 2 focus on how the romances of Sidney, Spenser, and Shakespeare provide subtle illustrations for the emergence of what Julie Crawford has called a "marvelous Protestantism."[62] These chapters also explore how the religiously charged crisis of genre brought with it a troubling gendered dimension. To call a text feminine became yet another way to identify it as Catholic. Building from the work of Frances Dolan, who traces how the pejorative epithet of "the whore of Babylon" comes to define unruly, and often Catholic, women, and that of Helen Hackett, who explores the feminization of romance, I reconstruct a rhetorical fait accompli that equates romance with Romanism, Romanism with the feminine, and the feminine with romance.[63] A pejorative understanding of women's relationship to romance, of course, does not begin with Protestantism, but it was deepened by it.

The second part of the book, "Superstitious Readers," focuses on how the failed, or at best incomplete, textual reformation prompted a turn toward reforming reading practices. It looks at how early modern theories of memory, understanding of affect, and gender practices drove writers like Sir John Harington, Edmund Spenser, and Lady Mary Wroth to define a hermeneutic that could be used to justify the reading of romance as a spiritual, and Protestant, discipline, fit reading for women as well as men. Medieval authors had provided famous examples of fallen romance readers; Francesca's damnation in canto 5 of Dante's *Inferno* began with her reading of Lancelot. The Middle English *"Mirror"* (1250–60), a collection of gospel narratives, includes a prologue dedicated to a noblewoman that warned her against reading "romaunces & gestes" such as "Tristrem" or "Gy of Warrewyk" and instead encouraged a more spiritually profitable reading of the gospel narratives the volume contained.[64] Thus, as medievalist Melissa Furrow argues, Catholic culture set the precedent for worrying over romance's effect on its readers, especially those believed to be most susceptible.[65] This already extant connection between discourses of gender and those of faith became acute under the growing pressure placed on reading practice within Protestantism.[66]

Cutting across gendered lines, Calvinist, Reformed, and Counter-Reformation debates over the right governance of the passions also play a role in the conversation about how to read romance. In much Reformation thought, the experience of reading was understood to be transformative. Foxe's *Acts and Monuments* points out numerous instances of conversion narratives in which hearing or reading catalyzed the individual soul toward salvation.[67] Affective response, often figured in explicitly sensory or somatic terms, is at the heart of these transformative encounters. To arouse a reader's affect, or in early modern terms, her "passions," opened the way for salvation—but also apostasy. Because so many Protestant indexes of romance credit the romance as being a more efficacious agent than scripture to summon readerly emotion, anxiety over affectivity intersects with concerns for habits of reading, which in turn consolidated a confessional identity. Extending the work of scholars such as Gail Kern Paster, Katherine Rowe, Mary Floyd-Wilson, Michael Schoenfeldt, and Christopher Tilmouth, I analyze how conceptualizations of the passions' role inflect how English authors write romance.[68] Chapters 3 and 4, on Spenser and Wroth, turn to how romance might help to inculcate good interpretive habits in its readers, thus proving an unlikely resource in the project of reform. Vindicating a reader's relationship to romance—both as figures within and outside the text—then becomes symbolic of the reformation of both.

The Countesse of Pembrokes Arcadia, *The Faerie Queene*, *Pericles*, and *Urania* convey the confusion as well as the zeal of individual authors who confronted the challenges posed in the wake of Reformation. Considered together, they emphasize something surprising and compelling. Their acts of erasure and transmutation engendered a literary canon that has come to shape our understanding of romance as one that looks quite different from an early modern perspective. We remember romance as it was negotiated within these exceptional, and now canonical, texts, forgetting the forest from which they emerged. As a case study of the interaction between literary forms and cultural pressures, this book establishes a rapport between romance conventions and religiously motivated castigation that together affiliate major works of Tudor-Stuart literature in a shared generic genealogy. In the chapters that follow, I will consider the context and pressures that drive these four texts to a dynamic, and particularly English, expression of reformation.

PART I

Fabulous Texts

"ROMISH" ROMANCE AND THE PROTESTANT DILEMMA

Why was English romance, post-Reformation, the object of such sustained scrutiny by religious polemicists and scarcely registered as a literary form by writers? At first glance, it might seem that the two discourses have little in common. After all, romances were popular secular texts and seemingly outside the religious disputes over catechism, books of prayer, and other devotional material. Yet the romance relied on complex rhetorical allusiveness that made truth claims by uniting otherwise disparate textual materials such as sermons, saints' exempla, and legendary English heroes. These claims to truth imbricate religious agendas with literary ambitions. Oft-repeated slurs align the genre with the Catholic, or the "Romish," in Reformation England: "Made in monasteries by idle monks," romance constituted the "fantasticall dreams of those exiled abbie-lubbers," the "trim work" of "idle Cloistermen, mad merry Friers, and lustie abbeye-lubbers" that kindled in its readers' hearts "the superstition of the elder worlde," with tales spun from a dark but "fabulous cloister."[1] This impulse to mark romance's inception with a disreputable parentage appeared in both earnest and satirical opinion. While the pejorative epithets frequently served a tendentious agenda, Lovel's dark, fabulous cloister, and by extension a medieval Catholic culture as the place of romance's inception, were not entirely fanciful genealogies. These popular epithets serve to foreground the problem hinted at in my introduction—that the past remained stubbornly, seductively visible despite its suppression. Friars may have been dissolved of duty, but their tales remained popular. In part I, I begin by taking stock of how and why romance was implicated as a troublingly active, even vibrant, remainder of medieval culture.

Romance, to sixteenth-century eyes, looked Catholic because of a long, complicated, and intertwined history of competition. The *Dialogus Miraculorum*, recorded in the mid-thirteenth century by Caesarius of Heisterbach, tells the story of Abbot Gevard, who, during a sermon to his English chapterhouse monks, noticed several brethren sleeping—some even beginning to snore. "Listen, brethren, listen," he cried out. "I have something new and important to tell you: There once was a king named Arthur." Seeing his somnolent audience rouse itself, he scolded them: "When I was speaking to you about God, you fell asleep," but "you all woke up and began to listen with eager ears" with the naming of Arthur.[2] Abbot Gevard's tactic to wake his sleepy audience by evoking the legendary romance hero Arthur raises a characteristic dilemma for abbots, clerics, preachers, and reformers alike: how could the appeal of Arthur's story be harnessed for Christian ends? For, as Gevard realizes, King Arthur's story compels greater alertness than the story of God. Faced with such arousing competition, many Catholic abbots, like Gevard, made the expedient choice to co-opt romance from the pulpit, rather than simply denounce it.

Abbot Gevard's evocation of romance heroes during the course of a sermon will become a familiar concession, and its blurring of the boundaries between sacred and secular narratives marks what will be both its appeal and its peril for later Protestant preachers. The medieval heritage of romance, in sixteenth-century England, marked the genre as a literary form interbred with pious and Catholic narratives. This intertwined history becomes a stubborn part of romance's reception among Protestant writers. Romance did not originate from the medieval Catholic world, but it was, as Geraldine Heng notes, "indelibly marked by it."[3]

Competing with popular forms of religious literature, English romances, medieval scholars Susan Crane and Helen Cooper demonstrate, absorbed religious values, embracing more pious, Christianized motifs than their continental counterparts.[4] The *South English Legendary* (ca. 1270–85), an important and widely circulated vernacular text, for example, provided medieval audiences with short narratives of the church calendar saints, including scriptural material and narratives of Christ as a type of knight for "Cristendom." Within the *Legendary*, saints as "Christ's knights" battle for the church militant in crusade narratives that parallel the conquests of romance heroes such as Arthur.[5] Abbot Gevard's sermon may suggest why such a symbiotic relationship developed between the religious and the romance hero. If properly marshaled,

Arthur's tale might be an efficacious surrogate for drawing an audience to "Christ's knights" and Christian truths.

Stories of medieval knights often exploit this potential, simultaneously modeling spiritual as well as secular ideals.[6] Because chivalry and religion worked in tension under the same conceptual framework, knights and saints frequently endured similar trials.[7] In both, the supernatural is omnipresent, and interventionist.[8] *Sir Isumbras*, for instance, tells of a hero who suffers Job-like loss of family and fortune when he forgets his duty to God. He loses his wife to the Saracens, his children to wild beasts, and his gold to an eagle. After he penitently labors for many years as a smith, an angel tells him he is forgiven. Shortly thereafter he finds his gold in the eagle's nest and is reunited with his family. His story resembles that of Saint Eustace, who also loses his family and fortune when he converts to Christianity. He suffers, but after regaining his fortune, he voluntarily accepts martyrdom for his faith. Likewise, Guy of Warwick's story begins with his chivalric slaying of dragons, while the second half portrays him as a penitent pilgrim and spiritual model journeying to the Holy Land. The story of the dragon and Guy of Warwick appeared in at least one sermon, evidence of the ready crosspollination between sacred and secular "romance" narratives.[9]

The syncretism between religious literature and romance, however, was not without its tension for Catholic writers. They too were wary of its popularity, but also of its pagan elements: magic, a pantheon of gods, and the capricious will of Fortune that undermined a providential understanding of history. Calling popular "gestes," such as that of *Guy of Warwick*, "bot vanitie," stories guilty of "veyne carpying," William of Nassington, for instance, distinguishes his translation of John of Waldby's *Speculum Vitae* (late fourteenth century) by promising his audience no "dethes of armes, ne of amours."[10] Earlier, romancer turned hagiographer Denis Piramus (writing in the late twelfth century) inaugurated a rivalry when he insisted in his preface to *Life of Edmund* that his tale of a saint exceeded those of the romance *Partenopeus de Blois*, matching it for pleasure and exceeding it for morals: "Si purrez les almes garir / E les cors garantir de hunte" (it is possible for it to cure souls and protect bodies from disgrace and shame).[11] Although, he admits, the *Lais* of Marie may have admirable "cuntes, chanceuns e fables" and *Partenopeus* may contain "dream-like" passages that ease sorrow, ultimately they occupy "memoires" only with pleasure; they do not cure souls.[12] The projected competition expressed by early hagiographers and early writers of romance implicitly registers how a medieval culture recognized, even if uneasily, a sympathy between those stories that ostensibly lead the reader to contemplate the heavenly and spiritual realms and those that champion idealized earthly knights, fealty, love, and courtly games.[13]

The grumblings of antiromance sentiment by clerics like Piramus and abbots such as Gevard, perversely enough, likely furthered the hybridization of Catholic religious narratives and secular romance. For, as their complaints make explicit, they recognize that frequently audiences were more emotionally aroused by the "veyne carpying" of romance, which sublimated example to pleasure. Abbot Gevard's monks were not the only ones moved from somnolence by the stories of romance. In the *Speculum Caritatis*, Ailred of Rievaulx (ca. 1110–67) writes: "Nam et in fabulis, quae vulgo de nescio quo finguntur Arcturo, memini me nonnunquam usque ad effusionem lacrymarum fuisse permotum. Unde non modicum pudet propriae vanitatis, qui si forte ad ea quae de Domino pie leguntur, vel cantantur, vel certe publico sermone dicuntur, aliquam mihi lacrymam valuero extorquere, ita mihi statim de sanctitate applaudo, ut si magnum aliqui ac inusitatum mihi miraculum contigisset" (In the stories fabricated by all sorts of people about some Arthur, I know not who, I remember that I was moved often to tears. But if by chance someone were to read piously about our Lord, or sing, or speak in a public sermon, and I am able to wring out some tears, I applaud myself for my sanctity, that so great and unusual a miracle had touched me .)[14] Ailred, like Augustine in his famous lament for how he wept over the story of Dido, shows how Catholics were wary of romance's efficacy to arouse the passions. But they both also suggest exactly why the church sought to exploit romance's potential, adopting its power for holy ends.

The *Gesta Romanorum*, a compendium of edifying stories first printed in 1472, shows just how successful such a merger could be.[15] The *Gesta* crosses a popular Latin collection of saints' legends with chivalric short romances, tailed by a moral and allegorical gloss. Although originally intended as a compendium of edifying stories for monks to use in preaching, the *Gesta* became popular entertainment as well as moral exemplum. Taking this Catholic adoption of the romance form a step further, Robert Chambers, an exiled English Catholic priest living under the reign of Queen Elizabeth, romances key moments of Biblical history in *Palestina* (1600) by turning Satan into the great "Enchanter" and Christ into a young prince, seeking to uncharm "the Lady, which was enchaunted by eating of the fruite of a tree."[16] *Palestina* shows the specific ways that Catholics tried to turn romance to good use. These compilers and authors recognized just how flexible romance narratives could be, allowing a discourse of religion to flourish alongside tales that kept audiences awake. By virtue of its popularity, its kinship to divine motifs, and its appeal to sundry constituencies (abbots as well as gentlemen, ladies as well as men), romance could be a vehicle uniquely situated to underwrite—and not just compete with—a projected religious as well as national community.

Arguing for how English romances became the genre of the English nation in the Middle Ages, Geraldine Heng shows the centrality of this genre in the projection of a national community, focusing particularly on how Arthurian romance furnished a crucial cultural authority for the fantasy of early overseas empires and the "military-religious experiment known in the West as the First Crusade."[17] Later, during the upheavals of Lollardy in the fifteenth century, readers, Helen Cooper argues, seem to have regarded romance as a stabilizing force for orthodoxy, as one compatible with forms of piety opposed to Lollardy.[18] In other words, despite certain reservations, Catholic culture had at various moments incorporated and even exploited the romance as a narrative form suitable to promoting a religious and communal identity. Romance's history, its complicated relationship to Catholic religious narratives, and its potential role in projecting a religious community made it simultaneously repellent and attractive to Protestants. If Catholics had successfully co-opted the pleasures of romance for didactic ends, how could reformers claim the same stories for new religious ends? This challenge is what I explore over the course of the following two chapters, mapping how post-Reformation English authors searched for an acceptable way to use Arthur and romance legend to marshal their sluggish audiences to a Protestant watchfulness.

"IN-BETWEEN": ROMANCE AND HYBRIDITY

But if romance's alleged popishness stemmed in part from historical development that hybridized sacred with secular narratives, what was it about the form itself that made it especially attractive for Christian purposes? As Gevard's sermon well illustrates, romance competed with the Bible for readers' attention, producing a version of what Northrop Frye once called "the secular scripture."[19] But where Frye sees the romance as sympathetically exhibiting a kind of formal emulation, I argue that romance's formal emulation of—and competition with—scriptural motifs produced real tension in its deployment by Christian authors.

Frye suggests that romance, through its presentation of wonder, seeks to awaken a readerly faith, a faith that in turn parallels Christianity's own wandering and recovery narrative. Although Frye reads this structural evocation of readerly faith as one parallel to Christian belief, reformers on the ground in the sixteenth century saw such arousal of faith via wondrous motifs as dangerously familiar to what they wished excised from, in their view, corrupt religious practice. For wonder too easily provoked religious adoration: Artegall's stunned fall " humbly downe upon his knee" when his knightly attacker is revealed to be a gorgeous woman encapsulates this romance motif, whereby he of his "wonder made religion."[20] The generalized "Christianity" produced in this effect was, post-Reformation, structurally read as Catholic by polemicists, in part, as I have suggested, because of Catholic religious culture's nurturing of romance. Romance, for later post-Reformation preachers, did not simply parallel scripture or even just compete with it; rather, it, like the proverbial wolf in sheep's clothing, sabotaged the faith it proclaimed. Just as the false healers of Ephesus cast aspersion on Paul's divinely sanctioned miracles, romance, with its "foolish lyes" and resurrected heroes, raised doubt over the veracity of its wondrous narrative.[21] Romance's frequent dwelling on the boundary between credible and incredible created acute problems for Protestants who wished to expose the ludicrousness of romance (and thereby Catholicism) yet simultaneously needed to uphold the literal truths of scripture—truths that had already been shown to read uncomfortably like the tales of romance. How could they discredit the magic of Arthur's story, and the miracles of saints, yet keep the miracles of Christ and his disciples? As Thomas Nashe quipped, atheists "talke as prophanely of the Bible, as of Bevis of Hampton."[22] How might an audience identify true from false wonder, biblical miracle from romance marvel, without losing all belief in the supernatural and thus becoming one of the unfortunate ungodly?

While Frye does not read romance as undermining Christian belief, he does identify a central motif that makes romance's claim for kinship to scripture so troubling following the Reformation. His theory points to a constituent aspect defined by a formal quality inherent to romance narratives. At root lies what we might call the "hybridity" of romance, a quality I shall argue that accounts for its attractiveness for Christian adoption, but also the quality that renders it subversive. By "hybrid," I refer to its etymological and biological origins, as a term to describe a half-breed, literally the offspring of two different species or varieties. Derived from heterogeneous sources, it is composed of incongruous parts. A composite of sacred and secular motifs, romance hybridizes these conceptual frameworks to produce a narrative story line that oscillates between natural and supernatural planes.[23] As a rhetorical strategy, it juxtaposes apparently incompatible material to make "fabulous" narratives, which extend beyond the usual range of fact.

The characteristic passage of romance narratives, the theme of roving knights who are in between geographic, temporal, as well as literary borders, is the literary equivalent of what postcolonial theorists describe as fusions of difference, cultural encounters involving conquest as well as less martial kinds of contact.[24] Errant knights, whether passively wandering (as more typical of Greek romance) or actively questing (as in chivalric tales), cross borders. They are thus often outside of the networks of classifications that normally locate them within a culture, rendering their identity ambiguous and malleable. Pyrocles and Musidorus, for example, adopt the personae of an Amazonian queen and a humble shepherd in order to woo Basilius's daughters during their Arcadian adventures; Britomart, in *The Faerie Queene*, cross-dresses as a knight to seek her love; Urania opens Lady Mary Wroth's text lamenting her unknown place in the world, lost to parents and society. Like these characters, romance heroes often strive from the margins (the illegitimate and the illicit) in search of their place within society. They pursue adventure or love, range the seas from Asia to Ethiopia (as Sidney roundly complains in his *Defence*), adopt and discard disguises, and cycle through serial conflicts whose underlying substance can take many forms but will frequently entail issues of sexuality and identity, whether gendered, national, or religious.

Such attention to "in between" spaces makes romance what Tom Bishop calls a "testing" genre, "one that exposes settled conditions to a kind of experimental derangement" and is consequently "prone to epistemological and other kinds of queasiness or instability."[25] Although the purported end of romance often reaches for a conservative formula (Guy of Warwick's eventual hermitage, Bevis of Hampton's final success to his inheritance, the marriage day of Pyrocles and Philoclea), its thematic attention to the "in between," amplifies its formal hybridity. Wandering, error and romance's dilation of desire, as scholars such as James Nohrnberg and Patricia Parker argue, make it a wayward and profligate form. Romance, Parker writes, "simultaneously quests for and postpones a particular end, objective, or object," and lingers "on the threshold before the promised end, still in the wilderness of wandering, 'error,' or 'trial.'"[26] Thus the hybrid, in-between dimensions of romance invites *errare* with all its concomitant associations of generic miscegenation, religious indeterminacy, wandering, contamination, and error.

Romance's hybridity contributes to the form's resistance and potential force but also its danger. It opens up a space that questions the fixity of as-

sumed binaries and identities, revealing interpenetration between allegedly
different categories as the fabulous in romance blurs heaven and earth, angels
and enchantresses. For within a hybrid landscape, boundaries appear malleable and identity flexible. The hybridity—the attention to the in-between, to
testing, to wandering, and even to error—makes romance a powerful vehicle
for exploring a confessional, religious identity, as the numerous examples of
knights as types for saints from medieval romances suggest.[27] The danger was
always, however, that the knight might not make the turn from wandering to
recovery or that the reader might miss the turn and proceed from wonder to
superstition.

The combination of admiration and fear that English reformers felt for romance reflected a broad wariness toward intermixed and potentially hybrid
identities—especially religious ones—at a time when Protestants were in need
of establishing, especially in the sixteenth century, a hard-line confessional
identity that demarcated them from what they liked to call the "papists." Because of its attention to the in-between, romance potentially undermined that
project even as it seductively lent itself to the erection of pious heroes worthy
of emulation. As the work of Mary Douglas shows, things that dwell between
classificatory boundaries are frequently regarded as polluting and dangerous.[28]
The frequent likening of romance to a disease, pollution, and contagion by
antiromance polemicists from Vives onward confirms romance's hybridity as
something both powerful and deadly in its transformative potential, at once an
efficacious agent and a determined contaminant. Romances, as Dering and
others reveal, were thought to be textual portals through which readers might
just as easily access the past as the present, the supernatural as the natural, the
imaginary as the real, foolish lies as truth—in short, "bewitching" readers to
miss the difference between them. Such practice broke down rather than wid-
ened a confessional divide.

Precisely for this reason, many preachers viewed romance with acute skepticism. It produced a fear that romance might well confuse, or even erase, the
boundaries they were working so hard to establish. For the romance, though
it had proven a useful ally in erecting a Catholic identity, also served as a
continual reminder of residual elements of paganism, showing how old habits
of thought still compelled attention. And, in what constituted a paradoxical
threat, while romance was perceived to blur boundaries that needed to be distinct, it retained its ability to sharpen or kindle the reader's attention and
memory. Aggravating such tension, romance was, if we trust the prosecution,
especially adept at stimulating not only alertness but also recollection and

memory through its rhetorical deployment of "fabulous" and erotic content. Engaged by a constant negotiation between illicit impulse and potential moral example, romance's hybrid nature would bedevil those who wished more simply to burn the offending stories and, along with them, the memory of an older, corrupted faith that they housed.

The two chapters in this section consider how English authors struggled in between the waves of reform to demarcate old, cloistered stories from new ones. The first confronts how Sidney's revised *Arcadia* and Spenser's deployment of Arthur's history in *The Faerie Queene* exemplify the Protestant struggle to keep the fabulous stories they inherited and yet distinguish their use from what those more polemical deemed the "superstitious" ends of "papists." The second considers how, because women served as proxies for the superstitious and Catholic dimensions of romance, male authors—in this reading, Sidney and Shakespeare—thought to reform the romance by restaging its female characters. This reformation involved retaining the qualities the heroines shared with virgin martyrs, such as constancy, fidelity, and rhetorical skill, but downplaying the role of the supernatural marvelous in their triumphs. Focusing on the dramatic qualities of Sidney's prose and the narrative qualities of Shakespeare's play, this chapter suggests how romance's formal as well as thematic hybridity offers a particular vantage or mode of investigation into Reformation controversies.

In what follows, the fabulous and hybrid matter of romance foregrounds the problem of reforming the English church, for what is superseded and suppressed calls into question the Reformation it is supposed to facilitate. Through Sidney's, Spenser's, and Shakespeare's composite romances, we can start to see that the past remains, not as a specter, but as an active and continuous palimpsest to the present. We can glimpse, through the narratives of these authors, the hybrid in-between nature of English religious and literary identity after the Reformation.

CHAPTER ONE

Fabulous Romance and Abortive Reform in Philip Sidney and Edmund Spenser

This chapter begins with a "ruined" book, a lavishly bound collection of the foundational works of the English church published in 1616. This particular volume includes the Psalter, a genealogy of figures from sacred scripture drawn by John Speed, a brightly illustrated edition of the King James Bible by the printer Robert Barker, and the Sternhold and Hopkins Psalms in English meter. Yet despite the orthodoxy of its contents, its binding bears traces of the confessional anxiety that repeatedly convulsed early modern England.[1]

Opulent, rich, red velvet, embossed with figures in gold and silver thread, the embroidered binding counters in small evidence for the thoroughness of an iconoclastic Protestantism, which had fitfully whitewashed illustrations from texts of religious devotion even as it had redecorated its church interiors. Indeed, this book and its binding show rather the contiguity of Christian confessional allegiance. For, although now faded and nearly illegible, embroidered Latin phrases frame both the front and rear cover images. This tattered Latin, "*Nova Facta Sunt Omnia*" (all this was made), "*Exista: Per Mosem Data*" (as given by Moses) recalls the Vulgate, and for Protestant England the Catholic Holy Scripture that the Protestant English Bibles superseded, as it encloses an Old Testament tableaux. On the front, an embroidered Moses and Aaron hold between them the tablets of stone containing the Ten Commandments superimposed over a cross threaded by a golden snake. The central images remain remarkably well preserved. The embroidered scene with its Old Testament heroes surrounded by a Latin frame suggests a coexistence of competing orthodoxies, of Latin and vernacular, of image and word, of Catholic and Protestant.

Embroidered binding on the back of a 1616 Bible (New Testament). *The Holy Bible*. (Imprinted at London, by Robert Barker, 1616), HEH438000:070, STC (2nd ed.), 2245. Reproduced by permission of the Huntington Library, San Marino, California.

But when the volume is turned over, there is a striking reminder that readers were preoccupied still with Christian confessional boundaries despite the emerging ideal of an Anglican *via media*. For the rear binding, which illustrates the two Marys worshipping at either side of the crucified Christ, has had its central image, the crucifix, carefully excised, leaving the two women to mourn the outline of the familiar, but now absent, icon.[2]

The suspicion toward the Catholic marked through this act of erasure tells a story that maps in a very material way the varied confessional allegiances of England's Christian readers. It vividly illustrates a central claim of this chapter: that in seeking to come to terms with the instability of the period's religious culture, readers as well as writers struggled to reconcile past and present forms of belief in ways that were sometimes violent, frequently contradictory, and often characterized by small painstaking gestures with disproportionately large symbolic resonance. The crucifix's effacement from this volume of orthodox Anglican devotional books offers a material testament of other more subtle acts of erasure that happened between the covers of narratives almost as familiar as those of Moses, Aaron, the Marys, and Christ over the period of England's long reformation.

Nearly three decades earlier, a remarkable excision of story sets apart two English vernacular romances, Sir Philip Sidney's revised *Arcadia* and Edmund Spenser's *The Faerie Queene*, marking them with the conflicts of faith. In Sidney's case, the omnipresent de rigueur motif of the duel between knight and supernatural foe remains only as an ellipsis. Spenser does not shun dragons nor other supernatural antagonists, but he too calls attention to the outline of a familiar but altered icon. In his explanatory letter to Ralegh, Spenser writes that his subject will be "the historye of king Arthure."[3] But he then proceeds to neglect, almost entirely, many of its most famous episodes, including the quest for the Sangreal. These two seemingly insignificant textual elisions emblematize a larger pattern within both works that reckon with what for Protestants had become a troubling dimension of the romance: its invocation of the supernatural marvelous with its powerful memorial qualities. Yet like the ghostly outline of the offending crucifix, these textual elisions raise more questions than they efface.

What we see at work in these textual erasures embodies the conundrum of English reform. Sidney's one lone monster is illustrative. Occupying less than one page in a nearly four-hundred-page romance, the only prowling monster in *Arcadia* exists as a simile. "Of most ugly shape, armed like a *Rhinoceros*, as strong as an Elephant, as fierce as a Lion, as nimble as a Leopard, and as cruell as a tigre" (Dd7ʳ), he hovers between an imaginary existence and a physical one.[4] The Arcadian monster can be glimpsed only through comparison, which, paradoxically, grounds him in a world of familiar, if exotic, animals. Sidney's hesitation in presenting a wholly imaginary beast suspends the *Arcadia*'s monster, neither a towering dragon nor a Dantean wolf, in generic, as well as species, limbo. His descriptive ambiguity intensifies when the battle between this "monstrous beast" and the hero, Pyrocles, gets relegated to a brief description:

"I undertooke the combatte: and (to make shorte, excellent Ladie, and not trouble your eares with recounting a terrible matter) so was my weakeness blessed from above, that without dangerous wounds I slewe that monster" (Dd7ᵛ). Reduced to sequential past-tense verbs that are the only concession to a heroic narrative—"undertooke," "was blessed," and "slew"—the text refuses to amplify the hero's might, the monster's fierceness, or the perilous struggle in which he was vanquished. Indeed, nearly half of the account is parenthetical, an interjected apostrophe to the reader. Instead, Pyrocles assures Philoclea, and by extension Sidney assures his readers, that he will "not trouble" her "eares" with such "terrible matter."[5]

I take as my point of departure in this chapter the questions raised by Sidney's deliberate act of diegetic erasure. The effect of his textual eclipse, like the redecorated roods and shifted altars or the "blotted" crucifix on the embroidered binding, works through an implicit recognition that something familiar has changed or gone missing. Just as crucifixes became a flash point in Reformation rhetoric because of their ready familiarity and association with Catholic worship, monsters were readily identifiable staples, or "memes" (the habit of repetition and recycling within a genre that mimics the behavior of genes), of romance who, after the Reformation, came to symbolize the genre's troubling connection to Catholic stories.[6] To put it another way, at a time of complex renegotiations over the efficacy of rituals and material objects, romance motifs were imbued with a similar symbolic status to other objects of church reform, and were thus subjected to a new scrutiny.

Although it is impossible to know who took the time to excise the crucifix from the cover of the 1616 book of religious texts, or their motives for doing so, the evidence points to the legacy of confessional conflict that could produce contradictory results: if this was an act of iconoclasm, why purge only the crucifix but leave the cross, the Latin words, the Marys, or even the richly embroidered binding? Similar questions emerge within the romances of Sidney and Spenser: Why banish the monster but keep the romance? Why keep the story of Arthur but leave out one of its defining quests? How are we to account for these omissions?

As my introduction argues, for many reform-minded Protestants, Edward Dering's solution to the Catholic "spiritual enchauntmentes" of popular stories was simple: burn them.[7] Yet despite his and others' exhortations, Saint George, Arthur, and Bevis along with a host of old romance heroes continued to thrive in stories that seemingly ignored the turns in religion. In between the calls for a literary auto-da-fé and the nonchalance of romance publishers and printers, such as William Copland or Thomas East, lie the romances of Sidney and Spenser. Although both draw from a medieval English and continental romance heritage—with its familiar legends of charmed boats, errant knighthood, distressed dames, courtly jousts, oracles, marvels, chimeras, hermetic rings, and a capricious Fortune—each selectively effaces other common motifs.[8] Their stories, as a result, look quite different from the corpus of other contemporary romances.[9] Through their selective acts of remembering and forgetting, they define a larger struggle of a culture reckoning with its past. This chapter will present and examine the implications posed by romance's post-Reformation reputation as a genre perpetrated by Catholics, identifiable by its "coniurationes, magicall artes, false miracles, [and] lying wonders," or what I call the supernatural marvelous, an aspect of romance that purportedly aroused and engaged readerly memory through a mode that appeared uncomfortably sympathetic to Catholic habits of faith.[10]

The problem arose from how the supernatural marvelous was believed to be a powerful ally for remembrance, as an aid to both individual recall and communal memory. To erase the marvelous, with its concomitant hold over memory, risks oblivion, a concern that runs throughout the anxious establishment of a new religious identity in the sixteenth century. At a time when Protestants were most assiduously rehabilitating icons of worship, and of memory, substituting new martyrs for old saints, Sidney and Spenser broach romance in order to work out the theological irritants of an avidly popular genre. Sidney's absent yet present monster thus emblematizes a literary effort to confront and correct an institutional memory, preferring to salvage rather than demolish the acts, objects, and meanings of a literary form that had come to represent a crisis in faith.

In making this argument, I observe continuity between texts that range from prose to poetry in which the marvelous and its memorial effects plays a central role. These two works inform my argument not because they are representative of early modern romance but because they are exceptional, anomalous works that go against romance as it was being published, printed, and written during the latter half of the sixteenth century. The pointed erasure of romance's dragons from what critics call the revised or the *New Arcadia* looks very different from the looming dragon toward which Spenser's hero the Redcrosse Knight pricks. Yet *The Faerie Queene* too pays attention to how the presence of the supernatural shapes the story of Arthur, Spenser's legendary controversial hero. Both authors were drawn to how romance's "fabulous devices" enhanced memory, thus complicating for each an easy dismissal of a superstitiously tinted supernatural.[11] By repurposing the romance marvelous, Sidney and Spenser buck the genre's most compelling and memorable aspect, threatening to unravel the form even as they sought to reconstruct it. What follows will be occupied with how the supernatural marvelous within romance poses a representational problem to the construction of memory and identity, both individual and collective. I make this argument by examining, first, the recurring and shifting but also unexpectedly central role that romance plays in theories of memory and religious affiliation, an examination I extend to Sidney and Spenser's texts as they produce a debate over the roles of books, reading, the marvelous, memory, and pious practice.

"OVER-BUSY REMEMBRANCE" AND ROMANCE

When Sidney revised *The Countess of Pembrokes Arcadia* during the 1580s, the concept of a Protestant English romance remained controversial.[12] In his influential *The Schoolmaster* (1570), even the less radical Roger Ascham, a humanist with a forward Protestant stance, lambasted England's own *Morte Darthur* as having been composed in "monasteries by idle monks or wanton canons."[13] Moreover, much mid-sixteenth-century romance originated in the Catholic strongholds of Italy and Spain, a point not lost on Ascham, who also inveighed against "merry books" procured from abroad and distributed "by subtle and secret papists at home."[14] If chivalrous and continental romances were encouraged to be read, romances would "soon displace all books of godly learning" and cause readers to think ill of "all true religion."[15] Ascham influentially erected a binary that set "godly learning" and "true religion" on one side and "merry books" and papistry on the other, thus perpetuating romance's controversial status for "the godly" in early modern England.

Yet the concentrated attacks on the dangerous heritage and habits of romance highlight its characteristic seductive appeal: readers prefer—and better remember—the "merry books" that stimulate pleasure and arouse wonder.[16] Just as the "enchantments of Circe" made Ulysses's men forget their homeland, Ascham argues, reading romance induces a "forgetfulness of all good things learned before."[17] Ascham's analogy suggests that, like Circe, romance fills the memory, leading one to forget what should properly occupy it. Similarly, in *A Sparing Restraint of Many Lavishe Untruthes* (1568), Dering accuses Catholics of captivating the people's minds with tales of "Gui of Warwick and Beuis of Hampton & such like," while "not one among a hundred could tell a lyne" from Paul, Peter, James, or John.[18] Both men fear romance will crowd out "good things" from readers' memory. For Sidney and his contemporaries, memory plays a crucial role in increasing knowledge and encouraging virtuous action. One of the earliest and most influential Tudor treatises on memory, William Fulwood's translation of Guglielmo Gratarolo's *The Castel of Memorie* (1562), defines memory as much more than a mere repository of images; rather, it actively shapes opinion and, hence, judgment.[19] Romance was dangerous, then, partly because of its papist past, but, even more alarmingly, it posed an ongoing threat because of the ways its supernatural and wondrous incidents held such a compelling effect on memory that they eclipsed "good things," such as scripture.

Unlike many of his contemporaries who viewed readerly pleasure with profound skepticism, in his *Defence of Poesy* (1595) Sidney argues that a writer should follow Christ's example of teaching moral principles through pleasurable stories that enlist delight and wonder to better inspire virtue: "For as the Image of each Action stirreth and instructeth the mind, so the loftie Image of such worthies, moste enflameth the minde with desire to bee worthie" (F2^r).[20] If the reader will but inscribe "in the tablet of . . . memory," he continues, the story of Aeneas or the Psalms of David, these might be "founde in excellencie fruitefull" (F2^r). In sum, Sidney argues that reading's highest end should be "an enriching of memorie, enabling of judgement" that encourages virtuous action (C3^r). These two examples—classical and scriptural—accord with Ascham's canon of acceptable readings. Sidney's *Defence*, however, gives a more extensive list of recommended texts that include romance, texts most famous for ranging into the chimeric realm. He argues that *Orlando Furioso* might well instruct a soldier (G3^r). And even that most excoriated of long romances, *Amadis de Gaule*, has "hearts moued to the exercise of courtesie, liberalitie, and especially courage" (E2^r). The romances so censored by Ascham and Dering, in other words, earn Sidney's praise for their instructive qualities.[21]

Sidney's concern with the effect of pleasurable tales on memory, throughout the *Defence*, finds even more pointed expression when he revises *The Countesse of Pembrokes Arcadia*. When he returned to the *Old Arcadia*, critics have argued, he did so partially to make it more didactic.[22] I contend that, instead, as he revised the Arcadian material into a more romance-like story, he sought to distinguish his romance from those so castigated by his fellow Protestants. Sidney's own religious convictions suggest a cosmopolitan outlook; he was friendly with Catholics and read widely even of those romances condemned by his tutors.[23] Yet in his fiction, he is chary of issues that drew Protestant opprobrium. Urania, the shepherdess-muse in the revision, whose memory sparks the opening dialogue, provocatively gestures toward a continental, Protestant stance on imaginative writing.[24] Urania had recently been proclaimed the new Christian muse of poetry by the influential Huguenot Guillaume de Salluste du Bartas. In his first publication of religious poems, *La Muse Chrestiene* (1574), Du Bartas recounts how the muse Uranie (in classical tradition, the muse for astronomy) appeared to urge him to turn from secular to sacred writing. Sidney's decision to name the figural muse of the *New Arcadia* Urania thus links Du Bartas's sacred Huguenot poems and Sidney's own prose romance as Protestant appropriations of classical and Catholic forms.[25] The invocation to Urania boldly insists that a Protestant muse might inspire—and even condone—a romance for its pedagogical and spiritual effect on readers' memory.

Whereas the *Old Arcadia* opens descriptively, showing Arcadia's landscape and detailing how its king, Basilius, tried to escape an oracle's prophecy by sequestering his family in shepherds' huts, the revised version begins dialogically with a debate over Urania's effect on the memory of the two shepherds, Strephon and Claius.[26] Though this dialogue is often read by critics as an introduction to the Neoplatonic themes of the *Arcadia* or to its epic pretensions, I contend that it pointedly engages with the rousing polemical debates over the bewitching effects of romance on readers' memory.[27] As the story begins, the "hopelesse" shepherd Strephon bemoans how he and Claius "are so called" by "over-busie Remembrance" of Urania to the sands against the island of Citherea (B^{r-v}). Consciously playing off the opening to the Spanish Jorge de Montemayor's *Diana* that begins with the shepherd Syrenus, whose tormented memory of absent love reduces him to languishing on a riverbank, Sidney's opening Socratic dialogue overturns Syrenus's bootless complaint and provides an alternative to idleness for memory's effects.[28]

Strephon cannot forget Urania, nor can he remember anything else. For "over-busy remembrance—remembrance, restless remembrance," he complains, "claims not only this duty of us but . . . it will have us forget ourselves" (B^v). In contrast to his wretched state of "over-busy remembrance," other, more carefree shepherds delight in watching their sheep "nibble upon the short and sweete grasse," never losing themselves to a "restless" remembrance (B^v). But for Strephon, who recalls how meeting Urania made him "blush and quake," the memory of her beauty ("where she stayed, where she walked") haunts him unceasingly (B^v). It drives him and his similarly afflicted friend Claius to leave their sheep and return to the very place where they last saw her depart—a place that in turn intensifies memory, giving "newe heate to the feauer of our languishing remembrance" (B2^r).

Strephon's nearly obsessive remembrance, his "forgetfulness" of himself and his sheep, as well as his restless memory, call to mind what antiromance polemicists feared an over-busy remembrance might foster in its readers. They will remember only Circe's enchantments and forget "to feare when they spie wooloues" (B2ᵛ). Strephon's encounter with Urania, who functions both as the object of the shepherd's romantic interest and the figural embodiment of a new kind of romance, occupies his memory, renders him a negligent shepherd, and, crucially, leaves him vulnerable to wolves' attack. Wolves, as John King shows, were rhetorically linked in much Reformation polemic to Catholicism.[29] The fear that wolves might sneak into the fold while the shepherd sits absorbed by idle memories engages the fear that romances, like wolves in sheep's clothing, provided Catholics with cover for an attack on English readers by diverting their attention elsewhere.

Despite the trenchant agony of Strephon's complaints, Claius disagrees. He argues that the "racking steward remembrance" may have just the opposite effect (B2ᵛ). Rather than being made idle, neglectful, and vulnerable because of his memories of Urania, Claius believes his memories "serve as places to call to memory more excellent matters" (B2ᵛ). He further describes how his memory stimulates virtue: "Let us think with consideration, and consider with acknowledging, and acknowledge with admiration, and admire with love, and love with joy in the midst of all woes" (B2ᵛ). Syntactically, Claius's use of anadiplosis with each new clause maps a trajectory that begins with remembrance and ends in a philosophical state of endurance, even in the "midst of all woes." He proudly contends that while other shepherds "marke their sheepe, we do marke ourselues" (B3ʳ). Claius directly counters Ascham's fear that romance crowds memory, making one forgetful of those Catholic wolves, precipitating a slide into lust and ultimately heresy. Remembering Urania prompts him to look beyond the physical world of tending sheep and to study the interior self. Because of Urania's memory, he tells Strephon, their thoughts might be raised "aboue the ordinary leuell of the worlde, so as great clearkes do not disdaine our conference" (B3ʳ). Claius articulates the hope of many humanist scholars that a well-read man might counsel a prince.

Claius replies not only to Strephon but also to critics who accuse romance of idly engaging memory and inciting dangerous fantasies. He reforms those idle fantasies into action: he credits his "over-busy remembrance" of Urania with the impetus "to runne ouer learned writings" and to throw "reason upon our desires" (B3ʳ). For Claius, remembering Urania does not inspire a turn away from other types of intellectual benefit but serves as an incitement toward them; rather than encouraging credulous desire, the remembrance of romance enables reason. The revised *Arcadia*'s opening postulates an alternative trajectory for romance's effect, for Claius's remembrance of Urania, and by extension the reader's, leads first to an inward focus and then outward, eventually facilitating reasoned counsel to great men.

Sidney returns in the *New Arcadia* to the question of what effect stories might have on a reader's memories and actions when Prince Musidorus describes his and Pyrocles's education. The shepherd Dorus (actually Prince Musidorus) recounts to Princess Pamela his own ideal education as a boy, recalling how worthy "images" were "delivered to their memory" by reading (S2^r). He credits the remembered delight of tales for instilling virtue: "The delight of tales being converted to the knowledge of al the stories of worthy Princes, both to move them to do nobly & teach them how to do nobly; the beautie of vertue still being set before their eyes, & that taught them with far more diligent care" (S2^r). Dorus's recounting of how the princes learned noble behavior from "the delight of tales" sets an ambitious metanarrative standard for Sidney's own tale of "worthy Princes." It further accentuates a marked contrast in Sidney's attitude toward the pleasures of romance from many who shared his religious inclinations.

Through Strephon and Claius's debate, Dorus's praise of "the delight of tales," and the inclusion of many romance motifs, Sidney argues that romance's enchanting power over memory might be harnessed for legitimate Protestant ends. Yet, as Sidney realized, to harness romance required fundamental revision of one of romance's defining features and its most notorious method for garnering readers' attention: the supernatural marvelous. Post-Reformation polemicists, as I have shown, considered romance popish partly because of its Catholic past. Even more damaging, however, was romance's manipulation of supernatural marvels calculated to arouse a reader's memory. Gratarolo's treatise suggests why. "[N]ewe or wonderfull thinges do make a stedfast infixion or impression in the Memorie," it advises in a section on how to best stimulate memory.[30] Believing that wonder-invoking scenes make a "stedfast" impression in the memory, polemicists were alarmed that such scenes depicted in romance often recalled Catholic genres, especially saints' lives, brimming with "lying wonders" that embedded themselves in memory.

The first wave of English reformers had worked hard to establish the idea that false wonders and feigned miracles were Catholic. William Tyndale, for instance, set the tone for later generations. Tyndale argued that the late medieval Catholic Church relied heavily on painted forgeries of real worship to arouse an audience's delight and credulity: wondrous relics, lavish ceremony, and, in particular, the Mass. Helen Parish convincingly documents how, during the 1530s, the repeated intrusion of the supernatural into the material realm (whether in the saints' lives, in devotional materials, or in the wonders surrounding the consecrated host) became a polemical weapon used to condemn Catholicism as a faith founded upon the fraudulent manipulation of its believers' credulity through "false" wonders.[31] In *The Co[n]futacyon of Tyndales Answer*, Thomas More argued that miracles were an essential sign of the true church. Tyndale, in his *Answer Vnto Sir Thomas Mores Dialogue*, countered that true miracles ceased once the scripture had been fully received; the Catholic Church's miracles, he thundered, were an attempt to legitimize new items of faith that had no basis in the scriptures.[32] And once the claim that the age of miracles had passed had gained polemical ground, it was a short rhetorical leap to suggest that all subsequent wonders had their origins in falsehood and deception. Such a dismantling of the supernatural had the added polemical advantage of conflating anti-Christian illusion and human deception, facilitating the representation of the Catholic Church as built from, as Parish writes, "fictions, promoted by forgeries and accepted by a congregation of fools and hypocrites."[33]

Later reformers expanded the category of false ceremonies condemned by Tyndale, indicting literary forms as well as the rituals of the Mass and religious relics. As Arthur Dent writes in *The Plaine Mans Path-way to Heaven* (1605), romances "were deuised by the Divell, [and] seen and allowed by the Pope" so that "men might be kept from the reading of the Scriptures."[34] "[E]ven as a Lapwing, with her busie cry, draweth men away from her nest," he continues, "so the Popish generations, by these fabulous devices, draw men from Scriptures."[35] Dent clarifies how the "fabulous devices" of romance resembled the "lying wonders" of relics and miracles, adjudging both to be the devices of deceitful, popish sympathizers. Another critic who wished to separate his astrological practice from the counterfeit prophecies of "lustie Abbey-lubbers," John Harvey, in 1588, contends that stories like *Guy of Warwick*, *Orlando Furioso*, and *Amadis de Gaule* "busie the minds" of readers, averting their attention from "serious, and graver matters" such as religion "by delighting their fansies with such fabulous and ludicrous toyes."[36] Even more pointedly, Edward Dering blasts romances as "spiritual enchauntmentes" that "bewytched" readers in the same manner as did the *"Legendawry"* and "Saintes lyues."[37] His rhetorical conflation of romance's effects with those of saints' lives offers an instructive window into why romance seemed irredeemably Catholic. Romance, like the legends of saints, "bewytched" readers by rendering porous the border between the material and supernatural worlds and by thus inviting readers into an in-between space. Both featured a geography where supernatural visitors routinely punctured borders between worlds. Romance's inclusion of magic and the uncomfortable proximity of that magic to the miracles of the saints made romance a seemingly fit vehicle for the perpetuation of superstition.

In *An Easy and Compendious Introduction for Reading All Sorts of Histories* (1648), Mathias Prideaux (son to John Prideaux, who staunchly opposed Archbishop Laud) makes a similar point and sums up over a century's worth of Protestant antiromance polemic. He castigates romance for stuffing the reader's "Fancy and Memory with ridiculous Chimerah's, and wandering Imaginations" and for transporting and deluding the affections with "languishing Love, impossible attempts and victories, stupendious inchantments, wherewith the weake Reader is often so taken, that he makes himself (as it were) a Party in the business."[38] The "impossible" and "stupendious inchantments," whether magical or miraculous, catalyze for Prideaux the "weake," or we might say "Quixotic," reader, possessing his memory and, consequently, dictating his behavior. Prideaux's metaphor equates the effect of romance reading to a kind of devil possession from which the reader must be rescued by a textual exorcism. He reads readerly possession or enchantment, moreover, as a direct identificatory link between the romance character and the reader of romance. Such a mimetic link between character and reader drives the engine of reform even as it indicts both text and reader as guilty parties.

REFORMING ROMANCE IN PHILIP SIDNEY'S *NEW ARCADIA*

In contrast to the line of reasoning espoused by Prideaux and his earlier polemicists, Sidney, as I have argued, defends romance's efficacy for compelling memory. On one hand, Sidney advocates narratives, such as those of romance, that "delight" because "delight" "hath a great affinity to memory" (F4^r).[39] On the other hand, he critiques its reliance on what Prideaux identified as "stupendious inchantments" and "ridiculous Chimerah's," thus engaging the credo of antiromance polemic to drive his reform. To negotiate this tricky position, he had to redefine what merited marvel and garnered readers' attention and their memory.

"The hero of romance," Northrop Frye writes, "moves in a world in which the ordinary laws of nature are slightly suspended," a world where enchanted weapons, speaking beasts, and "talismans of miraculous power" violate ordinary rules of probability.[40] Frye's definition shows how supernatural motifs permeate romance, as indeed is the case for Sidney's precedents for the *Arcadia*. Arthur, for instance, wields his magic sword throughout the Arthurian legends; the Greek *Aethiopian Historie*, which inspired many Arcadian episodes, features a gymnosophist diviner. Both Ariosto's *Orlando Furioso* and Montemayor's *Diana* depict powerful enchantresses. Even Jacopo Sannazaro's largely pastoral *Arcadia*, from which Sidney draws his title, devotes books 9 through 12 to the magic practices of an old wise woman, Massilia, and her son Ergasto, who practice many things "wondrous to tell," such as the tale of two dragons who licked the ears of Enareto, who then could understand the language of birds.[41]

A frequently reproduced image of a knight battling a three-headed dragon illustrates the fungibility of supernatural dragons and their duels with heroes. This image, taken from William Copland's 1557 edition of *Kynge Arthur* also appears in an illustration for *The hystory of the two valyaunte brethren Valentyne and Orson* (1555, 1565) as well as in Stephen Hawes's *Pastime of Pleasure* (1555).[42] In this instance, a reader has personalized the stock image by writing in "Sr Lancelot du laik" and "the serpent fell." The reproduced image suggests what readers of romances already knew: that one dragon battle could look quite like another. The marginalia, furthermore, points to how at least one reader read romance as Christian allegory: the "fell" serpent invokes the arch nemesis to humankind detailed in Genesis. The familiarity and interchangeability demonstrate the reiteration of story motifs and suggest again how Sidney might exploit such familiarity to draw attention to its transformation in his story.

These instances of miraculous power and the battle against supernatural foes, or what Prideaux might call "stupendious inchantments," foster wonder, or at the very least, they court it. Helen Cooper exposes how in medieval romance what frequently appears as supernatural and marvelous (like the scabbard of Excalibur, which prevents its wearer from losing blood) often baffles reader expectation for its lack of efficacy: "When the critical moment arrives, it fails to work."[43] This critical insight seems to have been lost on the early reformers, however, who likely felt that failed magic was just as pernicious as a feigned miracle. For a Protestant, the problem was less whether the magic talisman worked but that people believed it or were distracted by it, regardless of its proper functioning.

Sidney's skepticism of narrative techniques that invoke the supernatural supersedes his loyalty to his literary sources and reinforces Protestant wari-

Three-headed dragon from Thomas Malory's *The story of the moste noble and worthy kynge Arthur*, A[2]6ᵛ. (Imprinted at London, by Wyllyam Copland, [1557]), HEH 60094, STC (2nd ed.), 804. Reproduced by permission of the Huntington Library, San Marino, California.

ness of such ridiculous chimeras, feigned or unfeigned. The *New Arcadia* does portray marvelous and wonderful events. However, the strain of wonder advocated by the *Arcadia* stems from either love or physical beauty—not from dragons whose tongues perform miracles.[44] Thus, while Pyrocles wonders at Philoclea's beauty, it bears no relation to the supernatural. Indeed, those who do connect beauty with the supernatural are derided for their mistake. For example, just after Strephon and Claius's dialogue, the sight of Pyrocles clinging to the vestiges of a sinking ship arouses readerly sympathy. Full of "admirable beautie," Pyrocles hangs to the mast decked in his shirt "wrought with blew silk & gold," wildly waving his sword about his head (B5ʳ). Musidorus, intent on rescue, convinces the fishermen who saved him to sail toward the sinking vessel. Just as the fishermen draw near enough to throw a rope, the sight of the majestic prince stupefies them: "Their simplicity bred such amazement, & their amazement such a superstition," that they sailed by him, "held up their hands," and "made their prayers," leaving Pyrocles stranded on the ship's mast (B5ʳ). The fisherman's simple amazement grows to "superstition" as they mistake Pyrocles for a deity, leading them to abandon their rescue mission. Because the reader knows that Pyrocles—all too human, if extraordinarily beautiful—faces drowning, the fishermen's superstition seems a tragically ignorant response.[45] The paralysis caused by their superstition confounds their ability to see the truth. Distracted by the wonder, they fail at the rescue.

This complicated portrayal of wonder—evoked by the mistaken belief in an appearance of a supernatural anomaly in the material world—epitomizes Sidney's wariness of the supernatural.[46] While Sidney criticizes those who, like the "superstitious" fishermen, mistake a wonder of the natural world for one that is supernatural, he more pointedly provides a direct indictment of the naive reception of the supernatural marvelous later in *Arcadia*, in the travestied romance begun by Mopsa in book 2. Mopsa, the doltish daughter of the shrewish Miso and the foolish shepherd Dametas, wins the drawing of straws (or cuts), thus earning the privilege to tell a story—much to Zelmane's (the disguised Pyrocles's) chagrin.

Her story within a story draws derision even as she begins to speak with rude gestures, "wiping her mouth, as there was good cause" (Y5^r). Her never-completed story deserves closer scrutiny than her listeners give, in part because it is original to the *New Arcadia*. Mopsa tells how a beautiful princess falls in love with a knight. Eluding the watch set by her parents, she steals forth from the castle by night with her chivalrous hero. As they journey together, "often all to-kissing one another," the knight tells her how he was "brought up among the water Nymphes" who had "bewitched him" (Y5^v). If she ever asks his name, he warns her, he will vanish. Of course, the beautiful princess cannot hold her tongue; she asks the fatal question and immediately her knight "vanished quite away" (Y5^v). Remorseful, desperate, and seeking remedy after five days and five nights of pining, the princess travels "over many a high hil & many many a deepe river" until she comes to an aunt's house (Y6^r). In pity, the aunt gives her a nut, telling her not to open it until she is in the greatest extremity. The princess continues on her journey and "never rested the evening, wher she went in the morning," until she reaches another aunt, who gives her a second nut (Y6^r). Mopsa's potentially endless version of romance, populated with a suffering knight, a desolate wandering lady, magic nuts, and a never-ending quest of desire, gets interrupted by Philoclea, who pleads: "good Mopsa at my request keepe this tale till my marriage-day" (Y6^r). As Mopsa's supernatural tale threatens to meander into increasingly repetitive, supernaturally marvelous, dilatory amplification—how many aunts and magic nuts might there be?—Sidney abruptly cuts the tale, almost in midsentence. We never learn what the magic nuts might contain because Philoclea's wedding day, perhaps intentionally, never arrives in the unfinished revision. Mopsa's version of romance establishes exactly what Sidney's is not.

Philoclea's impatient, rough interjection likely stems from the tale's homely rendition, which sounds like a debased version of courtly, chivalric romance brimming with an unquestioning belief in the supernatural marvelous.[47] Mopsa's interrupted tale—well stocked with wonder-working nymphs and talismanic nuts—opens Sidney's own narrative to romance's repertoire of supernatural elements. Yet Sidney dismisses the tale with the same derision its teller inspires in Philoclea, at once employing and rejecting the supernatural marvels in her romance. Following Philoclea's impatience, we as readers are led to regard the story with the same bemused condescension as the primary, aristocratic characters. Why should we wish to hear such a foolish tale told by a silly, credulous female narrator? Those uncracked nuts, I suggest, are symbolic of a larger pattern in the *Arcadia* itself, which steadfastly refuses to open a bag of old narrative magic tricks. By locating the few instances that hint at supernatural or magical intervention within the purview of less-than-credible characters, Sidney discredits such romance motifs as belonging to common, superstitious tales.

Sidney creates similar moments throughout the text where the supernatural might leak into the narrative, only to guard subsequently against its intrusion. As my opening section to this chapter argues, Sidney's mutant (and the truncated battle to slay him) calls attention to the narrative's *lack* of such creatures: no dragons, hippogriffs, or magic sea monsters patrol the *New Arcadia*. The only talismanic objects—Mopsa's nuts—remain uncracked. Just as Sidney criticizes the inclusion of such supernatural elements by Mopsa, he also actively reformulates potentially providential and supernatural moments from the *Old Arcadia*. To cite one example, as he revises, he supplements an incident where the sudden twinned attack of marauding wild beasts—a bear and a lion—could be interpreted as supernatural and shows it to be the work of a human. The *Old Arcadia* offers no explanation for their appearance, making their materialization from the woods resemble a providential omen sent to prove the disguised princes' mettle.[48] In his revision, Sidney pointedly provides a very human origin, telling how the ever-scheming Cecropia, sister-in-law to King Basilius, keeps these beasts caged and hungry for the purpose of unleashing them on the unsuspecting princesses so that her own son Amphialus might inherit the throne of Arcadia. Thus, what could be read as a providential omen or supernatural intervention turns out to be no more, and no less, than simple, malicious human, and female, manipulation.

All of these episodes debunk the supernatural motifs that so saturate Sidney's sources.[49] The reader sees the superstitious fishermen, "assuredly thinking it was some God," mistake a distressed man for a deity (B5^r); Mopsa's magical nuts inspire only derision from the noble characters; and Cecropia's machinations reveal the intrusion of two vicious beasts to be the work of human, not divine, intervention. Playing on generic expectations for romance's conventional deployment of supernaturally laden wonder, the text refocuses wonder toward the discovery of fraud. Sidney thus demystifies what seemed supernatural. As he does so, he redirects readerly pleasure away from the supernatural itself and toward the revelation of its mechanisms. Taken together, these narrative moments cumulatively undermine readers' belief in supernaturalism. By locating the supernatural impositions where he does, Sidney questions the validity of a supernatural marvelous and emphasizes the human agency—and indeed corruption—required to produce and to believe such wondrous-seeming effects. He insists romance can supply precedents to support the active remaking of what merits remembering, thereby offering one mode for salvaging what others had condemned to destruction.

By making the "superstitious" supernatural a literary conflict as well as a material one, Sidney diagnoses a set of conditions that become volatile after the Reformation for the reading of secular texts. I have considered how Sidney assiduously denies the credibility of either monsters or Mopsa's magic nuts, putting the monster into parentheses and interrupting her tale midsentence, a rhetorical coup that whitewashes offending aspects of romance. Yet Sidney's reformation, like the excised crucifix, appears halfhearted, or at least conflicted, in its zeal, providing only a partial reformation. Much of the "Catholic" romance remains. Other aspects of romance that had raised moralist hackles, its presentation of erotic "bold bawdry" in the entangled desires of its main characters and violent delight in "open manslaughter," figure large in Arcadian adventures.[50] Sidney's efforts at reform vividly illustrate my central contention that reform within English churches and texts frequently resulted in a strangely hybrid work, much, ironically, like Sidney's single monster: neither wholly reformed nor wholly Catholic. The fate of Mopsa's tale, moreover, proves prophetic for that of the *Arcadia*, which too will be interrupted midsentence, leaving an incomplete text, an unfinished monument to the English Reformation.

ARTHUR'S ANTIQUE HISTORY AND THE MATTER OF "JUST MEMORY" IN *THE FAERIE QUEENE*

In contrast to the lone monster so quickly dispatched by Pyrocles, or the fore-shortened length of Mopsa's tale of magic nuts, the heroes of Spenser's *Faerie Queene* frequently combat dragons, witches, sorcerers, and blatant monstrous beasts who look very similar to their counterparts in Catholic romances. Red-crosse's dragon looks quite like the one that fights Bevis of Hampton, and the witch Acrasia behaves much like Armida (from Tasso's Italian tale) or the be-witching Lindaraza (from the *Mirror of Knighthood*), to cite but two exam-ples. My focus here will be to study the baffling but crucial moments within Spenser's tale when the text erases rather than allegorizes its marvels. These textual gaps show that Spenser too mitigates the supernatural while trying to preserve memory. The cultural memory enshrined within romance stories, specifically within the figure and legends of Arthur, allegedly "full of Papist-rye," becomes a focal point of selective erasure within a text that in so many other respects follows the conventions of the marvelous romance.[51]

Throughout most of *The Faerie Queene*, rather than derogating the problem-atic marvelous, as Sidney does, Spenser, John King argues, transforms it by "adding layers of moral, religious and political allegory."[52] Spenser does so—he himself claims, in his letter to Sir Ralegh—where he defends his "darke con-ceit," to ward off "gealous opinions and misconstructions," thereby making allegory the mode of *The Faerie Queene*.[53] This ethos of allegorical plotting that *The Faerie Queene* develops throughout book 1 shares close intellectual ties with the emergence of a post-Reformation reading practice that, as Jennifer Summit observes, "aimed to separate (Protestant) 'plain truth' from (Catho-lic) 'feigned fable.'"[54]

My analysis focuses on episodes where I see Spenser's winnowing of Prot-estant truth from Catholic fable falter. In my reading, book 2 confronts the problem of exploiting the marvelous against the hazards it allegedly posed. In chapter 3, I analyze how book 2 addresses this problem by instructing its read-ers in controlling their passions and transforming their reading of "painted forg-eries." Much of book 2, then, concentrates on a reformation of reading practice, a process I address further in part II of this book; that reformation begins with an act of erasure in Alma's library, where this chapter focuses.

What happens in Alma's castle is relevant to our discussion of how Protes-tant authors dealt with the problematic marvelous in how it rewrites Arthurian legend. Arthur's life and legends, as symptomatic of romance, more generally serve as a touchstone to the paganism residual in Catholicism and the Catholicism residual in Reformed England. Catholics had worried that romance, and even Arthur, smacked of the pagan, but for the hotter sort of Protestant, such as N. Baxter, "the booke of Arthur's knights" was doubly denounced for its paganism and for its "being full of Papistrye," a sentiment that reiterates Ascham's earlier judgment of it as a story corrupted by England's papist past.[55] The prosecution of "Papistrye" might be dismissed as a simple substitution of one pejorative epithet for another, neither of which dimmed Arthur's popularity. But this substitution, like the replacement of images on the rood screens, was not an indifferent matter. Arthur was troubling because he represented a specifically "English" past, but he also held inextricable ties to Catholic narrative forms, in part because of the grudging propagation of his legend by generations of church clergy. For these reasons, his adoption by Edmund Spenser as the presiding hero of *The Faerie Queene* brings to life the issues at stake in creating a new kind of literary culture built on the foundations of the old, even more vividly than had Sidney's *Arcadia*, which offered new, rather than antique, heroes to its English readers. Spenser's romance thus interrogates and complicates England's relationship to its own history.

The presiding deus ex machina in all six books, Arthur saves the foundering knights and their respective virtues at critical moments of their adventures. In the earlier *Shepherd's Calendar*, E.K. glosses the April eclogue and condemns the propagation of Arthur's legend "not many yeares since" by "certain fine fablers and lowd lyers . . . who tell many an unlawfull leasing," a sly referent perhaps to the diatribes that condemned Arthur's stories for being too pagan and "full of papistrye."[56] Polemicist ire did little to dampen the Tudor vogue among chroniclers and others seeking favor from the monarchy for tracing genealogy back to Arthur, but Spenser takes pains to separate the "unlawfull leasing" of this antique history, in ways that result in a story that shares more with those in *Acts and Monuments* than with those in Caxton's Malory.[57] For Arthur's history, as we read in *Briton moniments*, noticeably evacuates the marvelous, a narrative erasure whose absence would have been remarkable. Although Malory's *Arthur* appeared in only one reprint edition, published by Thomas East (1582), during Elizabeth's reign, its version of *The storye of the most noble and worthy kynge Arthur* kept the old tale current for "howe that the quest of the Sancgreall was begoun" along with the "mervaylous adventures" of Arthur's knights, Lancelot and Tristram.[58]

The proem introduces the central crux for a post-Reformation author wishing to revive the "Mervaylous adventures" of Arthur's legends:

Right well I wote most mighty Soveraine,
That all this famous antique history,
Of some th'aboundance of an ydle braine
Will judged be, and painted forgery,
Rather then matter of just memory. (2.0.1)[59]

These opening lines, and the book they introduce, pivot on a persistent problem: whether post-Reformation writers can exorcise romance, with its story matter steeped in a medieval, Catholic tradition. The proem's narrator tries to preempt an indictment, only to find that he names what he most fears. Seeking to deny that the poem originated from a fecund "ydle braine," the first verse underscores the link between this book and condemned books, those "painted" forgeries, by adapting the terms and language of familiar Protestant polemic against famous antique "histories." Calling the poem an "antique history," rather than "an historicall fiction" (as Spenser will do in his letter to Walter Ralegh), provocatively raises the tensions between the literary form of romance and its projected Protestant sovereign and audience.[60]

Even more strongly than Philip Sidney's *Arcadia*, Spenser's proem makes explicit to us that the romance bore a privileged relation to the past, preserving and remembering a culture ruptured by the English Reformation, which transformed both stories and how they were read. The adjective "antique" commits the poem to a backward gaze; literally, it invokes memory of former times, of olden days. Gower, the later choral figure who introduces the play *Pericles* as a "song that old was sung," will herald the play's affinity with the "ancient" medieval world he represents, just as Spenser here invites comparison to old tales of medieval chivalric romance.[61] For "stories of old times," George Puttenham tells his English readers in *The Arte of English Poesy*, are those of Bevis, Guy, Arthur, and other popular romance heroes—stories, Spenser's audience would know, that consistently made the Protestant index of dangerous books.[62] Aurally, moreover, the adjective anticipates what Spenser wishes to deny, that what follows is a "painted forgery." For "antique" might also be spelled, as well as pronounced, "antic," a word that, in the Renaissance, also connoted the grotesque and the fabulous. Elsewhere in Spenser, "antique," "antic," or "antick" often bears troubling overtones of overly "ornamental representation, purposely monstrous, caricatured, or incongruous" imagery, as it does, for instance, in Mammon's garments ("Woven with antickes and wyld ymagery") or the arras in Busirane's hall (2.7.4, 3.11.51).[63]

Ostensibly, Spenser invokes the past in order to *distinguish* his heroes from their forefathers. Much, however, rides on the implied differentiation; while *The Faerie Queene* might look like—and even be judged as—one of those old painted romances, it is *not*, insists the proem. The particular language of the proem's opening lines sketches an argumentative arc that engages much more than an anxiety of influence: "ydle," "just," and "memory" rally the language of abuse. The word "idle" held a special place in Protestant attacks on romance writers, often followed closely by the pejorative epithet "abbie-lubber": that is, a lazy monk, a term of opprobrium frequently invoked by polemicists following the Reformation.[64] As the modifiers tinged by Reformation debates pile up in the proem's opening stanza—"antique," "ydle," and "painted"—a favorable judgment feels less assured. Can an "antique history" replete with marvelous "antick" matter provide material for what the proem insists is "matter of just memory"?

The proem's concern that readers judge it to be "matter of just memory," indeed reckons with William Tyndale's warning that allegory's beguiling qualities could persuade to a false matter as readily as a true. "Beware of allegoryes," William Tyndale writes, "for there is not a more handsome or apte a thing to begile withall than allegory, not a more sotle and pestilent thing in the world to persuade a false mater than an allegorye"; yet if marshaled rightly, Tyndale continues, "there is not a better vehementer or myghtyer thing to make a man understand with all then an allegorye."[65] Allegory might usefully turn a three-headed dragon into a "serpent fell" and symbol for the devil, but its success depended on a reading process capable of such a transformation.

The proleptic struggle engaged by the proem, to balance the power of "painted forgery" over "matter of just memory," receives explicit treatment in the final cantos of book 2 when the knights Arthur and Guyon read two books of "their countreys auncestry" in the house of Alma, "burning both with feruent fire" (2.9.60). The scene takes place in the room of Eumnestes (Good Memory), and their reading is usually understood as their engagement with a national and mythical past. But Spenser takes pains to challenge this single, memorial interpretation. Arthur and Guyon make their way through not one but three rooms, each of which holds a sage: Phantastes (Imagination), who "could things to come foresee"; the unnamed Reason who "could of thinges present best aduize"; and Eumnestes (Memory), who "things past could keepe in memoree" (2.9.49). The three-room turret of Alma's castle follows a standard period model of the mind, with memory always located in the hindermost part.[66] Spenser, however, manipulates this familiar conceit. More than mere allegories for the mind, the three sages anatomize a hierarchy of literary kind: in their chambers, we see the competing generic impulses that haunt the proem mapped onto a corporeal model that locates generic effects quite literally deep within the mind.

Phantastes's "dispainted" room buzzes with the stuff of romance: centaurs, lovers, visions, "all that fained is" (2.9.50). The "idle thoughtes and fantasies" dismantled by Sidney in the *Arcadia* and anxiously banished from the proem flourish here (2.9.51). By contrast, in Eumnestes's library, where things past are kept in "memoree," "old records from auncient times" are "hangd about" recalling the "plain matter" Protestant's favored for "just memory" (2.9.50, 49, 57). Between them, an unnamed figure, Reason "did them meditate" to render a mind—and poem—"right wise, and wondrous sage," providing the very balancing act Spenser's own poem attempts to achieve (2.9.54).[67] Most resonantly for our purposes, it is here in Alma's brain turret that Spenser carefully reconstructs Arthurian legend through the reading of "antique histories." Readers of book 2 have seen it as deeply engaged with the Reformation as with the matter of Britain—matter integral to the struggle to change a literary form that was instrumental in transmitting communal memory.

Eumnestes's library houses the stories of "just memory." It represents a crucial locus for the processes of remembering and forgetting in order to arrive at the truth of British history, that, according to Jennifer Summit, husks "fictitious elements" from "truthful ones."[68] This process, she argues, recalls the antiquarian work of Leland and Bale who too sought to erect, through a process of selection and distinction, a memory of England's past stripped of its more incredible, fabulous, and Catholic, aspects. Summit's focus is historical, but I believe this process to be a literary one as well. Arthur and Guyon, after all, confront their lineage in a scene of reading that conscientiously appropriates their histories, but it also transforms their generic habitat of romance. One effect of this recovery is the reclamation of Arthur's romance along lines that accommodate a Protestant sense of what was a worthy object for memory and a fit subject for romance.

Just as Sidney highlights how he transforms the marvelous motifs of his continental and classical sources, Spenser calls attention to his departure from Ariosto's genealogical chronicle, told in *Orlando Furioso*'s third book. In *Orlando Furioso*, Merlin's follower, the enchantress Melyssa, conjures a procession of sprites. The sprites parade before Bradamante, foreshadowing the illustrious line she will bear that culminates in Ariosto's patron, the Duke d'Este.[69] The conjured spirits who tell their story recall the shades from the underworld in Virgil's *Aeneid* who shadow forth Aeneas's descendants to him. Notably, both of these literary antecedents feature supernatural means—conjuration and a journey to the underworld—to relate a prophetic genealogical history. Spenser, however, frames the story in a manner more reminiscent of Philip Sidney or John Foxe than his continental or classical models, as he eschews any magical narration. Instead, he foregrounds the process of reading. The book itself may be supernatural, but Arthur is not.

In Eumnestes's library, "there chaunced to the Princes hand to rize / An auncient booke, hight *Briton moniments*" (2.9.59). In similar manner, "*Sir Guyon* chaunst eke on another booke / That hight, *Antiquitee of Faery* lond" (2.9.60). Spenser's verb choice, in this sequence "chaunced," is canny. "Chance" might appear to be a version of a pagan Fortune; however, as a verb it also identifies a central strand of religiosity among Protestants. In her study *Providence in Early Modern England*, Alexandra Walsham, for example, quotes a Protestant divine, Andreas Geradus, who writes, what "we call chaunce" is "nothing els, then that whose course and cause is hidden from our eyes."[70] Harry Berger too sees "chaunce" as suggestive that it is God's will, as opposed to magic, that guides Arthur and Guyon to their chronicles.[71] Chance, moreover, guides the two knights to *read*, not simply to look. Even the more prophetic second genealogical chronicle of book 3, the parade of Britomart's illustrious line, begins with Glauce asking that Merlin "read" what he sees (3.3.25). Neither Britomart nor Glauce view the progeny that Merlin foretells. Merlin narrates them. Likewise, Guyon and Arthur read their ancestry from the books in Eumnestes's library. Such nonmagical revelation shears away the fabulousness of Virgil's and Ariosto's presentation, privileging providential "chaunce" and the act of reading over supernatural intrusion.

Spenser culled his material from a large repertoire of Arthurian genealogy. From Malory, Geoffrey of Monmouth, Hardyng, Holinshed, and Stow to the *Mirror for Magistrates* among others, Spenser actively reshapes Arthur's memory.[72] As he rehearses the genealogy, Spenser, stanza by stanza, elides or rationalizes the more marvelous moments; again and again the account valorizes rulers who worked with their human skills to govern. "Incidents in Geoffrey which might tend to distract the attention—such, for instance, as the stories of Rowena, the founding of Armorica, the death of the eleven thousand virgins," Carrie Anna Harper notes, "are rigorously excluded."[73] Likewise, *Briton moni-*

ments depicts failure as resulting from moral (and mortal) weakness, not from malicious or superior magic—or even interceding miracle.

Monsters, for instance, are as scarce here as they are in *Arcadia*. According to various chronicle sources, the ancient king Morindus died while battling a fierce sea monster. Holinshed records how "at length this bloudie prince heard of a monster that was come a land out of the Irish sea, with the which when he would néeds fight, he was deuoured of the same."[74] Similarly, in the *Ânnales*, John Stow records how "out of the Irishe Seas in hys time came for the a wonderfull monster, whyche destroyed muche people: whereof the king hearing, woulde of his valiaunt courage, needs fight with it, by whom he was clean devoured when he had raigned eight yeares."[75] The *Mirour* too records "Morindus . . . at last was devoured vy a monster."[76] Morindus's gruesome death in the scaly monster's belly, as he vainly tries to stab it with his dagger, makes for a gripping story. Yet Spenser only recounts how Morindus's increasingly "cruell rancour dim'd his valorous / And mightie deedes" (2.10.43). Here the monster is inferred to be a king grown tyrannous, thereby emphasizing human failure rather than supernatural combat when it eclipses the duel to death with a "wonderfull monster."

Even more pointedly, the Stonehenge of Spenser's chronicle holds little magical lore. Geoffrey of Monmouth's legendary account recorded how Merlin's magic transported Stonehenge (the Giant's Dance) from Ireland. Yet in Arthur's book, Stonehenge represents only "dolefull monuments" to "th'eternall marks of treason" committed by Hengist (2.10.66). Like Morindus, Stonehenge is remembered not for its marvelous properties, but for its lasting testimony to human error. Associating this monument with infamy rather than great feats of magic, Spenser derogates the most famous of all British monuments.[77] Similarly, the marvelous properties of the "boyling Bathes" "Which seeth with secret fire eternally" created through the "wondrous faculty" of Bladud, who practices "artes" learned abroad, are downgraded in Spenser from marvel to moral lesson (2.10.26). While credit for the "secret fire" goes to Bladud's "sweet science," such dabbling, we learn by the stanza's end, inspire in him "fond mischief" to "excell / The reach of men," resulting in a spectacular Icarus-like fall when his man-made wings fail him. The culminating alexandrine follows the *Mirour for Magistrates*, which recounts how Bladud's shade sorrowfully informs Morpheus how "Magicke . . . seemid sweete, / And full of wonders" so that "For many feates I thought it meete, / And pleasaunt for a Prince to use."[78] The stanza's careful framing of magic, "full of wonders," as ending in "fond mischief" drains Bladud's legend of its wonder, celebration, and excitement, directing reader attention instead to the mortal peril of play-ing with magic.

Spenser's culling of Arthur's marvelous past is manifested most sharply in his shaping of the Holy Grail legend, a touchstone in the polemic that sought to eradicate the "fables and lies" of Catholic legend from English memory (2.10.53). N. Baxter, a voice for reformed religious sentiment, damns the "vile and blasphemous, or at least of prophane and frivolus bookes, suche as are that infamous legend of K. Arthur . . . with the vile and stinking story of the Sangre-all."[79] For Baxter, Arthur's legend is synonymous with the "vile and stinking story" of the grail; they are both "frivolus," "prophane," and "blasphemous."[80] Yet the Grail legend held crucial details for establishing a link between the early Christian church and that of England, as it introduces Joseph of Ari-mathea, an important early church figure, into English history.[81] The "matter of just memory" in the Grail legend called for a salvage effort, one that sys-tematically eradicated its more "blasphemous" elements in order to preserve its truth.

After rehearsing how Coyll and good Lucius "first receiued Christianity," the stanza doubles back in time to recount how "long before that day," Joseph of Arimathea brought the "holy grayle" to England (2.9.53). Qualifying the statement with a parenthetical "they say," Spenser leaves his reader to judge the veracity of this famous incident told in medieval romance (Malory re-ported that Joseph carried it to Glastonbury Abbey).[82] The inclusion of this link, however, made through potentially corrupt Catholic sources, allows Spenser to trace a direct line from the ancient church through Joseph who "preacht the truth" to England, thus cleverly bypassing the corruption of the Roman church.[83] The stanza's positioning of Joseph of Arimathea performs a Foxean rhetorical coup: just as Foxe's *Acts and Monuments* sought to create a spiritual lineage between Protestantism and the early church martyrs, *Briton moniments* traces an alternative spiritual genealogy for the "sacred pledge of Christes Euangely" that reaches beyond the Catholic golden legends to the early church in order to reclaim that history for a Protestant ancestry.[84]

In the 1563 edition preface "Ad Lectorem," Foxe attacks *The Golden Legend* specifically for containing lying "fabellis."[85] Foxe's language anticipates Na-thaniel Baxter's and E.K.'s concern for the "fine fabling" enshrouding Arthur's past:

I haue oft tymes before complained that þe stories of Sainctes haue bene poudered and sawsed wyth dyuers vntrue additions and fabulous inuentions of

men, who eyther of a superstitious deuotion, or of a subtill practise, haue so mingle mangled their stories & liues, þᵗ almost nothyng remaineth in them simple
& vncorrupte . . . wher in, few legends there be, able to abyde the touche of history, if they were truely tryed.⁸⁶

Foxe's equation of history, "poudered and sawsed" with the "fabulous in-
ventions" of men of "superstitious devotion," condemns the Catholic versions of English saints and heroes in order to correct them with one "simple &
vncorrupte"—one suited for a reader rightfully more concerned with constancy "truly tryed" than with marvels.⁸⁷ Stripping away the "fabulous," *Briton
moniments* orders the stanza to emphasize how Joseph of Arimathea should
be remembered: not for his bringing of the Grail—that most sacred and holy
relic in Catholic medieval romance—but for his preaching of the truth.⁸⁸ By
emphasizing Joseph's preaching, Spenser downplays the talismanic and relic-
like significance of the Holy Grail. Arthur's *Briton moniments* erects a new
reading of the past, one that seeks, like Foxe's *Acts and Monuments*, to reclaim a
popular English mode of storytelling by sanitizing it of miracles, abbeys, and
Catholic "superstitious devotion[s]." Arthur, as a new kind of Protestant
reader, responds appropriately with a "wonder of antiquity" that grows from
learning of the "royall offspring of his native land," rather than a wonder generated by encounters with supernatural marvels (2.10.68). Neither dragons,
secret arts, nor talismanic relics are what leave him "quite rauisht with delight" (2.10.68).

The seventy-odd "dread" cantos of Arthur's history, however, seldom leave
students of Spenser as ravished with delight as Arthur himself appears to be.
Herein, I think, lies the challenge to Protestant authors seeking to reform—
rather than incinerate—the romance. Spenser's tripartite model for the mind
suggests why completely stripping the romance of its marvelous motifs might
not be the most efficacious way to redefine a genre. As even the apoplectic Baxter knew all to well, readers are less likely to remember—or buy—tales with
less sauce and powder. Arthur's ancestors prove difficult to keep in memory.
Described by successive verbs that emphasize their impermanence, they rise
and succeed and are deposed, restored, overthrown, chosen, and dethroned
in an almost indistinguishable cycle. It seems a fit volume for Eumnestes's library filled with "canker holes," which appears to be in perilous desuetude.⁸⁹
Though he is described as a "man of infinite remembraunce" with his "immortall scrine," his catalog of biblical, classical, and mythical history omits the
titles that might make the Protestant index. Yet his "infinite remembraunce"

enfeebles rather than invigorates him, and he totters about nearly buried by his "worme-eaten" records (2.9.57). Eumnestes, "halfe blind/And all decrepit in his feeble corse," appears perilously fragile (2.9.55). More is amiss with Eumnestes than the books "laid amis" that his aid Anamnestes must seek. Books are "oft" "lost," and a disturbing undertone creeps into the verbs that describe his almost fretful "tossing and turning" of his books "withouten end" (2.9.58). Such "tossing and turning" of books unsettlingly recalls the tossing and turning of characters through Arthur's stripped and cored history, lost to all but the antiquarian.

Guyon's *Antiquitie of Faerie Lond*, with its recuperation of fabulous material excluded from Arthur's history, sharply contrasts with the chamber that preserves it and throws into relief the figure from the forecourt of Alma's tower Phantastes, whose name alone conjures precisely the dangerous fabrications of romance believed to so successfully transmit Catholic habits of imagination: "deuises, dreames, opinions unsound,/Shewes, visions, sooth-sayes, and prophesies"; in other words, "all that fained is, as leasings, tales, and lies" (2.9.51). Directly translating the proem's anxieties about being judged "th'aboundance of an idle braine," Phantastes's "infinite shapes" "dispersed thin" call to mind George Puttenham's caution regarding the "phantasticall." The fantastic is necessary because "the inventive parte of the mynde is so much holpen as without it no man could devise any new or rare thing," but "phantasticall" visions need attentive restraint: for otherwise "it breede[s] Chimereres & monsters in mans imagination."[90] The alluring—yet false— visions and tales emanating from the first chamber that "encombred all mens eares and eyes," illustrate the allure but also the dangerous potential of the "phantasticall" and, by extension, of romance itself (2.9.51). It overloads sensory input, leaving little room in the reader's mind for judgment. Just as Archimago's false visions deceive Redcrosse, Phantastes's "devices," "shews," and "visions" share the worst characteristics of the discredited past in that they can deceive readers, even those who think that they pursue virtue. They are the beguiling allegories warned against by Tyndale.

Guyon's *Antiquitie of Faerie Lond*, as critics like Andrew King have noted, retells a romance-inspired genealogy, one that, like Geoffrey of Monmouth's chronicle, commingles a "phantasticall" legend with British history. It follows a mythical lineage of elves and "Faeryes" across an exotic landscape stretching from the East to the New World to the seat of Gloriana. Giants and magically enhanced "golden" walls and bridges of "bras" that endure in "renowmed fame" conjure up the fabulous devices of supernatural forces and interven-

tions (2.10.72, 73).[91] Guyon's book thus fully reengages the supernatural marvelous. The return to a marvelous narrative mode suggests that while one
might winnow what Foxe terms the "simple & uncorrupte" from the fantastic, the latter cannot be completely erased. *Antiquitie of Faerie Lond* tells the
stories that E.K., when glossing the June eclogue in *The Shepherd's Calendar*,
complainingly notes "sticketh very religiously in the myndes."[92] E.K.'s grudging admission encapsulates the Protestant dilemma: the "painted forgery" of
Phantastes's visions stick "religiously" in the memory, while the unembel-
lished "simple & uncorrupte" history risks the canker holes of forgetfulness.

The two books read by the knights represent the extremes residing at either
end of Alma's brain-like turret: at one the imagination, the "phantasticall,"
false visions and shows, qualities linked to Catholic modes of storytelling; at
the other, a library depowdered and desauced, decidedly antimonastic and
Protestant. Anatomizing them in Alma's harmonious castle, Spenser acknowledges the desideratum of each and proposes they be mediated by "goodly reason," the unnamed middle sage, who draws the admiration of both knights
and, who, significantly, "his disciples both desyrd to bee" (2.9.54). Alma's tripartite model refuses the binary choice between "merry books" or "painted
forgeries" and "just matter" as proposed by many Protestant reformers. However, its success depends upon that middle sage who "did them meditate" and
separate simple and true from the fantastic and the false (2.9.54). That labor,
the final cantos of book 2 will suggest, proves unsustainable. As I argue in
chapter 3, Guyon's desecration of the bower of bliss dims the fantasy that romance might be reformed without being little more than a "ruined choir" or
scorched remainder.

MARVEL-LESS ROMANCE AND PATCHWORK REFORM

The 1616 Bible, which encloses its compilation of Anglican religious texts
within a suggestively mutilated binding, that opened my chapter also closes it.
For while one might ask what a *Book of Common Prayer*, a Bible, and a Psalter
had to do with romance, all constituted the most popular and perhaps familiar
of texts to an early modern reader. Each of these texts was changed, rewritten,
repackaged, and altered by the various reform movements across the sixteenth
century. Moreover, these foundational religious texts were never far afield
from Sidney or Spenser. Sidney had a manifest interest in translating Psalms
himself, and the genealogy of scriptural figures made by John Speed reflects
Spenser's own keen attention to genealogical trees in his recounting of Ar-

thur's story. Finally, I have been arguing that Sidney's and Spenser's texts mount an exploration of how diegetic motifs interact with religious identity, thus enacting within a literary field what Julie Crawford has called a "marvelous" Protestantism, one which takes much from the old faith but seeks to reframe its effects.[93] Their consequent appropriations and transformations of romance significantly fracture and reinvent a literary form, resulting in hybrid works almost unrecognizable as romance. The singularity of their texts, with their enigmatic ellipses and foreclosed tales, document the haphazard, unfinished, and recursive nature of reform in England as baldly as the effaced crucifix haunting the cover for the Church of England's religious texts.

For although Sidney's and Spenser's texts grapple with reforming the marvelous within romance, most printed and published late sixteenth-century romances continued blithely to exploit marvelous machinery. The Famous Historie of Chinon of England (1597), for instance, tells of adventures concerning the "Knights of King Arthurs round Table" (title page). The element of magic and marvel nearly overwhelms any other narrative development or concern. Likewise, Emanuel Ford's numerous romances, including Parismenos (1599) and Parismus (1598), delight in enchanted castles, golden towers, monsters, and fair sorceresses and portray a landscape dotted by Catholic-seeming houses such as Saint Austin's Chappell.[94] Only one late sixteenth-century romance exhibits a similar concern for the marvelous. Pheander the Mayden Knight (1595) maintains the ideal of chastity and eschews any machinery of enchantment or marvel, and its debt to Sidney's romance is marked.

Thus, in one reading, Sidney's and Spenser's efforts to reform romance do little to transform the actual field of early modern English romance. Yet, from another perspective, their critical impact cannot be underestimated. Their texts shifted reception of the genre, making an acceptable canon out of what had been a blacklist or index.[95] For instance, in a section entitled "A choice is to be had in reading books" from Palladis Tamia (1598, the second installment for a series of literary commonplace books), Francis Meres lists several romance titles "accordingly to be censored."[96] Twenty-four titles follow, listing the usual catalog of blacklisted romances: Bevis of Hampton, Guy of Warwick, Arthur of the Round Table, as well as the recent Famous Historie of the Seven Champions of Christendom (1596) by Richard Johnson. Sidney, on the other hand, receives only praise for his "immortall Poem, The Countesse of Pembrookes Arcadia," and Spenser's depiction of Elizabeth in The Faerie Queene is likened to Homer's Achilles.[97] In Apology of the Power and Providence of God (1627), George Hakewill, a staunch conformist Calvinist, cites Sidney's Arcadia as proof that England excels all previous eras in cultural achievement. Implicit in his narrative is the triumph of the Reformation over the dark ages of superstition and what he terms the days of the "antichrist."[98]

Some polemicists persisted in thinking the romances of Sidney and Spenser more immoral than immortal, as did John King, who, in his sermons on Jonas (1597), fulminated that "frivolous stories" such as the "Arcadia, & the Faery Queen, and Orlando Furioso" constitute the preferred reading for "wanton students of our time."[99] In another instance, Wye Saltonstall's portrait of a maid in *Picturae Loquentes* imagines how wanton reading may breed wanton readers.[100] Saltonstall describes how a maid "reades now loves histories as *Amadis de Gaule* and the *Arcadia*, & in them courts the shadow of love till she know the substance."[101] It should be kept in mind, however, that Saltonstall's verbal portraits are satirical, and the satire might just as well be mocking the sensibility of polemical readers like John King. They ape an exaggerated point of view, one, perhaps, that mocks the belief that reading romance might so influence action—as much as expressing true pious concern. More to the point might be the puritan minister Samuel Torshell, whose warning seemingly lumps the *Arcadia* among *"bad bookes"* that belong on a pyre, not on a shelf.[102] Even Torshell, however, makes a distinction between "your *Amadis of Gaul*, your *Palmerins*, your *Mirrour of Knighthood*," texts he categorically condemns, and "your deare *Arcadia*," which he suggests might be read in moderation, as long as it does not "steale away your hearts" from scripture.[103]

One final example will serve to illustrate how Sidney's and Spenser's romances were often an exception to a rule of condemnation. Mathias Prideaux dedicated his *An Easy and Compendious Introduction for Reading All Sorts of Histories* as a guide to education for the "towardly young sons" of the Reynells.[104] Among other things, the manual classified books. He categorizes "romances, or the bastard sort of histories," not by "uses" but by "abuses": (1) "Rude" (*Huon of Burdeaux, Valentine and Orson, Arthur of Little Brittaine*); (2) "Endlesse" (*Amadis de Gaule, Palmerin, Mirrour of Knighthood*); (3) "Depraved"; and (4) "Superstitious" (*John Capgrave*).[105] At the list's end, Prideaux concedes that some romances may constitute worthwhile reading and includes a fifth category: "Morall." In this new category, he lists "Spensers *Fairy Queene*, Sir *Philip Sydnies Arcadia*, with other pieces of the like straine may passe with singular commendations for morall *Romances*."[106] Categorizing Sidney's and Spenser's romances as "morall," Prideaux vindicates their place in a child's reading.

For the modern reader of Sidney or Spenser, who is likely to be a scholar, this image of a boy or an eager young woman reading these "morall" romances may be rather amusing. Such a child might be drawn to monsters, but in Sidney's curious version, he would hardly find the typical creature of romance, nor would he find the Arthur of old legend in Spenser's tale. Pruning and grafting "memes" drawn from multiple pagan and Catholic sources reveals just enough of the expected motifs to enable the educated reader to recognize the old motif and thus to pay attention to its reformation. In this way, we can see how "the delight of tales" might move readers "to do nobly" by setting before their eyes "the beautie of vertue" without reliance on the so-called lying wonders, or what Prideaux called the "miracle mongers" feared by Protestants (S2^r).[107] They keep the seductive appeal of romance, transmitting its glamour and excitement while making it useful for a new religious context. They thereby convert what more apoplectic polemicists believed only the flames could reform. In so doing, they offer a dramatic illustration of this chapter's central argument: that in the contentious post-Reformation period, the romance attained a new cultural significance, not as a passive genre for the preservation of and nostalgia for the past, but as a site where the past was actively reshaped through diegetic modes. Their texts used old forms to express new content and in turn illuminated the cultural continuities and discontinuities— the hybridity—eroding the ostensible historical and confessional divisions created by the Reformation.

While the reception history of these two romances arguably exonerates them from the slur of an "abbie-lubbing" past, the texts themselves reveal less optimism. In Sidney's dedicatory letter to the Countess of Pembroke, his sister, he uses a telling word. The *Arcadia*, he writes, had to be "delivered" because its "many fancies" otherwise "would haue growen a monster."[108] The letter's language suggests that the *New Arcadia* might be, inadvertently, the monster that the tale itself excised. Sidney's hybrid, simile monster may be a stand-in for Sidney's own textual creation, creating a monster while wanting there not to be one. The author of *The Faerie Queene* too will find it increasingly more difficult to control the allegories its monsters represent. When the most fatal monster, the Blatant Beast, eludes capture in book 6, he takes tales of scandal out into the world despite the best intentions of the Faerie Queene's knights. The textual blotting enacted in Sidney's monster simile and Arthur's "uncorrupt" history as recalled in Eumnestes's library provides us a glimpse into a literary form split in its loyalties, regardless of the ostensible imposition of a new religious ideology. If the marvelous in romance fostered a memory for the past, the works of Sidney and Spenser reveal that its tenacity may be the condition for remembering.

CHAPTER TWO

Saint or Martyr?

Reforming the Romance Heroine in the
New Arcadia *and* Pericles

The Champions without more words disrobing themseues from their Pilgrims attyre, euerie one selected foorth an armor fitting to their portely bodyes, and in steed of their Ebone staues tipt with siluer, they welded in their hands the steeled blades, and their feete that had wont to indure a painefull pilgrimage vpon the bare ground, were now redy prest to mount the golden stirrup.[1]

In the extract above taken from *The Seven Champions of Christendom* (1596), Richard Johnson's champions transform from holy pilgrim to knight, exchanging "Ebone staues" for "steeled blades," shedding holy robes for steely armor. The quick "redy prest" easy transformation of pilgrims to champions provides a useful departure point for understanding the troubling fungibility between hagiography and romance in early modern England. Catering to an eager readership, Johnson exploits rather than condemns such a conjuncture of genre. He dubs Saint George the English hero (from Coventry), leader to an international band of Christian saints, the titular "champions of Christendom" who "mount the golden stirrup" and perform knightly deeds.[2] Thus, while the Protestant divine Edward Dering viewed the conflation of Catholic saints' lives— which "so defiled" the festivals and "high holydaies"—and the tales of romance as part of a popish plot to "bewitch" English believers into "superstition," polemicists were not alone in making use of the analogy.[3] This chapter takes as its focus texts that confront the hybrid aspects of "Catholic" romance inspired by the lives of saints. Dering's verb choice "bewitched," with its feminine connotation, raises a second related thread in this chapter's focus: women as proxy for the "superstitious" and Catholic dimensions of romance.[4]

The stories I consider in the following pages are ostensibly romances, but their texts repeatedly crisscross saintly and knightly motifs. In chapter 1, I show how the cloistered heritage—and its consequent adjectival relationship of the "fabulous" or the supernatural marvelous—was a source of tension for romance authors after the Reformation. I demonstrate in what follows how that same vexed history could also be mined for a new spiritual benefit. Structuring my investigation will be the ambiguity between women, as dangerously efficacious carriers of the Catholic past manifested in their sorcerous, frequently fraudulent power to perform marvelous feats, and the powerfully redemptive figure of the female saint, who was also marked by supernaturally miraculous motifs.

Although Johnson's saintly champions seem untroubled by their dual identities, Edmund Spenser's Duessa vividly personifies the problem of the reciprocity of the feminine, the false church, and romance women bruited about after the Reformation.[5] "The author," the transmogrified Fradubio of Spenser's *Faerie Queene* moans, "of all my smarts,/Is one Duessa a false sorceresse,/That many errant knights hath broght to wretchednesse" (1.2.34).[6] As a "false sorceresse," she doubles as the Whore of Babylon, who for Protestants symbolized Catholicism. She seduces the Redcrosse Knight away from Una, the true reformed church, and takes him far into the forest of romance, Error's woods. The struggle between these two female characters emblematizes a larger pattern of early modern romance, in which male authors sought to reform the romance of its Catholic taint by reforming its women, in this case by transforming Duessa into Una.

Especially attentive to their female heroines, Philip Sidney's *New Arcadia* and the play *Pericles* reveal how the persistence of hagiography (specifically that of the virgin saint), as troublesome kin to romance, offers these writers a charged template for a literary and gendered recuperation. The princesses' trials, especially in the most thoroughly overhauled third book of the *Arcadia*, elevate women to paragons of virtue, nearly eclipsing masculine heroics. Their martyr-like suffering throws into stark relief Sidney's reformulation elsewhere of supernatural marvels along the lines of Protestant belief. Like Sidney's *Arcadia*, *Pericles* stages a daughter as the crucial agent of a narrative—and generic—redemption; Marina works rather than prays her way out of the brothel, redirecting the miraculous (and hagiographic) motifs of romance toward a less supernatural wonder grounded in a very human constancy. She, like Pamela and Philoclea, labors with words and relies on a rhetorical dexterity for preservation rather than any Egyptian-like healer, miraculous lightning bolt, or other deus ex machina. Borrowed from the iconography of hagiography, these hero-ines, like the new model virgin martyrs of John Foxe's Protestant martyrology, become the star agents of a reformation aimed at reinvigorating the romance through the establishment of a model female piety predicated on a distinctly Protestant sensibility.

My argument in this chapter recovers the continuities between forms of ro-mance often separated from one another in critical discourse: prose fiction and the dramatic romances of Shakespeare's late plays. I do so in order to fore-ground overlapping thematic and narrative concerns.[7] But the texts them-selves also invite formal continuities. The narrative quality of *Pericles* is an oft-noted stylistic feature, and Sidney's *New Arcadia* stages dramatic moments, especially in the final book. Cecropia affords a further link: she becomes a stage director in the extended captivity episode, making Sidney's third book directly concerned with issues of theatricality and staging. Finally, both texts con-scientiously transform the romance seductress into a pious heroine by draw-ing from the sedimentary model of the Catholic virgin saint. Their examples make it possible to see how, in Reformation England, the "stories of old time" were simultaneously sites of castigation and emulation, across the literary spectrum. I conclude by suggesting that while these two works posit a genera-tional change for generic transformation, their palimpsest threatens to un-ravel the denouement of each story, thus complicating any narrative of trium-phant reform.

SAINTLY CHAMPIONS AND VIRGIN MARTYRS IN POST-REFORMATION ENGLAND

Johnson's saintly champion George keeps company with other early modern hybrid heroes. Spenser's Redcrosse Knight, for example, is revealed to be none other than Saint George. These early modern knightly saints follow medieval tradition, for after all, Malory's *Le Morte Darthur* concludes with Guinevere becoming a nun and Lancelot expiring piously in *odor sanctorum*, essentially becoming a saint. Woodcut illustrations visually reinforce the ready textual crossover. In William Copland's 1555 imprinting of *The hystory of the two valyaunte brethren Valentyne and Orson sonnes unto the Emperor of Grece*, we find one of the text's eponymous heroes, the "meruayllous" Orson, pictured as "an hermyte in a great wodde."[8] The image depicts Orson habited in monk's robes, his head shadowed by a double nimbus, holding in his right hand what might well be an "Ebone staue" and in his six-fingered left hand a rosary. The woodcut adorned every edition of the romance that Copland reprinted (1555, 1565). Cataloged by Ruth Luborsky and Elizabeth Ingram as the "monastic saint," the representation visually testifies to the ready hybridity between a Christian knight and a Catholic saint, as Orson, here represented, transforms in the opposite direction from Johnson's knights, doffing armor for holy "hermyte" weeds.[9] The woodcut's material history further illustrates the composite nature of hagiography and romance texts. It appeared as early as 1506, accompanying the *Contemplacyons* of Richard Rolle, the hermit of Hampole, and in 1519, it featured as the cover image of Wynkyn de Worde's edition.[10] The material recycling of this image, to fit both a saintly narrative and a popular romance, raises the question, What exactly was the English perspective on celebrating and recounting the lives of the saints post-Reformation?

"The Romish Doctrine concerning Purgatory, Pardons, Worshipping and Adoration, as well of Images as of Relics, and also Invocation of Saints," the Thirty-Nine Articles of 1564 reads, "is a fond thing, vainly invented, and grounded upon no warranty of Scripture, but rather repugnant to the Word of God."[11] The 1564 wording captures official policy that grew out of the actions of Henrician reform under the guidance of Thomas Cromwell, who had, during the more zealous moments of reform, abrogated many traditional saints days, or "holy dayes."[12] Queen Elizabeth famously refused a New Year's gift of a new service book from Alexander Nowell, the dean of Saint Paul's, because it had cuts "resembling angels and saints."[13] "Have you forgot our proclamations," she demands of her dean, "against images, pictures, and Romish relics in churches?"[14] In keeping with this official denunciatory rhetoric, reprinting of the popular medieval collection of saint's lives *The Golden Legend* ceased after Wynkyn de Worde's 1527 edition, although its stories and heroes remained in the popular imagination.[15] References to saints, for instance, dot plays and poems, as when Henry V tells his loyal soldiers to cry "for Harry, England, and Saint George," or a little later when he invokes Saint Crispin to mark the upcoming battle.[16] These contradictions, prohibitions at odds with popular circulation, are telling, for they serve to underline the pressure—and frequently the gap—between theology and practice in early modern England.

The Reformation, with its official expulsion of saints, brought with it a renewed fascination in them. Previous centuries had created saints whose actions and cults of worship were profoundly antithetical to the Reformed church. Yet, as Johnson's saintly heroes demonstrate, depictions of saints con-

The hystory of the two valyaunte brethren Valentyne and Orson sonnes
unto the Emperor of Grece, C4ᵛ. (Imprinted by William Copland, 1555),
HEH 12925, STC (2nd ed.), 24571.7. Reproduced by permission of the
Huntington Library, San Marino, California.

tinued to hold a powerful authority. It is not surprising then, that despite official Protestant skepticism, enterprising reformers mined the medieval saints'
lives, reinterpreting and rewriting them to reflect changing attitudes toward
the marvelous and miraculous within devotional models. The staunch Protestant John Foxe, chief amongst the revisionist martyrologists, for instance,
looked back to these models of sanctity with as keen an interest as Johnson in
his *Seven Champions*.

The 1563 *Book of Martyrs* includes a "kalender" that converts the former
saints' holy days to days in remembrance of martyrs. The utility of this history
sought to shift the focus of commemoration away from saints' relics (along

with their marvelous miracles) and toward their holy, steadfast lives, the narrative of which followed. Foxe's substitution of martyrs for saints institutionalizes a reformulation of the old for new ends. As it did so, it elevated English figures to the same heroic status as their Biblical counterparts: so, for instance, Mary Magdalene appears on July 22 just across from Elizabeth Folkes, "Mayde," who heads up August 26. With this calendar, Foxe impresses a distinctly English sensibility over the pantheon of holy-day saints, turning what had been Catholic into English Protestant. This table, available in churches throughout England, represents the spread of Protestant belief. It also reveals, however, how the tools used to effect it were sometimes almost indistinguishable from those they sought to replace. In narrative terms, maid martyr Elizabeth Folkes had a very similar story to the virgin martyrs recounted in *The Golden Legend*. It is precisely the evident interchangeability between martyrs and saints, between saints and romance figures, that makes the framing of difference key to this subtle but crucial identity shift. Borrowing Foxe's rhetoric, I read, in what follows, a parallel appropriation as happening to the champions of romance. In both cases what Gower calls in the prologue to *Pericles* "Songs that old were sung" find a new audience.[17]

CECROPIA'S "SUBTLE SLIGHTES" AND ROMISH WOLVES IN THE *ARCADIA*

I begin with Cecropia, a character whom I read as an important swing figure, embodying Protestant anxiety regarding the too-Catholic figure of the romance enchantress and her hagiographic double. From the dedicatory epistle to Mary Sidney, the *Arcadia* folio volume projects "a worthy sanctuary" of feminine virtue, built with "good judgement," that sits alongside the text's masculine heroes (A4^r).[18] The *Arcadia* highlights the feminine virtues of Pamela and Philoclea by placing them in opposition to a woman who, like Spenser's Duessa, symbolizes the corruption of romance seductresses as a Catholic metaphor for falsehood. Just as Una stood as the redemptive figure to Duessa, so Pamela and Philoclea will overcome against Cecropia. Pamela and Philoclea's behavior, I argue, remembers the virtuous lives of female saints and virgin martyrs, and Sidney draws on this iconographic religious model, recasting his Protestant heroines from an existing mold. They embody the qualities for which the shepherds praise the absent Urania, exercising her salutary effect to move minds toward virtue. By sharp contrast, aligned with charlatan illusions,

July hath 31. dayes. The Moone, xxx.

	Day		Dayes of their death	Yeare of our Lord
g	1	Henry Woz, John Sleh, mar.	1	1522
A	2	John Frpth, Andrew Helvet, mar.	4	1533
b	3	Antony Verso, Rob. Testwood, W. Flinemaze, mar.	18	1543
c	4	Tho. Bradford preacher, mar.	1	1555
D	5	John Leafe. Jone Polley, mar.		1555
e	6	wylliam Coyng minister, mar.	2	1555
f	7	Richard Hoke, mar		1555
g	8	John Blands preacher, Thoa Franke, mar	12	1555
A	9	Humfrey Middleton, mar.	12	1555
b	10	Nicholas Shetterden, mar	12	1555
c	11	w Ellis Dighel, mar		1555
D	12	Dicick Carner, mar	12	1555
		John Launder, mar.	23	1555
e	13	Thomas Iuelon, mar.		1555
f	14	Nicolas Haule, mar.		1555
g	15	John Aleworth, confel.		1555
A	16	John Ca. les. cof.	1	1556
b	17	John Ewyn, Julins Palmer, Schelemaller and Iskine, mar.	15	1556
c	18	Wa. Carwches Paratine Gaffpe, & her child not one howser olde, & Guplrempne Gilberts. mar.	17	1556
D	19			
e	20			
f	21	Tho. Dungate, Tho. Fozman, Anne Tree, mar	18	1556
g	22	Simo Miller, Eliza Coper, mar.	13	1556
		Mary Magdalene.		
A	23	Richard Yeoman minister, mar.	10	1558
b	24	willia Pikes, mar.	14	1558
c	25	James Apostle.		
D	26	Stephen Cotton, mar.	14	1558
e	27	John Slade, mar.	14	1558
f	28	Stene wight, mar.	14	1558
g	29	Rob. Milles, mar.	14	1558
		Rob. Dines, mar.	14	1558
A	30	Tho. Benbzick gen	9	1558
b	31	tleman, mar.		

August hath xxxi dayes. The Moone, xxx.

	Day		Dayes of their death	Yeare of the Lord
c	1	Leonard Kepler, mar.	16	1527
b	2	James Abbes, mar	2	1555
e	3	John Denly gentleman, mar.	3	1555
f	4	John Newman, mar.	28	1555
g	5	Patricke Patyngham, mar.	28	1555
A	6	william Coker, mar.	23	1555
b	7	william Hopper, mar.	23	1555
c	8	Henry Laurence, mar.	23	1555
D	9	Richard Collier, mar.	23	1555
e	10	wyllia Stere, mar.	23	1555
f	11	Richard wryght, mar.	23	1555
		Elizabeth warne, mar.		1555
g	12	George Tankerfield, mar.	26	1555
A	13	R. Smith, mar.	8	1555
b	14	Stephen Hozwod, mar.	30	1555
c	15	Thomas Fulle, mar.	30	1555
D	16	william Hail, mar.	31	1555
e	17	william Hail, mar.	31	1555
f	18	Robert Samuell preacher, mar.	31	1555
g	19	Jone Watt, mar.	1	1556
A	20	wylliam Bongeoz, mar.	2	1557
b	21	Robert Purcas, mar.	2	1557
c	22	Thomas Bennold, mar.	2	1557
D	23	Agnes Siluerstyde, alias Smith, mar.	2	1557
e	24	Barthelmew Apost.		
f	25	Ellin Ewzyng, mar.	2	1557
g	26	Elizabeth Folkes mayde, mar.	2	1557
A	27	wyllyam Munt, mar.	2	1557
b	28	Alice Munt, mar.	2	1557
c	29	Rose Allyn mayde, mar.	2	1557
D	30	John Johnso, George Egles, mar.	2	1557
e	31	One Fryer and the sayde George Egles mar. fister.	2	1557

Kalendar for July and August from John Foxe's *Acts and Monuments*. (Imprinted at London, by John Day, 1563), HEH 59840, STC (2nd ed.), 11222. Reproduced by permission of the Huntington Library, San Marino, California.

Cecropia symbolizes the corrupted woman and church, promulgating a false wonder that must be rebuked by a steadfast faith and the rhetorical confidence of Basilius's daughters.

The wariness toward the supernatural that I discussed in my first chapter undergoes more elaborate treatment in the *Arcadia*'s most completely overhauled book, the third, where Sidney dwells extensively on his female characters. Cecropia appears less as a supernatural figure than a wickedly fraudulent one, and her practice establishes her as the antithesis to Sidney's heroines. From her first appearance, duplicity defines her. Gynecia, wife to Basilius and mother of the princesses, heartily (and rightly) mistrusts her "because shee had heard much of the divellish wickednesse of her heart" (M5^v). Cecropia seems to be concerned for the safety of Basilius's family in Arcadia, and her words disguise her maliciousness, but Gynecia's suspicions prove prescient: Cecropia increasingly works mischief, releasing the bear and lion (we learn in the revision) who threaten the princesses in book 1, fomenting rebellion in book 2, and in book 3 ambushing and imprisoning Zelmane, Pamela, and Philoclea. Through the figure of Cecropia and her fraudulent performance, Sidney confronts—and revises—a complex allusive network of romance motifs. Scholars have noted how the Catholic Mary Queen of Scots and Catherine de Medici inform Cecropia's portrayal; more convincingly, Barbara Brumbaugh suggests that Sidney associates his villainess generally with the papal church.[19] Most important, all of these pejorative Catholic dimensions reveal that Cecropia's threat lies less in her magic skills than in her practice of false magic and manipulative stagecraft, destroying Arcadia's peace.[20] Cecropia carries with her the freight of suspected Catholic ideologies and purported insidious plots; she is indeed the wolf Strephon should fear.

Cecropia's papist associations make her practice of fraudulent marvels all the more pointed. Moreover, her uncanny resemblance to stock romance enchantresses complicates her Catholic resonance in a manner similar to Duessa. Sidney's description of Cecropia's dwelling place, early in book 3, establishes her place in a genealogy of romance enchantresses. Her castle, deemed by most men an impregnable fortress, sits in the "midst of a great lake upon a high rocke," constructed partly by art "but principallie by Nature" (Kk2^r). Its clever fusion of art and nature, its inaccessible height, and its island-like remoteness, liken it to a conventional sorceress's dwelling. Alcina, Ariosto's enchantress, lives atop a narrow and stony hill surrounded by a bog; Montemayor's Felicia resides in a thick woods between two rivers; and Sannazaro's Massilia dwells on a hill between two springs; Circe too, of course, inhabits an inaccessible island. Like her romance predecessors, Cecropia jealously guards access to her fortress, and just as Alcina fabricates a facade to distract her "guests," Cecropia masterminds illusions to torment hers.

Cecropia differs from her romance heritage, though, in important ways. Although we are led to expect magic, Cecropia, we soon learn, has no actual magical power. She utters no spells to bind her prisoners, concocts no lover's potion to drop into Philoclea or Pamela's eyes, and performs no enchantments to deceive her prisoners. She works entirely within the material world, physically locking Zelmane, Philoclea, and Pamela in separate cells, and mustering all her rhetorical, rather than magical, wiles to move their affections to suit her ends. Yet, although she lacks magical skills, Cecropia adeptly performs illusions. For weeks, she attempts to woo first Philoclea and then Pamela to accept Amphialus's marriage proposal. Determined that one of them will marry her son and thus secure Basilius's throne, she urges Amphialus to rape Philoclea and force her submission. Furious because he refuses, Cecropia switches from rhetorical persuasion to violence against her prisoners, "giving them terrors, sometimes with noices of horror, sometimes with suddaine frightings in the night," and threatening the princesses with a rod and "matching violent gestures" (Tt6^v). When even her violent techniques only further harden the sisters' near saint-like resolve, she mobilizes her ultimate weapon: theatrical illusion. By leaving theatrical illusion as the last, most horrific tool in Cecropia's arsenal of persuasive tricks, Sidney presents it as the most pernicious. By having it function in the place where the reader might expect magic, Sidney substitutes wonder at magic with wonder at the fraud created by an adept illusionist. Through this rhetorical sleight of hand, he presents magic as smoke and mirrors, illusion, and trickery exploited by an adept Catholic medium.

Determined to intimidate Philoclea with Pamela's death, Cecropia prepares "her eies for a new play" (Vv2^v). Pulling the cell curtains so that both Philoclea and Zelmane might view her "play," she erects a scaffold "covered with crimsin velvet" (Vv3^r). To her audience's mounting horror, Pamela is made to kneel down with her head on the block. Philoclea, "opprest . . . with a storme of amazement," falls into a deadly trance when the sword performs "his cruell office upon that beautifull necke" (Vv3^v). Cecropia then threatens Zelmane that she must convince Philoclea to marry Amphialus, or else Philoclea will share Pamela's fate. Philoclea refuses all Zelmane's pleas as resolutely as she refuses Cecropia. One morning soon after, a noise awakens Zelmane to a ghastly sight: "a bason of golde, pitifully enameled with bloud, and in the midst of it, the head of the most beautifull *Philoclea*" (Vv8^r). With no screen of dramatic irony, readers experience Cecropia's tortures of Philoclea through Zelmane's great distress. Only after Zelmane dashes her head against a wall in suicidal desperation does Sidney unveil how the audience—and the reader—has been played.

Philoclea later tells Zelmane how "the mischievously suttle Cecropia used slightes" to stage a convincingly real vision of a fake execution (Xx2ᵛ). A simple maid, Artesia, was forced to wear Pamela's apparel. From afar, she looked like Pamela, leading Zelmane and Philoclea to believe in Pamela's death. Even more cunningly staged, Philoclea's "execution" shows how simply an audience might be deceived. Led down below the scaffold, Cecropia and her servants thrust Philoclea's head through a hole they had made in the scaffolding floor. About her neck they put "a dishe of gold, whereout they had beaten the bottome, so as having set bloud in it"; she tells Zelmane, "you saw how I played the parte of death" (Xx3ʳ).[21] The culminating effect of Cecropia's "suttle" slights shows the dark potency of an illusion crafted, like Arthur Dent's "fabulous devices," to draw the viewer from the truth.[22] Cecropia's Catholic allusions, combined with her deliberate cunning sleight of hand, question the efficacy and truth of supernatural wonders. By pulling the curtain on Cecropia's theater, Sidney underscores the material nature of the two princesses' seeming resurrections. Cecropia's illusions, designed, Philoclea says, "to have wrested our mindes to the forgetting of vertue," illustrate the high stakes for a reader who might mistake such wonders for reality (Xx2ᵛ). Cecropia's literary and historical resonance with both Catholicism and romance casts doubt on the validity of either's respective invocation of the supernatural. She is the wizard behind the curtain.

Cecropia thus epitomizes what could be wrong in a genre with a bent for false wonders. Her sex connects her to Eve, and her behavior simultaneously links the romance sorceresses and fraudulent Catholic perpetration of "lying wonders."[23] For she, like Duessa, engages the supernatural as a manipulative force to convince her audience of falsehood, confirming the worst fears that romance began by exciting lust, then heresy, and, finally, damnation. Her skill at producing false wonders is but an outward sign of a further inner corruption; the false wonders do indeed indicate a heretical mind. We shall soon see, as she reveals to Pamela in the famous debate concerning Providence's role in human affairs, ignorance and superstition underlie what appear to be miracles. Wonder too, she declares, is an affect ripe for those clever enough to manipulate it. As Roger Ascham understood, once supernatural agency had been called into question through false use, the next step was "to think nothing of God himself."[24] Cecropia's cavalier, even jaded, attitude toward wonder exposes a peculiar difficulty for a Protestant writer. Protestantism did not obliterate belief in the supernatural: to do so, its divines and polemicists realized, would be to open the door for abolishment of the divine. Yet the separation of wonder from superstition, of faith from fraud, relied upon a system of belief that was highly subjective, making one woman's wonders look like another woman's superstition.

"It is the right nature . . . of Beautie, to woorke vnwitting effectes of wonder" Cecropia tells Pamela. For such "unwitting effectes of wonder . . . will bring foorth feare, and their feare will fortifie their loue" so that a woman's "lippes may stande for ten thousand shieldes, and tenne thousand vneuitable shot goe from her eyes" (Nn7^r).[25] Such "unwitting effectes," she continues, ought to be harnessed, for thus might a beautiful woman manipulate men and so conquer "lives without venturing" (Nn6^v). By suggesting that beauty with its unwitting effects be used to control men, Cecropia shows how even the most simple response of wonder might be corrupted. Through this subtle argument, she reveals the difficulty of Sidney's attempt to separate benign (wonder after natural effects like beauty) from malign forms (wonder after supernatural effects), as her viewpoint categorically scorns "the good effects of verture" as deriving from "fearefull ignorance," which was the "first inventer of those conceates" (Nn6^r).[26] Her perspective colors Sidney's suggestion elsewhere in the *Arcadia* that wonder produced by physical beauty might be positively transforming. Strephon and Claius claim that their wonder after Urania's beauty leads them to higher forms of contemplation; by Cecropia's logic, it just makes them easier sheep to herd.

What at first appears to be an aesthetic debate over the nature of beauty and wonder quickly turns into a religious concern. Pamela refutes Cecropia, denying that her beauty should be used for "croked bias" (Nn8^v). So Cecropia raises the stakes, telling Pamela that her love of beauty and its concomitant virtue denies the true nature of wonder's potential. For, she argues, in so honoring the good effects of virtue, Pamela denies the fact that these effects are little more than the result of "foolish feare" and "fearefull ignorance" (Nn8^v). "For, when they heard it thunder not knowing the naturall cause," Cecropia argues by analogy, "they thought there was some angrie body above . . . Wherof they knew no cause that grewe straight a miracle" (Nn8^v–Oo^r). In a quick turn of logic, Cecropia moves from arguing that physical beauty and the wonder it engenders ought to be used for advantage to proposing that *all* things seemingly wonderful derive from ignorance. Wonder in response to seemingly natural "miracles" like thunder differs little from naive wonder after beauty and its purportedly associated "virtue." In short, once she proves that wonder generated by beauty is a force open to manipulative use, she dismisses the possibility that supernatural wonder could be free from similar manipulation. Both forms of wonder, she implies, are tools to control the ignorant. Thus, she concludes, because man, "by the pregnancie of his imagination . . . strives to things supernaturall," "thinke that those powers (if there be any such) above, are moved . . . by the eloquence of our prayers," and are thus fools (Oo^r). The supernatural, by her terms, springs from an overactive, pregnant imagination. At a time when atheism was anathema, Cecropia espouses extreme heresy. She illustrates the slippery slope that Ascham feared: deep skepticism regarding wonder or "miracles" can result in dismissing the numinous—a position untenable for any Christian. The development of her argument suggests, that her atheism grows directly from an understanding that equates wonder with fraud, a point that Sidney's own text seems at pains to illustrate in its dismissal of the supernatural marvelous.

Cecropia's rejection of the supernatural marvelous and consequent atheism complicates any straightforward reading that sees Sidney wanting to strip the supernatural completely from his romance world. While profound wariness marks Sidney's use of it, Cecropia shows how a too-strident skepticism also poses a grave risk. The conflicting impulses of Sidney's regard for the supernatural found in the *Arcadia* reflect Thomas Moffet's memory of how, as a young man, Sidney loathed astrology, for being well schooled, "excellent and inspired with true religion, he feared lest, too receptive to the fables of soothsayers, he might in rashness diminish the Divine Majesty."[27] Moffet's adverb "too" is telling, as it suggests that even in boyhood, Sidney was simultaneously receptive to and wary of supernaturalism. He does not want to misplace his faith—to put it into astrology and the "fable of soothsayers"—and thereby "diminish" and deny "the Divine Majesty." Although Moffet's recollections should be regarded with some caution, their sentiments capture the quandary of one "inspired with true religion" (i.e. Protestantism), who must believe in one form of supernaturalism while guarding against a too-ready reception of another. Cecropia's subtle "slights" and wonders might be dismissed as fraudulent, but the manifestation of Divine Majesty still held a clear place in *Arcadia*.

Sidney's complex portrayal of Cecropia provides exceptional insight into the cultural significance of the sixteenth-century linkage between representations of women, fraudulent wonder, romance, and Catholic practice. Her fall, I argue, illustrates the emergence of a newer understanding of how that triangle might be reconfigured, as the *Arcadia* adapts protocols of representation developed in the pages of John Foxe's *Acts and Monuments*. For Foxe develops a methodology that erects confessional difference by adaptation as much as expurgation. Foxe wrestles the legends of saints from their Catholic taint by redefining the terms of wonder rather than desanctifying those legends entirely as does Cecropia.[28] Cecropia's error will be corrected by the example of the patient and adamant Pamela and Philoclea, whose models of female piety will overwrite her negative exemplum.

PAMELA, PHILOCLEA, AND PROTESTANT MARTYRS

The manner of Cecropia's defeat matters to Sidney's genealogy of correcting her faults and those of romance more broadly. Significantly, Cecropia suffers defeat from no man; no knight confounds her, captures her, or rescues her prisoners. Typically, a romance enchantress loses her prisoners through the intervention of another stronger, more faithful knight. Trebatio's son, the Knight of the Sun, frees him from Lindaraza's pleasurable bower; Tasso's Rinaldo requires rescue from Armida by a team of knights; even Spenser's Verdant must be saved from Acrasia by Sir Guyon. Against Cecropia, however, Sidney's princely heroes prove ineffective. Pyrocles remains emasculated under the dress of Zelmane, capable of little more than wailing and banging her head against her cell wall; Musidorus, outside the fortresses, proves equally helpless despite his sallies against the walls. No knight triumphs in Cecropia's final inglorious tumble from her own tower. Instead, the sisters' sharp resolve prevails, shaming Cecropia to her son, for whom she wagers everything. Such a seemingly simple plot substitution holds manifold repercussions for how the *Arcadia* redeems romance.

Pamela's righteously inflamed retort to Cecropia's scorn of miraculous or wondrous providential intervention is one of the text's longest uninterrupted speeches. Its sermonizing casts her in the mold of a Protestant heroine, capable of defeating her persecutor through an erudite, theological rhetoric.[29] Her cheeks "died in the beautifullest graine of vertuous anger, with eies which glistered forth beames of disdaine," Pamela silences her captor, "Peace (wicked woman)," and deconstructs Cecropia's godless vision of "Chaunce" and miracle (Oo^r). Pamela asserts "an all knowing God whose insight reaches into man's heart," whom, she triumphantly concludes in a fit of prophetic rage,

Cecropia will know "as the instrument of her destruction" (Oo^r–Oo4^r). Pamela's speech espouses a providential accounting of cause and effect that counters the twin outcomes of Cecropia's logic—superstition or atheism—with a lively devotion.

Pamela's dauntless, aggressive rhetoric within the context of incarceration, coercion, and torture calls to mind something more than a romance heroine. Both Pamela and Philoclea, during the captivity episode, outgrow their earlier, more static roles as pursued and chaste princesses of romance. Neither becomes the intrepid, cross-dressed heroine like Ariosto's Bradamante, or even Spenser's Britomart, who defeat enemies with a charmed lance. Nor, however, is either damsel rescued by the strength of a knight's sinewy arm. Instead, the two sisters take on increasingly saint-like roles as book 3 unfolds, an identity that Sidney's language subtly enforces.[30]

The female saint turned martyr provides a template for how, in turn, an "abbie-lubbing" romance heroine might become a pious Protestant example. The striking cover image used by the staunch reformer John Bale suggests how, in a seemingly quick substitution, a female Catholic saint might be transformed into a champion of Reformation belief.[31] The woodcut recasts the familiar iconography of Saint Margaret of Antioch. Here the traditional martyr's palm of the medieval dragon slayer becomes Anne Askew triumphantly treading on the papal dragon, defeating him not with the sign of the cross but significantly with a book titled *Biblia*. The remaining palm branch and the familiar halo surrounding the figure's head, however, slyly hybridize this "godly" woman, showing her to be a composite figure recognizable to both Catholic and Protestant eyes. The interpretation of her symbolism relies on the framing narrative to explain which confessional camp she champions.

John Foxe provides numerous verbal examples that offer a similar Catholic-to-Protestant translation of the now godly virgin martyr. Saint Eulalia (who does not appear in Caxton's version of *The Golden Legend* but instead in accounts by Prudentius and Bede, among others), a Spanish martyr living under the persecution of Diocletian in the early fourth century, provides an exemplary reformulation. Although accounts vary, most agree that as a young woman of twelve or fourteen, Eulalia, convinced in her heart of the truth of the new Christian religion, by her own volition went to the tribunal to confess her faith. After her confession, which included a scathing indictment of the Roman pagan gods and idolatry, legend has it that executioners tortured her

Anne Askew and the Papal Dragon. John Bale's *The First Examinacyon of Anne Askewe*, title page. (Imprented at Marpurg in the lande of Hessen [i.e., Wesel: printed by D. van der Straten], in 1546), HEH350444, STC (2nd ed.), 848. Reproduced by permission of the Huntington Library, San Marino, California.

with iron hooks and then held lighted torches to the open wounds until her hair caught fire. Stifled by the flames, she died. Reportedly, as she expired, a white dove flew out of her mouth toward heaven. As further marker of her righteousness, a miraculous, out-of-season snow fell to cover her naked body, left where it lay in the forum.[32] Her story encompasses a typical narrative arc for a Catholic virgin martyr: she offers a godly confession, refuses to let worldly favor sway her belief, endures brutal torture, and has her death marked by a miraculous sign of providential favor.

"No less admirable and wonderfull was the constancy also of women and maydens," Foxe proclaims, opening a section of the *Book of Martyrs* (1576 edition) that rehearses several old legends of virgin saints, including Saint

Katherine, Saint Agnes, and Eulalia.[33] Foxe institutes a rhetorical move that will typify his retelling of the deeds of these maiden saints. Shifting the focus from the miraculous wonders that accompany a virgin's trial and death, Foxe directs the reader's admiration to the "wonderfull" constancy exhibited by female martyrs. Similarly, in his narrative itself, Foxe works to relocate wonder's source. According to Foxe's version, the noble-born, twelve-year-old Eulalia refuses honorable, great marriage and "gorgeous apparel," concentrating instead on her heavenly reward.[34] Driven by her belief, she leaves home to condemn the idolatry of the ruling Romans at the public tribunal. Incensed by her daring accusations, but perhaps moved by her youthful beauty, Maximanius first offers "fayre perswasions" to dissuade her from her holy zeal.[35] "Doth not the glisteryng and golden pompe of thy bryde bed moue thee?" he wheedles.[36]

Sidney undoubtedly knew his Foxe, and the trial structure of the captivity episode unfolds along parallel lines. Pamela and Philoclea's narratives use similar imagery and language, revealing the hagiographic palimpsest to both sisters' experience. Philoclea declares her resolution to remain true to her beloved, Zelmane, determined, she tells Cecropia, "to lead a virgin's life to my death, for such a vow I have myself devoutly made" (Ll5[v]). Cecropia, here a kind of Ephesian figure for the pagan tyrant as well as the duplicitous back-slid church, woos Philoclea first by promises of a golden bridal bed to be shared with her son Amphialus, going so far as to stage musicians to sing to her dulcet promises of wedded bliss, "with fair promises if they would promise fair" (Ll7[r]). Later, Philoclea will recall to Zelmane how " having in vain attempted the fardest of her wicked eloquence . . . (accompanied with great flatteries and rich presents)," Cecropia failed to dissuade her from her virgin end (Xx2[v]).

Philoclea's avowed virgin intent establishes her as a quasi-religious figure even in her secular story, a representation that gains ground in the text's description of her sister Pamela. Failing to move Philoclea, Cecropia turns to Pamela, whose posture in her cell of supplication for divine grace Sidney details with pictorial exactness: "therewith kneeling down even in the same place where she stood," she sends "to heaven from so heavenly a creature" a prayer with

such a fervent grace, as if devotion had borrowed her body to make of itself a most beautiful representation; with her eyes so lifted to the skyward that one would have thought they had begun to fly thitherward to take their place among their fellow stars; her naked hands raising up their whole length and, as it were, kissing one another (as if the right had been the picture of zeal, and the left of humbleness, which both united themselves to make their suits more acceptable) (Ll8ᵛ).

Philoclea's kneeling posture, with naked upraised hands pressed together and eyes "so lifted skyward," fervently pleading divine intervention, recreates verbally the pictorial form of a host of female saints depicted in the *Legenda aurea*. As Karen Winstead notes in her study of virgin martyrs, visual representations were among the most important sources for religious information in the late Middle Ages. The saints and their stories were readily known through sculptures, wall paintings, stained-glass windows, and illuminated manuscripts.[37] Indeed, the *Legenda* included numerous illuminations that showed Saints Lucy, Euphemia, and others in postures of prayer and supplication under torture. Pamela's posture, along with Sidney's religiously tinged descriptors such as "grace," "devotion," "zeal," "humbleness," "wickedness," and "goodness," courts a striking resemblance to many of these saintly poses. Indeed, Pamela and Philoclea, who are described as having, respectively, "majesty of virtue" and "silent humbleness" in their characteristic epithets in book 3, harken to these earlier religious models more than to contemporary romance heroines such as Briana, Griana, or even Oriana from the newly popular imported romances, *Mirrour of Knighthood*, *Palmerin*, or *Amadis* series (Oo4ᵛ).

This tableaux produces "so strange a working power that even the hard-hearted wickedness of Cecropia . . . felt an abashment at that goodness" (Ll8ᵛ). Sidney, like Foxe with his virgin martyrs, leads us to wonder at the constancy exhibited by Pamela and Philoclea. Their refusal becomes an icon of virtue as opposed to a miraculous delivery. The visual quality of this "image" of Pamela, offers what Sidney in his *Defence* refers to as a "speaking picture" that paints her virtue in religiously explicit terms.

As book 3 unfolds, the similarities between virgin martyr narratives and the trials of Pamela and Philoclea build. In Foxe's account of Eulalia, the reader follows Philoclea from her rejection of her captor's "fayre perswasions," to marry or receive worldly wealth, to torture.[38] While Foxe eschews some of the more graphic descriptions of her torture, he does recount how the hangmen perform a "terrible harrowyng of her flesh" and how she, eager to embrace her fate, swallows the flames that burn her in order to die more quickly.[39] Similarly, once Cecropia realizes she cannot move the sisters with fair promises, she withdraws "all comfort both of servants and service from them," and her physical tortures escalate into psychological as she "pursued on her rugged way, letting no day pass without new and new perplexing the poor ladies' minds and troubling their bodies" with "sometimes . . . noises of horror, sometimes with sudden frightings in the night, when the solitary darkness therof might easier astonish the disarmed sense" (Tt6ᵛ).

The bodily descriptions of the tortures recall the language of Foxe's mishandled virgin. Eulalia's "white and fayre skinne" is both mangled and bathed, "as out of a warme fountaine," with her own "fresh bloud."[40] Likewise, Sidney's analogy of Cecropia's assault on Philoclea as akin to kites attacking a "white dove" equates his romance heroine with the symbol used often to mark the virgin saint (as in the Catholic Eulalia legends): a white dove (Tt6ᵛ). Nature responds to Cecropia's scourging "that most beautiful body" with the sun "[drawing] up to hide his face from so pitiful a sight, and the very stone walls did yield drops of sweat for agony of such a mischief" (Tt6ᵛ). Pamela also did "suffer the divers kinds of torments they used to her," bearing all "with so heavenly a quietness and so graceful a calmness" that she appears like the sun beaming through the "clouds of affliction" (Tt8ʳ). With both sisters, more than secular heroism shines through the narrative language. Pamela, at the conclusion to her godly confession that refutes Cecropia's heretical disbelief of miracles, horrifies Cecropia: awestruck Cecropia observes "so faire a maiestie of vnconquered vertue" in Pamela, who, it appears to her, glows halolike with "a light more than humaine" about her (Oo4ʳ⁻ᵛ). This marvel of a beautiful light that shines about Pamela places her within the tradition of saints and martyrs who, as Helen White details, are frequently lit up by miraculous lights: the light of innocence about Saint Agnes in the Roman brothel, Saint Genevieve's miraculously lighted candles, as well as the shining tree of Saint Kenelm.[41] To this Catholic list we might add the bright halo surrounding Anne Askew's titular figure on John Bale's Reformation propaganda.

Other characters respond in ways that confirm these readings of Pamela and Philoclea as near-saintly heroines. Pyrocles, when confronted by his beloved who he had believed to be dead, says incredulously: "I saw your head—the head indeed, and chief part of all nature's works—standing in a dish of gold, too mean a shrine, God wot, for such a relic" (Xx2ᵛ). His comparisons of her to a "shrine" and a "relic" invoke the trappings of a *Legenda aurea* virgin, whose shrine and relics worked miracles. Amphialus too treats Philoclea as his saint, for when his friends discover him nearly bled to death from his attempted suicide, "there fell out Philoclea's knives (which Cecropia at the first had taken from her and delivered to her son, and he had worn them next his heart as the only relique he had of his Saint)" (Xx7ʳ). Like Pyrocles,

Amphialus treats Philoclea's material memory, in this case her knives, like an amulet or bit of bone fragment to remind him of his "saint." That both lovers should refer to the mortal princess Philoclea as their "saint" reinforces the patterns of martyrdom that shadow Sidney's secular romance heroines.

Yet, however closely Pamela and Philoclea may limn the stories of virgin martyrs in these closing scenes, crucial details are missing. Although the two sisters are awarded descriptions analogous to virgin saints, while they suffer equally and steadfastly defend themselves rhetorically like martyrs, no intervening deus ex machina delivers them or even seemingly answers their prayers. Helen Hackett, in her reading of the Arcadian heroines, argues that Cecropia's false executions further recall resemblance to saints' lives, where rape always remained a threat only, since exceptional virtue "earned miraculous protection."[42] This, however, is precisely what Sidney's account denies: miraculous protection. What looms large in this comparison is how the narrative steadfastly denies them any miracle, or timely rescue, even as it deliberately calls up a narrative expectation for it. Pamela's halo signals her saintliness but works no miracles. When the text abruptly ends midsentence a few pages later, both sisters still remain captives in Cecropia's palace, even though the wicked illusionist herself has fallen from the leads propelled by her guilty conscience.

I return to Foxe's opening statement that precedes his account of virgin martyrs drawn from Catholic sources and to his all-important shift in where the reader's wonder and amazement should focus, for herein lies one explanation of why Sidney tells his story as he does. Foxe frames his entire tale of Eulalia's legend with Protestant skepticism regarding some of the stranger, more miraculous aspects of her story. After finishing her story, he writes, "The said Prudentius, and Ado, also Equilinus" tell of "a white doue issuyng out of her mouth at her departyng, & of the fire quenched about her body, also of her body, couered miraculously with snow, wt other thinges more."[43] Foxe differentiates his version from the earlier Catholic ones by throwing into doubt such miraculous details, exhorting "wherof let euery reader vse his owne iudgement" to determine their veracity.[44] Denying that such miracles undisputedly attest to her holiness, Foxe emphasizes instead her faithfulness and able, godly defense. His suspicions thus downplay the miraculous aspects of her story, while simultaneously venerating her for her constant death, "worthy of prayse and commendatiō[n]."[45] Such a rhetorical shift accompanies subsequent accounts, as the marginal gloss next to the following legend of the virgin martyr Agnes alerts the reader that "Straunge and vnnecessary myracles [are] omitted."[46]

The omission of "strange and unnecessary miracles" from Foxe's recounting of virgin martyr legends resembles Sidney's care throughout the *Arcadia* to downplay and throw into question what appear to be supernatural, marvelous occurrences. As Foxe here suggests, the omissions draw attention to what has been suppressed or erased from the narrative. When Philoclea appears to Zelmane in a seemingly miraculous resurrection, he addresses her with wonder as "Most blessed angel!" She, however, quickly corrects him: "Do not deceive thyself . . . I am no angel, I am Philoclea" (Xx2ʳ). Philoclea's negative response, "I am no angel," grounds her firmly within the material world. Her following explanation, moreover, for her seeming resurrection illustrates the fiendish cleverness and devilish manipulation of one who would seem to work wonders, a rhetorical unveiling that recalls the earlier exposition that I have argued, revealing the fishermen to be superstitious fools for mistaking Pyrocles as divinity. Like Foxe's reader, one is drawn to wonder at the marvelous strength and endurance shown by such young women, not at any divine or angelic manifestation.

Philoclea and Pamela, like Foxe's rehabilitated virgin saints, deliberately draw from an old reservoir of motifs to call attention to their reformation. Furthermore, by showing romance heroines to be as constant, faithful, and rhetorically savvy as the virgin martyrs dotting the pages of Foxe's monumental guide to Protestant devotion, Sidney undercuts critiques about romance's "bewitching" overly eroticized women and their effect on credulous readers. From the beginning, the saints' and martyrs' legends were powerful instruments for engendering devotion, propaganda designed to convey wonder and excitement in order to convert and inspire pious living. Sidney uses these religious templates to redeem the genre of romance through its most vilified figures. Although their story remains unfinished in the incomplete 1590 revision of the *Arcadia*, Pamela and Philoclea already operate on a different erotic trajectory than in the shorter *Old Arcadia*: the consummation of Philoclea and Pyrocles's love never happens, and the interrupted, near rape of Pamela by Musidorus seems far off from the revision's narrative arc. Sidney subsumes these unruly erotic passions, harnessing them instead to a devotional model that venerates chastity and rewards steadfastness, qualities both heroines have in abundance during the captivity episode. While Pamela and Philoclea's suffering can invite a sadistic voyeurism, and while one might question the appropriateness of using an iconography of religious ardor to describe a secular passion, these saintly narrative motifs raise the romance heroine in stature above their masculine counterparts in a manner markedly different from either the *Old Arcadia* or from other contemporary romances. Through the trials of the two sisters, Sidney experiments with a new paragon of feminine virtue, one whose influence—even when contested—testifies to its appeal. Although not all later readers agree about the *Arcadia*'s merits, its prevalence in debates over right reading indicate its centrality to questions that were being simultaneously asked of gender as well as genre in a changing religious climate. Pamela and Philoclea's triumph over Cecropia signals how a new generation of romance heroines might outshine their sorcerous and Catholic-tainted predecessors, thus appropriating the old modes for new ends.

FROM THAISA'S "GREAT MIRACLE" TO MARINA'S "GENERAL WONDER" IN *PERICLES*

Cecropia's subtle theatrics that are supplanted by the Foxean sisters' performance offers a narrative template for how a dramatic romance might also be repurposed. I now turn to another text that enacts a generational change— from saintlike mother to martyred daughter—in its presentation of female heroines: the play *Pericles*, a dramatic romance that Shakespeare helped to shape.[47] "The dramatic genre on which the saint's life exerted greatest influence," Michael O'Connell argues, "was the romance."[48] Of all Shakespeare's dramatic romances, the self-conscious medievalism of *Pericles* constitutes the most explicit acknowledgment of this cloistered lineage: the resurrected Gower, the miraculously revived Thaisa, and Marina's heroic virtue invite a vexed affinity with hagiographic conventions.[49]

The prologue to the play, spoken by the medieval Gower, courts these older conventions, framing the tale within a pre-Reformation milieu of cyclical religious celebrations: "ember eves and holy ales" (1.0.6).[50] Ember eves were quarterly celebrations marking seasonal changes and festivals, "ordained by Pope Calixtus," as William Caxton's translation of *The Golden Legend* tells us.[51] Codified in the old church calendar as three-day religious cycles of fasting and prayer, they invited ritual renewal by encouraging reflection on the mystery of redemption.[52] The tradition of celebrating "ember eves" reaches back to pagan holidays stemming from the Latin *quatuor tempora* (four times) of Roman agricultural practice that used religious ceremony to implore the gods' blessings for crop seeding and harvesting. With its overtones of both a pagan ritual for natural renewal and agricultural fertility that became Christian markers of spiritual re-creation, Gower's evocation of "ember-eves" sets a richly allusive tone for a tale set in a pagan world that nonetheless contains rhythms of the Catholic calendar.

Restoring the long editorial tradition of emending "holy ales" to read "holy-dayes," as in the sixteenth-century quarto text, furthermore, sustains Gower's extended allusion to old church festivals and narratives. The vociferous, zealous reformer John Bale, in his *Pageant of Popes*, includes in his reader address a list of papist traditions that pointedly names, among the "paxes, beades, tapers and crosses," the "holye dayes, imber dayes."[53] Indeed, as Eamon Duffy has shown, saints' holy days were some of the most hotly contested aspects of the Reformed calendar. Under Thomas Cromwell, the Crown radically amended the traditional pattern of religious observance in local festivals for church holy days, suspending a number of saints' days celebration, including those of Saint Mary Magdalene, Saint Anne, Saint Katherine, and Saint Agatha.[54] Gower's "holydayes" recalls the intense battles over calendrical reform enshrined within John Foxe's "kalender" whose substitutions I marked at this chapter's opening. Finally, the term "holyday," with its rich allusions to saints' days, completes the pun at the next line's end: "And lords and ladies in their lives" looks back to "holydays" to suggest a dual reference to reading saints' lives as well as to the lives of the "lords and ladies" (1.0.7–8).

Gower, then, calls attention to the mottled source history of secular, pagan, and Catholic medieval traditions behind *Pericles*. In doing so, he recapitulates the play's intertexts: the ancient tale of Apollonius of Tyre, a version of which Gower tells in book 8 of his *Confessio Amantis* (ca. 1393; reprinted 1554 by Thomas Berthelette); Laurence Twine's *The Pattern of Painful Adventures* (ca. 1594), a nearly contemporary prose romance based on the 153rd story in the Latin *Gesta Romanorum*. The *Gesta*, much like *Pericles*, mixed hagiography, romance-like tales, and moralized Catholic exempla.[55] Gower's self-conscious didactic narrative role throughout thus invokes such Catholic exempla; he promises a play not only to "glad your ear and please your eyes," but also to be a spiritual "restorative" (1.0.3, 4). Channeling the poet chorus of saints' plays and the moral conclusions to *Gesta* tales, Gower revives stories fallen from official favor, such as the disappeared saints' plays like *Saint Christopher*, the other play performed with *Pericles* at the recusant Sir John Yorke's Christmas celebrations, presented at Gowthwaite Hall by the Cholmley players.[56] I do not suggest here that *Pericles* is a mystery-cycle play, a saint's play, or even a crypto-Catholic play and cover for recusancy. Rather, I argue the prologue's reminder of ember-eve and holy-day narratives draws attention to the play's engagement with a central problem of romance within post-Reformation England: its sympathy with the saint's life.[57]

Gower raises, as a synecdoche, generic problems that the rest of the play takes up. Although the play's outward orientation, like that of Sidney's *Arcadia*, is secular and even pagan, its displacement of hagiographic motifs onto ancient pagan romance through the story of Apollonius of Tyre only highlights the resonance of that earlier conflict between Christians and pagans to that between Protestants and Catholics. This displacement emerges spectacularly in the differing ways that the play presents Thaisa and Marina, both of whose stories draw from the "old songs" heralded by Gower. I begin with Thaisa's story and Cerimon's "great miracle" of resurrection in Ephesus (5.3.58). Act 3 follows Gower's gaze backward, bringing to life how an ostensibly secularized stage might, with its physical testimony to miracle, vivify romance's origins among the spiritually restorative narratives of Catholicism.[58] In contrast to Sidney's Cecropia, whose Catholic dimensions underlie her fraudulent wonders, Thaisa testifies to the great affective potential within the cult of the saints whereby a romance heroine might be transmuted. Just as Paulina in *The Winter's Tale* exhorts her audience to "awake your faith," (5.3.95) in order to witness the miracle of Hermione's transformation from marble statue to living queen, Thaisa's story demands an audience's faith to believe its "great miracle" (5.3.58).[59]

THAISA IN EPHESUS

Gower broaches the religious tensions over saints and miracles in his prologue, and that tension deepens as the play takes us to Ephesus. Shakespeare had already imagined Ephesus as a site of mystery, magic, and transformative power in his earlier *Comedy of Errors*. His return in this late play to Ephesus revives the contradictory resonance that the city as a geographical site held for Catholics and reformers alike.[60] As my citation of Dering's earlier use illustrates, Ephesus recalled Paul's zealous preaching, the burning of heretical books full of the curious arts, and a people's turn from idolatry. Equally famously, it raised memories of iconophilia, false miracles, and the medieval cult of the Virgin Mary, whose legend flowered alongside that of the pagan virgin Diana.[61] In sum, Ephesus—much like romance—represented the potential to sympathize with the condemned elements of Catholicism—iconophilia, hagiography, and its "lying wonders" (to borrow William Perkins's phrase)—or to reform them as Saint Paul once did the citizens of Ephesus.

I dwell on Ephesus's complex religious resonance because its status crucially underlies the "great miracle" of Thaisa's story. Whether Cerimon, skilled as he is in the "curious arts," belongs to the "popish sort," like Cecropia, who works through "lying wonders," or belongs in the older tradition of Pauline miracle workers may explain why the play dwells extensively on his reputation and his study when other texts that feature Pericles award him only glancing attention. In all the major intertexts—Gower, Twine, and the *Gesta*—nowhere does Cerimon play such a complex miracle-working role as he does in *Pericles*, a role further complicated by its Ephesian context.

For many preachers, Ephesus became synonymous with Rome, specifically in its pejorative association between femininity and Catholicism and in its saintly resurrections as "lying wonders" indicative of false worship. From the pagan Diana to the Virgin Mary to Saint Drusiana, the city remembered Rome.[62] The gendered religious slur was driven home in many contemporary sermons: the Bishop of London, William Barlow, a more moderate voice than some, writes in his *Defence of the Articles of the Protestants Religion* (1601), the church at Ephesus was "as apparant in shew, as ceremonius for rites, as superstitious in deuotion, as glorious in temples, and as auncient for succession as the Romish Synagogue (since that faithfull citie became an harlot)."[63] George Benson, in a sermon before Paul's Crosse (published 1609), sees Ephesus as a symbol of an apostate church more concerned with the worship of its female idol than with Christian religion.[64] Such rhetoric culminates in outspoken John Vicars, who most explicitly links Diana and her city with a popish harlot; she is "Babylons Beautie" and the "Roman Catholicks Sweet-Heart."[65] Ephesus foregrounds why a "resurrected" romance heroine touches a cultural nerve, for it revives the fascination with "Babylons beautie" and its Catholic stories of miraculous resurrections.

The nature of Thaisa's "great miracle" in Ephesus goes straight to the heart of Protestant anxiety over saints' lives and their marvelous dimension.[66] In *A Discourse of the Damned Art of Witchcraft* (published 1608, 1610), a noted spokesperson for resistance to all that resembled Roman ritual, the puritan sympathizer William Perkins, uses the Ephesians story told in Acts to argue that a continued Catholic belief in miracles is like a false healer who is proved to be nothing more than a conjurer and sorcerer of the devil. Arguing that miracles ceased shortly after the time of the apostles, Perkins contends that the belief in miracles

> is at this day common and vsuall among the Popish sort. . . . For such were those Vagabonds which came to Ephesus, and tooke vpon them to cast out deuills by the name of Iesus, and Paul. . . . From which time many heresies beganne to spread themselues; and then shortly after Poperie that mysterie of iniquitie beginning to spring vp, and to dilate it selfe in the Churches of Europe, the true gift of working miracles then ceased, and in stead thereof came in delusions, and lying wonders, by the effectuall working of Satan, as it was foretold by the Apostles . . . of which sort were and are all those miracles of the Romish Church, whereby simple people haue beene notoriously deluded.[67]

The "lying wonders" that Perkins condemns as Romish heresy descend from the false healers of Ephesus, a legacy that troubles later stories concerning female saints, such as Drusiana and, I will argue, Thaisa. *Pericles* encourages such a religiously informed reading from the moment of the discovery of Thaisa's coffin, a scene that plays up both sorcerous and providential connotations, emphasizing the pun of Cerimon's name with "ceremony."

Pericles dramatically frames Cerimon's first appearance by the omen of the "turbulent and stormy night" (3.2.3), bringing a storm so severe that the "earth did quake" and "the very principals did seem to rend / And all to topple" (3.2.16–17). The stormy night, earthquake, and turbulence infuse the following scene with strange and foreboding signs of providential significance.[68] Cerimon enters in the wake of this portentous storm to claim that immortality attends "[v]irtue and cunning," "[m]aking a man a god" (3.2.27, 31). Marjorie Garber reads this speech as revealing the physician inherent in Cerimon; it establishes the naturalness—not the supernaturalness—of his art. For her, Cerimon's speech provides a natural, rationalist explanation for his talent as a physician.[69] While it is true that Cerimon's description of his art as both learning and practice suggests the increased use of experimental seventeenth-century medicine, his reference in the very next line to a "secret art" that makes a man a god implies his abilities go beyond the merely natural.[70] His "secret art" that he has studied "[b]y turning o'er authorities" calls to mind the learned men of Ephesus with their books of curious arts (3.2.32, 33).

As Cerimon confers with the two gentlemen, some servants enter bearing a chest. In the *Gesta*, Twine, and the *Confessio*, Cerimon and his servants find the chest while walking along the shore, bring it back, and open it to discover the body and a letter. *Pericles* increases the dramatic tension of this discovery. As the servants leave the chest, the second gentleman remarks, "'Tis like a coffin, sir," and Cerimon acknowledges, "'Tis wondrous heavy" (3.2.51, 52). The first servant adds that he "never saw so huge a billow, sir/As tossed it upon shore" (3.2.53–54). The additional description of the unnaturally "huge billow" that tosses the "wondrous heavy" coffin emphasizes its marvelous arrival. As Cerimon proceeds to examine the well "caulked and bitumed" coffin-like chest, he makes a startling observation absent from all the source stories (3.2.59). "Soft!" he says. "It smells/Most sweetly in my sense" (3.2.59–60). "A delicate odour," confirms the second gentleman (3.2.60). "As ever hit my nostril," Cerimon concludes (3.2.61).

Pericles's revision of this moment bears closer scrutiny. At this critical dramatic moment, as Cerimon looks down into the coffin, all of the play's source stories make Thaisa's beauty the scene's cynosure. The blazons describing her match the usual trope of extraordinary beauty that a romance heroine was suggested to possess. Twine's account tells us "the haire of her head was naturally as white as snowe . . . her eies were like two stares . . . her neck was like the white alabaster shining like the bright sunne beames."[71] Cerimon, instead of uttering the expected romance motif, solicits a hagiographic reading—the *odor sanctorum* was a hallmark of martyred saints.[72] The sweet odor could be rationally explained by the presence of spice bags lining the coffin. A coffin packed with bags of spices, most editors note, would have signaled incredible wealth, a wealth not out of reach for a man such as Pericles, who was traveling on the Mediterranean, a transport route for spices coming west from India. Indeed, such spices were being used as preservatives for dead bodies in the early seventeenth century.[73] Yet just as Cerimon's earlier reference to "blest infusions" contains a double possibility, Cerimon's words are richly suggestive. Carolyn Walker Bynum persuasively argues holy women were especially likely to be singled out and recognized by corporeal marks of sainthood because female spirituality was peculiarly bodily.[74] Although I do not mean to argue that Thaisa should be read literally as a saint, *Pericles*'s deliberate reworking of this scene elicits a hagiographical subtext to the dramatic romance. Cerimon's allusion to the dead queen's sweet-smelling corpse further enhances the sense that we witness a miracle, allying the tale with an older form of belief and an older form of storytelling.

Cerimon's preparations for waking her further build toward a miraculous reading. He explains to his attending servants that he has heard of an "Egyptian/That had nine hours lain dead, who was/By good appliance recovered" (3.2.83–85). Critics have speculated that this reference may come from Apuleius's *Golden Ass*, where an Egyptian man is revived to give evidence in a murder trial.[75] Yet the exact source for the reference may not be as important as its Egyptian resonance. Like Ephesus, Egypt bore with it the connotations of magic and curious arts. This reference to Egypt recalls the handkerchief in *Othello* that was given to his mother by "an Egyptian" who was a "charmer" and put "magic in the web of it" (3.4.54, 55, 67).[76] To place Cerimon in the tradition of Egyptian healers, who were thought to practice by magic rather than natural science, further locates Cerimon's healing outside the realm of explainable medical practice and connects him to the Ephesian healers who also practice "curious arts."

All of these details portend a miracle, and the play deliberately fosters such an interpretation. The source stories show Thaisa coming to life after vigorous stimulation with various oils and rough cloth. In Twine's telling (which closely follows Gower's), Machaon commands a fire to be lit, takes the queen from the chest, and carries "the body reverently in his armes, . . . bare it into his owne chamber, and layed it upon his bed." He administers "hote and comfortable oyles" that he warms "upon the coales" and dips in "faire wool" which he then foments "all the bodie over" until the "congealed blood and humours were thoroughly resolved."[77] Gower and Twine both portray Cerimon's clerk removing the body from the casket, stripping it of grave clothes, and laying it near a fire, while vigorously stimulating the congealed blood with rough cloths. Such labor exerted by an attendant argues Thaisa might indeed be awakened through medical intervention.

Pericles presents a different scenario. Although Cerimon commands a servant to "make a fire within" and "fetch hither all my boxes," what action he performs remains vague (3.2.79–80). The only explicit direction Cerimon utters is that the "rough and woeful music that we have / Cause it to sound" (3.2.87). As Elizabeth Hart convincingly argues, the adjective "rough" implies religious ceremony; its presence belies Cerimon's medical practice and instead invokes mystical sources of healing that, Hart argues, go back to the sacred mystery cults.[78] It also invokes Catholic ceremony and hagiographic miracles. Cerimon's only words, "How thou stirr'st, thou block!" which editors read as his rebuke to the servant who has left off playing the viol, suggests the music has as much efficacy as Cerimon. Only after the music plays does he announce, "This queen will live" (3.2.90, 92).

As witnesses onstage, the watching gentlemen provide the first interpretation of what has happened to Thaisa—and their language of wonder and miracle serves to frame the audience's response.[79] Thaisa's first words further confirm the witnesses' testimony. As she stirs, she says, "O dear Diana, where am I? Where's my lord? What world is this?" (3.3.103–4).[80] In both sources, Thaisa (Lucina in Twine's version) opens her eyes and warns Machaon not to touch her "otherwise than thou oughtest to do, for I am a Kings daughter."[81] Here, Thaisa's first words invoke resurrection: "Where am I? What world is this?" Thaisa believes herself someplace other than earth. One might also read "lord" not only as a reference to her husband, Pericles, but also as a Christian reference to the Lord Jesus Christ. The gentlemen's continued refrain of "Is not this strange?" and "Most rare" adds a chorus to a miraculous event (3.2.105). In short, the altered sensory details of a sweet-smelling corpse, ceremonial "rough music," and awestruck witnesses point toward a ceremonial and miraculous—not naturalized—explanation for her resurrection.

By altering small details of the Pericles tale, the play explicitly engages with romance's medieval heritage, steeped in the milieu of Catholic religiosity, miracle plays, and saints' lives. Its dramatic effect hinges on the very improbability of the event—its rupture of an earthly logical chain of cause and effect— just as the saint's life turns around the representation of a miracle, an event contrary to nature. Gower's prologue and Thaisa's resurrection invite the audience to be "restored" like Lazarus, by inhabiting the same imaginative space as those of lords and ladies of old who celebrated ember eves and holy days. Such a literary reenactment serves to animate and make accessible these contested beliefs.

MYTILENE MARINA

Thaisa's resurrection at Ephesus in act 3, I have argued, sympathetically recapitulates romance's similarity to stories from The Golden Legend, drawing dramatic tension from its contentious Ephesian context. By flirting with a hagiographical subtext, with its references to holy odors, "great miracle," and marveling witnesses, it draws on the great theatrical and affective power of miracle—and of romance—over its audience. Something quite different happens, however, in act 4 as Gower directs us to Mytilene, where the play exploits its hagiographical resonance in ways similar to Sidney's Arcadia, in sympathy with its largely Protestant milieu. Mytilene, too, held Pauline associations (Acts 20:14) but was also famous for its charismatic females, such as Sappho, a woman noted for her lesbianism and rhetorical skills as a poet. Yet this world, unlike Ephesus, feels far from Gower's medievalism and ember eves. A brothel scene double that of any source text, replete with newly contemporary characters and dialogue, the Pander, Bolt, and the Bawd, bring to the exotic romance geography of the Mediterranean region a strong flavor of the local London brothels then being paraded on the Jacobean stage.[82] Ephesus fostered a backward glance in time to recapture a deep religious past where miracles were possible—and even applauded—but Mytilene fast-forwards to the present world of 1609 London, where miracles seldom happened, and if they did, they were quite likely to be branded a "lying wonder."

Building on the audience's faith to accept great miracles during the first half of the play, Gower prepares us for yet another narrative of restoration heavily imbued with motifs drawn from old romance's generic kindred, the virgin saint's life: in chorus 4, Gower establishes Marina's reputation in Tarsus as one of "general wonder" (4.0.11). Marina's story, even more than her mother's, draws from a repertoire of hagiographic motifs, only, like that of Pamela and Philoclea, to engage them to a very different end. Like other virgin martyr saints (Agnes, Theodora, Serapia, or Denise, to name a small sampling), Marina's peerless qualities inspire intense jealousy and land her in "unholy service" at the brothel (4.4.50). But unlike act 3, act 4 disconnects romance from its medieval, Catholic heritage by excising the expected miracle. The wonder generated in act 4 grows not from a "great miracle" but from Marina's paradoxical status as both a marvel and a very human agent of transformation, who must work for her own, and others', redemption (5.3.58).

The story of Marina's life, as critic Lorraine Helms notes, has affinities with the life of Saint Agnes.[83] Saint Agnes's story becomes one of the few virgin martyr accounts retold by John Foxe in his *Acts and Monuments*, suggesting that her story—like that of Ephesus—compelled Protestant fascination as well as Catholic. Foxe's handling of the story, however, registers a crucial tonal shift that also underlies *Pericles*'s treatment of Marina. In the old Catholic version, as recorded in Caxton's translation of the *Golden Legend*, a pagan lord falls in love with Agnes. When she spurns his advances, he condemns her to be thrown to the "harlots and handled as they are handled."[84] To hide her shame, God causes her hair to grow long and sends an angel that "environed S. Agnes with a bright clearness in such wise that no man might see her ne come to her."[85] Clothed in such bright robes, she, as does Marina in the play,

> made of the bordel her oratory, and in making her prayers to God she saw tofore her a white vesture, and anon therewith she clad her and said: I thank thee Jesu Christ which accountest me with thy virgins and hast sent me this

vesture. All they that entered made honour and reverence to the great clearness that they saw about S. Agnes, and came out more devout and more clean than they entered.[86]

Agnes's power to turn her customers from lust to devotion parallels Marina's strange transformative effect on the men that enter Bolt's brothel; importantly, however, Marina dons no mysterious "white vesture," and no "great clearness" hovers behind her.

Although Foxe's Agnes looks much like Caxton's, the not-so-subtle narrator wrestles to distinguish his Protestant account from earlier Catholic ones. As I noted in the preceding chapter, Foxe condemns how the stories of Saintes "haue bene poudered and sawsed wyth dyuers vntrue additions and fabulous inuentions of men who eyther of a superstitious deuotion, or of a subtill practise" to the end that they "haue so mingle mangled their stories & liues" that little remains that is "simple & vncorrupt."[87] As we saw with Eulalia's legend, to differentiate his "uncorrupt" version from those "fabulous inuentions" of men of "superstitious devotion," he directs reader attention away from Agnes's miraculous preservation, her "vnspotted and vndefiled virginitie," and toward her steadfast resolve for which she "deserueth no greater prayse and commendation, then for her willyng death and Martyrdome."[88] He highlights her "willyng death" and steadfast belief rather than crediting "fabulous invention," like that mysterious clear light.

Yet even John Foxe, with the most godly of intentions, cannot quite strip Agnes's tale of all supernatural intervention. Despite his glossing interjections, the narrative lapses into hagiographic language. For instance, Foxe recalls vividly how one young man, part of gang of youths who craved Agnes as "ludibrious pray," received swift divine judgment: "fire lyke unto a flash of lightning" strikes "his eyes out of his head, wherup he for dead falling to the ground, sprauleth in the chanell durt."[89] Foxe's miraculous lighting bolt, for all his claims to the contrary, looks remarkably similar to the mysterious clear light that guards Agnes in Caxton's version. This contradictory moment reveals, I believe, what comes to define a Protestant hagiography or, indeed, romance in sixteenth- and early seventeenth-century England. The evident struggle and frequent failure to "de-powder and de-sauce" the "superstitious" from stories result in an ambivalent narrative. As we move into Marina's story, that struggle for redefinition reveals itself in a striking tonal shift. Whether intentional or not, the difference in register and attitude toward older source stories from act 3 to act 4 reenacts the crisis of reforming a literary form, whose identifying motifs get caught in between Gower's medieval Ephesus and Shakespeare's post-Reformation London.

The Agnes legend, as a type of virgin martyr and older narrative model, provides one layer to the sojourn of Marina in the brothel. But the text also seems to have learned something from a more recent narrative tradition: the Protestant interlude, specifically those featuring the other Mary, Mary Magdalene. My point is not simply that Marina's tale draws from numerous prototypes but that its doing so introduces real tension in the way the reader comprehends it and understands its import. Consider, for instance, how one Protestant, Lewis Wager, adapts an old saint's play, the Digby *Mary Magdalene*, into *The Life and Repentaunce of Marie Magdalene* (1566).[90] Wager's Mary Magdalene, despite her Biblical pedigree, conjures up the air of one who strolled the London stews of Southwark, and her lively banter with her "counselors"—Nobility, Honor and Utilitie, who are really Infidelitie, Malicious Judgment, Pride, and Cupiditie (about buttocks, face paint, pockmarks, and kissing)—leads to a rousing, scurrilous song whose language and tone anticipates that of the Bawd and Bolt.[91] The twist here, as John N. King shows, is how the crude puns confirm Nobility, Honor, and Utilitie as Catholic vice figures, operating as a vehicle for polemic against the Catholic church.[92] The Bawd, the Pander, and Bolt, with their salacious humor—jokes about the pox and the French knight—offer persuasions to Marina that mimic that of Nobility and his friends to the Magdalene, first appealing to Marina's vanity, calling her a "pretty one" on whom "the gods have done their part" and next promising "pleasure" and a wide sampling of fashionable gentlemen (4.2.61, 62, 72). "Dramatic bawdry," King argues, often symbolizes the "spiritual fornication" of "Roman ritualism."[93] Although King writes of an earlier decade when John Bale popularized the image of the Roman church as the Whore of Babylon, its association had by no means ended. In Thomas Dekker's *The Whore of Babylon*, likely performed only a year before *Pericles*, a bawd, whose red pimples betray her as having the pox, serves a lustful harlot, the empress of Babylon (i.e., Rome), garbed in robes of truth.[94] The extended brothel scene with Marina thus mixes a register of the virgin saint's life with a reformed tradition that combines dramatic bawdry, a Catholic "whore of Babylon," and the contagious pox to better portray Catholicism's vice. The updated local London slang, such as when the bawd cracks that Marina "would make a puritan of the devil" (4.5.18), moreover, brings religious politics to date, locating the audience in the familiar world of 1608 London, where such competing Christian registers were familiar.

In Thaisa's "great miracle," the dead queen's recovery evokes a Catholic template of miraculous intervention vis-à-vis the saint's life and religious theater to provide a touchstone for theatrical wonder. In Marina's story, that same palimpsest undergoes interrogation. Supplemented by echoes of Protestant interludes as well as contemporary stage references, it directs wonder away from any supernatural intervention to a simple but determined effort by Marina to save herself. Her redemption from the brothel happens through resourceful human agency. Wonder in Mytilene grows from Marina's day-to-day behavior and her ability to transform those around her through dexterous verbal skills and determined refusal.[95] Two gentlemen come to see her for "unholy service" (4.4.50), as Gower terms the work of the brothel in his proceeding chorus. Like Agnes's visitors, they leave without service, claiming that they are for "no more bawdy houses," "out of the road of rutting," and wish only to "hear the vestals sing" (4.5.6–9). Marina turns these brothel-bound men from concupiscence to virtuousness. Lord Lysimachus undergoes a similar transformation; he enters the brothel joking about "the deeds of darkness" and how much a "dozen of virginities" might cost him (4.5.38, 26). He leaves imagining that he entered without a "corrupted mind," "with no ill intent," and damns the doorkeeper, Bolt, for his house of "sink" (4.5.99, 114, 125). Supernatural forces do not intervene.

Marina's reliance on resourceful human agency rather than "great miracle" to escape the brothel shows dramatically near act 4's end. While she wishes "that the gods / Would safely deliver me from this place!" she immediately turns from hope of a godly deliverance to offer to pay off Bolt with coin: "ere's gold for thee" (4.5.182–84). In a most unsaintly gesture, she proposes to sing for her supper, as it were, by teaching others her arts. Marina saves herself without the aid of an intervening angel, miraculous growing hair, a bright light, or deadly lightning bolt. The only "bolt" that intervenes on her behalf requires a fee for his services. In Marina's actions, the play distances itself from the miraculous past and reflects a contemporary London critical of Popish mysteries.[96] By so doing, it serves profoundly to demystify the working of miracle for the altered religious context of Protestantism that did not entirely deny the miraculous but regarded it warily and sought to recast its presentation and efficacy.

Marina's human agency as a source for wonderful and transforming effects presages Pericles' resurrection—a resurrection pointedly wrought not through the efficacy of ceremonious music or supernatural intervention but through the very human medium of dialogue. Pericles doubts Marina's material, physical presence, suspecting that supernatural agency clouds his vision: "But are you flesh and blood? / Have you a working pulse and are no fairy?" he queries (5.1.142–43). Marina quells any such speculation, assuring him, "I was mortally brought forth and am / No other than I appear" (5.1.95–96). The dawning recognition—and reunion—between father and daughter happens through an increasingly stichomythic dialogue that climaxes in a linguistic paradox: "Thou that beget'st him that did thee beget, / Thou that wast born at sea, buried at Tarsus, / And found at sea again!" (5.1.185–89).[97] These chiasmic lines herald Pericles's resurrection. Recalling Gower's emergence from "ashes ancient" at the play's outset, Pericles rises from the ashes of his sackcloth and calls for fresh garments, reassuming his duties of kingship and his own identity as king: "I am Pericles of Tyre" (5.1.193). Marina's power, drawn from her verbal skills, reroutes romance's traditional strategies for soliciting wonder out of the contested landscape of miracles, with their saint-life analogues, into a world where miracle happens through determined human action and verbal resourcefulness. Pericles's resurrection testifies to language's power as restorative. The titular hero's revival revises the play's earlier presentations of resurrection—Gower's uncanny rise from ancient ashes and Thaisa's spectacular awakening—through the reforming, generational figure of the daughter, one indeed born for latter times. Marina, in crucial ways, resembles Pamela and Philoclea more than her saintly analogue Agnes, showing how a writer might adapt the genre's most controversial figure—the romance heroine—by supplanting her reliance on the supernatural marvelous with a model of piety that rewarded steadfast faith and rhetorical performance.

THE EPHESIAN RETURN

Thus far my reading has argued that authors such as Sidney and Shakespeare wrote romance self-consciously attentive to its troubled reputation, confronting head-on its saintlike aspects that made it, in the eyes of some, a "superstitious" genre. Their stories arguably engage with the ways that the dangerous fabrications of Catholicism translated into an anxiety in the discursive realm of romance. Their efforts to reformulate the rhetorical triumvirate of women, romance, and Romanism, can be counted as a kind of literary triumph, producing stories salvaged from the cloister that thrived within Reformation contexts. But while the reception shows a judicious handling of "fabulous" narratives to earn them a place on the Protestant shelf, the texts themselves come to seem less sanguine about the efficacy of reform. Their triumph looks as vexed as scholars now understand the Reformation to have been.[98]

In the end, after a tour through a reformist-hued Mytilene, the play returns to Ephesus. As it does so, the final act questions whether a narrative, once de-sanctified and cleansed of its "superstitious" taint, might still hold its power to rouse a somnolent audience. What substitute could a Protestant romance offer for the loss of the supernatural marvelous and "bold bawdry" that held such a compelling force over emotions and memory?[99] The strategies unfolded over the last two chapters suggest some answers, but they also threaten to unravel romance at its emotional core, rendering it a neutered, mutilated form, stripped of its most alluring aspects. For what likely awoke the sleepy chapter-house monks in Arthur's tale, or in the virgin martyr legends, were the very qualities under erasure.

The final act of *Pericles* stages the strain of reconciling the very different worlds of Ephesus and Mytilene, of London pre- and post-Reformation, and of telling a tale "that old was sung" in a new way. The play's reanimation of cere-monial effects, heralded by the reemergence of efficacious "music of the spheres," such as Pericles hears after recognizing the girl to be his "dead" daughter Marina, coincides with a dramatic deus ex machina; Diana descends and directs him to sail to Ephesus (5.1.217). Her abrupt vertical intrusion, puncturing his Jacobean-like Mytilene world with her supernatural one, brings us back to the Ephesian realm of act 3, where ceremony and "rough music" pro-duce great miracles (5.1.215). The strange "music of the spheres"—whether the director makes the choice for the audience to hear it also or not—moreover hints at a return to something primarily religious. Pericles's and Marina's ar-rival at Diana's famous pagan Ephesian temple conforms to a generic model where supernatural, religiously inflected wonder reconciles a romance's end. Sidney's unfinished text avoids the need for such a deus ex machina by suspend-ing Pamela and Philoclea in prison indefinitely, leaving an open question as to what it would have taken for them to escape in the revised version.

While it might be argued that *Pericles*'s final act, like those preachers who wished to gloss over England's Catholic religious past in order to access the early church of Ephesus under Paul, reaches for a third temporal alternative, one that skips back to pre-Christian roots in an ancient pagan temple. Peri-cles's continual hailing of "Pure Dian" and his offer to make "oblations" to her in the last scene poignantly refuse to relegate this pagan, but also Catho-lic, icon comfortably to the past (5.3.70). Yet, despite the romance-like return to Ephesus with its curious arts, I contend the competing trajectories of Ephesian miracle and Mytilene redemption diffuse a climactic ending and contribute to what critics point to as the "unevenness" of the play.[100]

I have shown how the play highlights the mysteries of Ephesus as the site of curious arts, saintly resurrections, and the virgin cult of Mary in act 3 through the "great miracle" performed by Cerimon. When we return to Ephesus in act 5, however, after passing through the post-Reformation, London-like landscape of Mytilene, the play accesses miracle only by memory. Dramatically, no marvel awaits the audience, who already knows that Thaisa lives in Ephesus as a vestal nun to Diana. Cerimon remembers the miracle of act 3:

> Early one blustering morn this lady was
> Thrown upon this shore. I oped the coffin,
> Found there rich jewels, recovered her, and placed her
> Here in Diana's temple. (5.3.21–24)

His account shears away the earlier details of the most strange and supernatural storm; the enormous wave that tossed the coffin to the shore; the sweet odor of the coffin; in short, the miracle of her resurrection. The declarative verbs—"oped," "found," "recovered," "placed"—stress Cerimon's actions as explainable, rational discovery. The human and the verbal overwrite the miracle. Cerimon simply observes in a flat declarative statement, "Look Thaisa is / Recovered" (5.3.28–29).

Here the wonder stems from the emotional reunion of family, emblematized by the symbolic discovery of the ring—an old trope of romance—uniting husband, wife, and child. Pericles recognizes that there has been a "great miracle," and desires that Cerimon deliver "how this dead queen relives" (5.3.64). The miracle itself, however, resides in the past tense. Its immediacy recedes through the mediation of narrative. Pericles longs to witness that former miracle, but he must be satisfied to *hear* about it through Cerimon's story. Unlike in *The Winter's Tale*, where resurrection, miracle, family reunion, and plot climax all occur in act 5, in *Pericles* we may end in a temple, but the "great miracle" exists as a tantalizing past event, one accessible only through language. The play's obsession with language's narrative power—evidenced in its acute attention to the medium and modes of storytelling—has been chronicled by T. G. Bishop.[101] Less noticed, however, is how the power of narrative to remember evolves in each successive resurrection, transitioning from the backward-looking, elder Ephesian realm of efficacious ceremony, as embodied by the phoenixlike Gower and Cerimon, to a forward-looking post-Pauline

Ephesus of efficacious language, where miracle, and indeed resurrection, happens through language.

My reading suggests that the play's sequential stylistic and formal disjunctions, shown in part through its very different presentations and attitudes toward the wonder of resurrection, bring to life the quandary of early modern romance. Like Ephesus itself, *Pericles* is a play of dual possibility. Just as Ephesus could stand for iconophilia or iconoclasm, for "true miracles" or "lying wonders," *Pericles* suggests that romance contains the potential to be mobilized for its hagiographic sympathies, as the "Roman Catholicks Sweet-Heart," or for its ability to demystify and reframe those old stories for an audience weaned on the Foxean martyrologies, in "latter times."[102] Its simultaneous access to the past, as well as its engagement with the present, might account for its popular theatrical appeal, just as Ephesus's contradictory associations lent it imaginative fascination.

Although more than two decades separate the *Arcadia* and *Pericles*, and one is a prose romance penned by a known Protestant, if cosmopolitan, writer, while the other is a dramatic romance by an author who held a hybrid if not recusant faith, they both reflect ways of working out how to wrest new interpretations from the bedrock of romance. If *Pericles* raises doubts about the efficacy of a reformed romance narrative by returning to Ephesus, that doubt is registered as a glimpse at the unfinished ending of Sidney's romance. Pamela and Philoclea, for all their modeling of a Protestant piety, never leave Cecropia's tower in the abruptly ended revision. The promised wedding day never arrives, and Zelmane, who in the final sentences "was fain to leap away" from her enemy, brings shame to herself in a breach of knightly conduct (Zz8^v). *Arcadia*, convulsed by factionalism, despite Basilius's attempts to storm Cecropia's tower, is hardly the golden world promised by Sidney in his *Defence*. The lack of a culminating, decisive battle, whereby a great dragon or evil might be definitively conquered, or an enchantress captured in a net or humiliated through the loss of her prey, strips the text of any triumphant or redeeming end. Instead, the story wanders to an indeterminate and diminished halt, undermining any privileged Protestant conclusion to the adventures won by such steadfast resolve and Foxean piety. It suggests a miracle might be needed to resolve its tensions. What would have happened had Sidney completed the narrative of his revised *Arcadia*? Again and again, the endings of "reformed" romances that confront the terms of the Protestant index show a creeping anxiety about the success and promise of their "Reformation." The reading I offer suggests the complex relationship of romance with its past, which con-

sists in partial preservation, some transformation, and a measure of disa-
vowal and disillusionment. Contemporary readers who read the *Arcadia* as a
Protestant triumph had a stake in the Reformation's victory, and their readings may reflect their own desires as much as the text's synthesis to fulfill
Gower's promise to reconcile old with new. As the texts falter in their optimism, offering diminishing success, writers turned to the reader as a potential
source of more transformative Reformation, and it is to those efforts that I
turn in the second part of this book.

Superstitious Readers

Having put the case for the rehabilitation of romance through a conscientious effort to transform its most Catholic elements, I move on in the following pages to examine a related riposte to its affective commemorative powers. The conflict over romance's "fabulous" legacy was deepened by its double commemorative affect. Put simply, readers remembered Arthur's stories while they forgot Christ's. This was because, as Augustine himself admitted, romance roused readerly emotion, or what the early moderns termed "passions," which in turn were believed to be a spur to memory. The consequent emotional agency, one might even say sabotage, of romance is illuminated by the specific exhortations against it throughout the long Reformation.

In *A Christian Directory, or, A Summe of Practical Theologie* (1673), the minister and religious writer Richard Baxter claims that English readers should "avoid the Reading of Romances and Love stories" because, "by representing strong and amorous passions," they "stir up the same passions in the Reader" that will cause them to "catch the *Feaver of Lust*, which may not only *burn* up the *heart*, but cause that pernicious *deliration* in the *brain*."[1] Baxter's imagery of a reader on fire flares back to Edward Dering's bonfire fantasies suggesting that Dering offered a homeopathic solution: burn the offending books, which would otherwise cause their readers to burn. Although writing after the authors I have discussed, Baxter's comment summarizes the religiously motivated attack on romance's affective force that flamed for well over a century. It reiterates, but also bookends, similar sentiments instituted by Juan Luis Vives, who, well over a century earlier, in *Instruction of a Christen Woman*, traced how reading the wrong texts arouses the wrong passions, which in turn consume the reader with a "contagion" or "feaver"—a fever that rages in the heart, the seat of the passions, but also in the mind.[2] Vives had warned, for instance, that amorous reading was a gateway that raised "the thoughts of love" and thus opened the way to "wanton luste."[3] Cognitive theorists today recognize that what and, especially, *how* we read shapes synaptic brain functions.[4] While early modern polemicists lacked the science, they recognized the effects. Appearing as they do within manuals dedicated to guiding Christian behavior, the language of these antiromance polemicists reifies Francesca's fall; they imagine the mimetic and erotic danger of reading romance to be intimately related to a religious one. "A woman should beware" of romances, Vives specified, as much as they would of "serpentes or snakes."[5] His readers would not likely have missed the analogy: to read amorous tales was to court temptation and error, a flirtation that had damning physical as well as spiritual consequences.

Although coming from opposite ends of the Christian spectrum, one Catholic and one Puritan, and written across the gulf of the long English Reformation, both Vives's and Baxter's attacks articulate an understanding of reading grounded in somatic erotic sensation and volatile affect. According to their formulation, one reads and falls through the body. The sympathetic relationship that Vives and Baxter stage between the romance and the body's passions represents an effort to eradicate those books likely to corrupt hearts by damning those books likely to arouse powerful feelings in bodies. Both, too, suggest that the moral problem of romance—its effective call to lust—had a spiritual dimension, one that could result in damnation. For Protestants, damnation did not include a stint in purgatory, but it did entail a fall into "false doctrine" and papist "heresy"—a state facilitated by the lure of romance.[6]

In part II, I take up the volatile affect romance was thought to engender. I focus on how the textual reformation of romance (dampening its supernaturalism and making its women pious) led to an inevitable extension whereby its readers and their interpretive practice might also be imaginatively reformed. I examine the construction of a reading practice in post-Reformation England shaped by authorial concerns that reading was inherently dangerous. My focus will be on the textual and paratextual methods that sought to encourage a self-reflexive reading experience. I suggest that this imaginative discursive realm explores the paradoxes and contradictions generated by the Church of England that had a real impact on the way men and women understood the act of reading.[7]

In this respect, Vives's and Baxter's brief but telling comments about ro-

mance reflect an ongoing effort to map—and control—the relationship between reading, the passions, and pious practice.[8] They reveal how even seemingly secular reading habits and religious practice were, in fact, overlapping
concerns. In the milieu of the Reformation, John Pendergast observes, as
Protestant spiritual and ontological paradigms provided new ways of conceiv-
ing texts and interpretation, literary and religious discourses were more con-
tiguous than distinct.[9] The Protestant Reformation "transformed expectations," as Alex Davis notes, of what reading might do "for the state of his or
her soul."[10] Reading offered salvation or damnation, and what James Kearney
refers to as a "readerly or textual conversion" was always a distinct possibility
and danger.[11] By mapping the various effects of romance's excitement of the
passions onto the body and the mind, romance's critics deploy a trope that
attends to other sources of disquiet, most notably the Reformation of individual subjects.

In his treatise *The Mysterie of the Holy Government of Our Affections*, which
was published in 1620, just one year before Lady Mary Wroth's *Urania*, Thomas
Cooper, a Church of England clergyman best known for his writings on witchcraft, usefully illuminates how a Jacobean reader might understand the relationship between "the affections" or "the passions," reading, and spiritual
discipline.[12] Passions are, Cooper writes, "the fuell to our desires, & bellowes
there unto" that figure forth the "desires of the mind, in the outward man."[13]
The passions' origins, Cooper acknowledges, were debatable. Some said bodily
humors drove them; others located the soul as the generative "bellowes."[14] In
short, did bodily humors or the soul ignite the passions? The passions' origins
matter deeply for concerns about reading and its influence over the body.
Cooper argues, "These *Affections* proceede from the Soule, and not the Bodie,
not the Humours."[15] If, as Cooper suggests, the passions proceed from the soul
to affect the body, which "accidentally sinnes," primary care needs to be given
to how passions are generated in the soul. Vives had already laid the ground-
work for how reading stirred the soul's passions, which then aroused the
body's. For as a reader reads a romance, even though physically not engaged
with what she reads—or as he puts it, "though she handle them nat"—the
reader nonetheless becomes "conversant . . . with hearte and mynde."[16] In such
manner, a reader's soul is first seduced by what she reads; the physical consequences follow, just as Francesca's reading of Lancelot's kiss led her to enact
the kiss that damned her and her beloved to the inferno.[17] In other words, reading awakens the passions produced in the soul, which, in turn, become the
"bellowes" to direct bodily behavior.

Although Cooper does not directly address the reading of romance, he does indict anything that excites the primary passions (love and hate) without providing them with a proper object.[18] Notorious for its incitement to "bold bawdry" and "open manslaughter," we can see how the romance invokes a pointed anxiety.[19] By arousing love as an erotic, "bawdry" force without a moral gloss, romance would arguably, by this logic, engender improper or "ungrounded" passions. If the passions, Cooper continues, "hath found Ground, and rely on the Word . . . Then are they spirituall: but if eyther ignorarantly or superstitously they are carried to any Object: this is rather the power of Tentation, then the Rectitude of Affection."[20] To put it differently, only "spiritual" passions grow from the "Word" or scripture; superstitious affections grow when other objects or sources prompt them.

Romance invokes primary passions of love and hate within its reader but does not ground them within the spiritual "Word," and such lack of grounding makes love lust and hate murder, spurring passion to action. That is, because it solicits the passions but does not provide a proper end or object for their release, it breeds temptation and error. Expressed in the concern over idle passion was the fear that reading romance texts was neither a scholarly nor an edifying act. For romances were, in the words of the anti-Catholic poet and avid colonial promoter William Vaughan, "idle and time-wasting Bookes" devised by the Devil, and reading them was imagined to incite desire without discipline.[21] The stress that polemicists place on affectivity—and its proper governance and training—via "the Word" (i.e., what is read and how it is read) coincides with a larger Protestant effort to redefine the act of reading as one where judgment channeled passion.[22] Such an emphasis on reading and on the proper management of the passions within Protestant discourse unsurprisingly met its greatest challenge in romance, the literary form renowned for its ability to rouse an audience, only to lead them into lust and error.

The deliberate incitement of improper passions, Cooper continues, smells of a "most desperate Policie in Poperie" to "detayne unstable and deceived soules in their damnable Errors."[23] The only hope to escape such "divellish illusion" lies in having an "inward motion" to "embrace the Truth."[24] In Cooper's treatise, guarding the passions—especially when reading—becomes a religious imperative for avoiding "damnable" and especially papist error. As the title page announces, such guarding is "very necessarie for the triall of sinceritie, and encreasing in the power of Godlinesse."[25] For Cooper, reading the Word, or scripture, provides an individual training for how to manage passions and thereby to increase godliness. By contrast, other books of powerful emotional effect were dangerous, and readers required guidance and discipline lest violent and louche behavior, heresy and Catholicism, tempt them to "divellish" error. For some English writers, reading romance, as I argue below, was imagined to teach similar strategies for a deeper understanding of, and better control over, their affections. They recognized and sought to harness romance's mimetic and erotic force to the project of reforming individual readerly habits, increasing thereby a kind of godliness.

Romance's emotional impact had not always been formulated in the negative. *The treasurie of Amadis of Fraunce* (1572), a printed edition that mimicked the style of a commonplace book, offered a series of extracts from that most excoriated series of books, *Amadis*, as instructive modules. In its dedication to the reader, it promises the following: "honest and virtuous lessons" to stir and move the reader to appreciate how those "depely" drowned "in sorrowe" are comforted with "godly and vertuous consolation"; to illustrate how "abundant teares" mollify and melt a hard-hearted paramour; and to picture forth how noble and worthy captains inspire courage.[26] Each one of Thomas Hacket's examples, in the paratext to Thomas Paynell's translations from *Amadis*, builds its force for instruction from its affective qualities: in other words, by raising the passions (sorrow, love, courage), *Amadis* teaches readers how to take profit from the text's characters or types. They work to "incourag[e] the bashfull person and covvarde to bee valiant, as the vvorthie ladies and damselles in their amorous Epistles, feruente complaintes of iniuries handled moste excellently."[27]

While *Amadis* is admittedly a curious and unique document, this dedication pointedly reverses the terms of romance attack, offering romance's emotional appeal to its reader as evidence for how one might transform oneself for the good by offering "forme" or templates of instructive behavior. It presents one of the few justifications of the romance as model humanist text, marshaling the emotional memory of its examples for character improvement, along the lines of Claius's argument over the effect of Urania's memory in Sidney's revised *Arcadia* (see chapter 1). In its defense of romance, *The treasurie of Amadis of Fraunce* reimagines its condemned qualities as its most useful. What both the attacks and the defense reveal, however, is that the romance, for better or for worse, illuminates the relationship between text and reader more explicitly than other literary forms; this quality may have been invaluable to the peculiar self-reflexivity advocated in Protestant modes of reading.

Many polemicists, Cooper and Baxter among them, considered romance, in part because of its strong sway over the passions, to be corrosive to Protestant reading practice, condemning it as a fiction altogether corrupt. Yet, as I demonstrate in the chapters that follow, the very property that condemned it—its efficacious arousal of emotion—drew authors to make romance the center of their project for thinking about and transforming reading practices in ways consistent with Christian, and especially Protestant, belief. The desired mode of reading involves an active reader who distills truth from the dross of fabulation. My third chapter studies Guyon as a model of this reformed reading process but concludes with some doubt about what reforming the reader costs. My final chapter turns to the first English romance written by a woman. When Lady Mary Wroth declares romance to be a "perfect glasse," she lifts terms that were routinely used to describe the negative effects of reading romance, effects believed to be especially dangerous to and visible in its female readers. The persistent link of passions with the weaker female body marked much discourse of the period; however, recent studies show that men's passions were also a source of much anxiety.[28] By foregrounding the "affections" and "passions" of its readers, the second book of Spenser's *Faerie Queene*, a book explicitly dedicated to a female monarch, and Wroth's *Urania*, investigate how their texts might reverse rather than enforce assumptions about readers of either gender too easily seduced into the wrong passions. Romance, Spenser and Wroth boldly argue, might encourage an active, reasoned interpretation rather than a naive, mimetic identification. It might, in other words, be appropriate training for Protestant readers rather than an invitation to a fiery destruction.

CHAPTER THREE

Glozing Phantastes
in *The Faerie Queene*

When the Griffeth horse flies off bearing with him the hapless Ruggierio in *Orlando Furioso*, it prompts its English translator, Sir John Harington, to gloss the episode in an extended exegesis as follows:

> We may understand the Griffeth horse that carried him, to signifie the passion of the minde contrarie to reason, that carries men in the aire, that is in the height of their imaginations, out of Europe, that is out of the compasse of the rules of Christian religion and feare of God unto the Ile of Alcyna; which signifieth pleasure and vanities of this world. (E^r)

A peculiarly didactic anxiety to pedestrianize Ariosto's winged horse pervades the gloss. It emblematizes concern for how readers will respond to what Harington elsewhere refers to as the "meerely fabulous" dimension of romance.[1] The gloss insists on a double reading to defuse a marvelous motif—whose contentious nature I discussed in my previous two chapters—as well as the emotions, or "passion," it might engender. Neatly sidestepping the marvelous nature of "Griffeths" (or impossible aerial voyages), the gloss invokes the Platonic metaphor of a man overtaken by passions, imagined as being on a wildly running (or flying) horse. Thus what is fabulous at the literal level becomes believable, as well as morally significant, at the allegorical. The gloss advises the reader to look beyond the "meerely fabulous" dimension of Ruggiero's voyage in order to recognize the real danger: belief in hippogriffs, or to put it in literal terms, naive engagement with fabulous motifs. For to do so "signifie[s] the passion of the minde contrarie to reason," a flight that, crucially, carries the hapless beyond the realm of "Christen religion" and "feare of God" to deposit them on a sorceress's isle.

This gloss included by Harington in his translation of that most excoriated of Italian romances proves illuminating to my reading of Spenser's second book in *The Faerie Queene*. For book 2 will be preoccupied by a knight who curbs his passion and who loses his horse, turning him into a pedestrian champion whose feet pace him on his quest. This chapter takes up Spenser's concern for how readers respond to romance as the instructive crux shaping book 2's adventures. The proem forecasts this concern in its hedging over how its most important reader (significantly, a female), the sovereign Queen Elizabeth, might judge Guyon's "antique history" to be an idle "painted forgery" rather than one pedagogical or "just" (2.0.3).[2] Guyon's adventures, long read for their epic contours, in my reading confront and meditate on the romance, especially its efficacy to rouse the passions.[3]

Critics read Guyon's precarious performance of Temperance, at his quest's conclusion in the Bower of Bliss, as a failed attempt to moderate passion.[4] The example of Guyon, who is more human than Arthur, suggests the difficulty of achieving a mind that does not, like Ruggiero, fly "contrarie to reason." My reading extends the ramifications of Guyon's actions. I posit that Guyon's questionable performance of temperance in the culminating canto compromises not only his victory but also undercuts the hope that romance might be reformed or its readers disciplined. Describing to Ralegh "his whole intention in the course of this worke," Spenser expresses his hope to provide "great light to the Reader."[5] Doubt over the optimism in his letter's proclamation, that his work's "end" would "fashion" a "noble person" in "gentle discipline," however, corrodes the triumph of book 1, leading to the defensively bristling proem to book 2 (which my first chapter analyzes as a parry against post-Reformation anxiety regarding romance's cloistral fabulousness). The conundrum of a temperate "gentle knight" who seemingly fails to learn from his adventures, brings into question the reported "whole intention" of Spenser's work as one that might fashion a "gentle" reader who, too, has been made "vertuous" by discipline (1.1.1).[6]

Book 1 reveals the dangerous path down which Redcrosse plunges, as his passions, initially raised by those "ydle" images of lust, bring him to the brink of ruin, leaving him vulnerable to Despair and tempted by the unpardonable sin of suicide (1.9). Here, as late as canto 9, Una must rescue him, snatching from his hand the "cursed knife" as he is again "dismaid" by "trembling horror" (1.9.50, 49, 52). Berating him for his continued behavior as a "fraile, feeble, fleshly wight" overmastered by passion, Una's remonstrance shows how little the knight has learned despite his trials (1.9.53). In the final two cantos of book 1, Redcrosse redeems himself by defeating the dragon, emerging as an exemplary hero of romance. But a troubling anxiety lingers. Redcrosse has slain the dragon, fulfilling the imperatives of a romance narrative, but his future actions in the poem indicate that he has learned little in the way of becoming a savvy manager of his passions or gaining interpretive control. He may fulfill the mandates of the romance hero, but his behavior raises grave doubts about whether he emerges as a disciplined reader.

Book 1, as Jeffrey Dolven has shown, raises the question of what it looks like to learn.[7] If Redcrosse misses the lesson-making of his adventures, what hope is there for the reader to learn how to control his or her passions or to learn effective listening and reading habits? Book 2 dwells on the problems posed by Redcrosse's failures in book 1, in particular the interpretive recalcitrance fostered by the Knight of Holiness's overly affective engagement with romance provocations such as monsters and dissembling damsels. Book 2, I argue, tackles this failure, exploring how a romance hero, and his readerly surrogate, might "manège" the passions. Quite literally, Guyon's challenge will be to master his horse, a metonym for his passions. Guyon must ride the extremes of affect that romance allegedly provoked in its readers: on the one hand, a temptation to idle, careless reading, and on the other, an incitement to overly passionate, mimetic engagement.

Engaged in the instruction of would-be knights with a "generall end" "to fashion a gentleman or noble person in vertuous and gentle discipline," Guyon embodies the hope that there might be a temperate, or we might say, disciplined, "fashioned" and Reformed reader, one whose discipleship to the middle sage in Alma's castle insures his own "goodly reason" (2.9.54).[8] His dual nature as chivalric hero and allegorical figure makes him precisely suited to reform knightly behavior—and simultaneously to model an interpretive approach governed by a muscular control of passions. The hero of Temperance walks the mean, or "in-between," way. As a hybrid figure whose name conjures a native English romance hero and penitent pilgrim, his battle to achieve a *via media* resonates powerfully with the struggle to erect a Church of England built from a new constituent of readers trained to take pleasure, and salvation, in their own hands.

GLOSSING THE "MEERELY FABULOUS"

Redcrosse Knight's failure frays *The Faerie Queene*'s initial confidence in allegory as a sufficient practice to justify its promise to "fashion" a reader in "vertuous and gentle discipline," for, it becomes clear, discipline (or holiness) cannot be learned without interpretive sagacity (714). If book 1 introduces allegory as a reading method capable of making an "antique history" worthy of "vertuous" readers, book 2 provides a lesson in how to read it. By harnessing romance and allegory together, Spenser's salvage project relied on readers who could pierce through its "darke conceit" "by certain signes here sett in sondrie place" (0.2.4, 715). Spenser's tantalizingly brusque elucidation of his allegorical method, in his letter to Ralegh, corroborates book 2's proem with its reference to "certeine signes" as being keys to a hermeneutical strategy to bend "the image of a braue knight" toward the aims of a "virtuous and gentle discipline."[9] Yet, as I demonstrate in chapter 1, William Tyndale's warning to "beware of allegoryes" reminded writers that allegory might be as beguiling as it is instructive.[10] The only way to assure correct reading, Tyndale implies, is to train a reader who can distinguish "false mater" from right understanding. Yet how was an author to ensure that the textual allegory was correctly construed, that Guyon, and his reader, learned what he was intended to learn?

We can glimpse the difficulty of distilling a lesson from the more fabulous "phantastic" dimensions of romance in the interpretive ingenuity of Spenser's contemporary Sir John Harington. He worked arduously to prove how romance, if read allegorically, would be more than "meerely fabulous" to a careful reader, even a reader of the Italian romance by Ariosto, *Orlando Furioso*, a text routinely named in the Protestant index (A[r]).[11] Whether or not the story of Harington's provoking the queen by passing to her ladies a translation of the immoral canto 28 (his punishment allegedly being that he was to translate the entire poem) is apocryphal, its subtext of anxiety remains for how it will be read.[12] Like Spenser's proem's address ("Right well I wote most mighty Soueraine"), which seeks to prove the "just matter" of the forthcoming work, Harington's anxiously courts approval: "If your Highnesse will reade it, who dare reject it? if allow it, who can reprove it? if protect it, what Momus barking, or Zoilus biting can anie way hurt or annoy it?" (ii[r]). Harington's and Spenser's care to preempt royal criticism reveals their awareness of the potential hostility their texts could generate. Allegory, for each, forestalls criticism; as Harington assures his readers, behind the "pleasaunt and pretie fiction" lies a "good and honest and wholesome Allegorie" (v[r]). Yet Harington's qualifying adjectives "good" and "honest" prove to be proleptic as they invite Tyndale's question whether allegory indeed might be beguiling or instructive.

For both Harington and Spenser, men of cosmopolitan literary tastes, the difficulty of bridling romance with an allegorical bit must have been keen. Sir John Harington was no hotter sort of Protestant; he jestingly referred to himself as a "protesting Catholicke Puritan."[13] Yet despite Harington's polyglot confessional allegiance, he recognizes romance's compromised reputation in Protestant England. Allegorical romance had reached a summit with Tasso's *Gerusalemme liberata* in Italy, but as both English writers realized, using allegory as a justification for fabulous and amorous tales might only narrowly placate critics wary that such motifs trailed "papist" agendas. From Harington's anxious, elaborate textual apparatus we can glean just how difficult such a project might be.[14] To begin, Harington argues in his "Briefe Apologie" that the burden for correct interpretation lies with the reader. Amoral reading, he writes, is the reader's problem:

> And first if any have this scruple, that it may be hurtfull for his soule, or conscience . . . as though it might alien his mind from vertue and religion, I referre him . . . to a litle brief treatise in the beginning of this booke, written by me generally in defense of poemes, and specially of this present worke, which I dare affirme to be neither vicious, nor profane, but apt to breede the quite contrarie effects, if a *great fault be not in the readers owne bad disposition.* (A^r, my emphasis)

Spenser articulates a similar sentiment when, in his own proem to book 2, he chastises the "witless man" who "so much misweene / That nothing is but that which he hath seene" (2.0.3). Harington and Spenser both would wish to blame the "readers owne bad disposition" rather than the text (or its author or translator), for reading that might be "hurtfull for his soule" or that might "alien" his "mind" from religion. Although each voices a seemingly cavalier denunciation of bad readers, perhaps mocking those antiromance polemicists with "scruple" who might view the "present worke" as "hurtfull" for the reader's "soule," both nonetheless avidly work to guide even the most dim-witted of readers to avoid error like Redcrosse's. Harington, of course, has no Redcrosse in his translation, yet he winnows an instructive lesson out of Ariosto's romance.

Textual glossing or commentary was associated from the start with the explication of scriptures, especially the Gospels, and in most sixteenth-century contexts is explicitly religious. Although designed to comment, explain, and interpret, "glossing" in its English context carried with it "a sinister sense" of "a sophistical or disingenuous interpretation," reflecting a wariness for biblical glossing, which grew out of a scholastic, Catholic tradition.[15] But just as they did with so many other Catholic traditions, Protestants sought to appropriate the practice to their own agenda. To late Elizabethan nonscholarly readers, the most famously glossed text available to them was the Geneva Bible. Attaching a Protestant agenda to an allegorical "gloss" thus had notable scriptural precedent, but its practice bore with it an antagonistic, loaded relationship between Catholic and Protestant habits of reading.

By printing a heavily glossed and annotated *Orlando Furioso*, Harington's text translates these religious tensions into a romance context. Swaddled in a four-fold schema for allegorical interpretation taken from Italian commentaries, Harington's reading guide follows Dante's justification for applying an exegetical framework to nonscriptural texts.[16] Not unlike the practice of the Genevan glossers, Harington draws from an Italian and Catholic model to make a distinctly English and Protestant interpretive claim. Harington here adopts a trend for Protestant romance glossing anticipated by Thomas Underdowne, whose translation of an ancient Greek romance by Heliodorus, *An Aethiopian Historie*, also encased its text in gloss.[17] Such a practice of glossing demonstrates a self-conscious attempt to deflect disruptive and, especially, Catholic motifs and to adapt an old practice, and an old genre, to a new religious context.

Stephen Dobranski's work on readers in early modern England suggests how the methods and traditions of both humanist and reformist reading practices underpinned active, interpretive practices.[18] These "practices helped to emphasize the *act* of interpretation over a text's *effects*," Dobranksi demonstrates.[19] Harington's multilayered interpretive glosses, dotting the textual margins, invite just such an active reading process, visually drawing the reader's attention from the tale to the margin. By breaking the reader's absorption in the story, the glosses check reader response. For instance, when the reader encounters in stanza 12 a hermit, who like Archimago, will be more than he appears, the marginal gloss forewarns the reader that the hermit represents "an unchaste hermit, or rather hypocrise, in whose person he showeth the holy Church men, that spend much devotion on such saints."

The Protestant slant to this gloss, which pejoratively aligns hypocritical hermits to Catholic monks and their devotion to the saints, finds further reinforcement in the way that the page visually mimics the heavily glossed Geneva Bible. It presents a sly visual suggestion that insists on romance's Christian,

10

THE SECOND BOOKE

8

When from Bayardos ouer furious might,
The Pagan had himselfe discharged so,
With naked swords there was a noble fight,
Sometimes they lye aloft, some times aloe,
And from their blowes the fire flies out in fight,
I thinke that *Vulcans* hammers beat more slow.
Where he within the mountaine Ætnas chaps,
Forgeth for Ioue, the fearfull thunderclaps.

A description of a cobus betweene two knights skelfull in their weapon.

9

Sometime they profer, then they pause a while,
Sometime strike out, like maisters of the play,
Now stand vpright, now stoup another while,
Now open lye, then couer all they may.
Now ward, then with a slip the blow beguiler
Now forward step, now backe a litle way:
Now round about, and where the tone giues place
There still the other presseth in his place.

10

Renaldo did the Pagan Prince inuade,
Striking at once with all the might he cowd,
The other doth oppose against the blade,
A shield of bone and steele of temper good.
But through the same a way Fusberta made,
And of the blow resounded all the wood:
The steele, the bone like yse in peeces broke,
And left his arme benummed with the stroke.

Fusberta was Renaldos sword.

11

Which when the faire and fearfull damsell saw,
And how great domage did ensue therby,
She looked pale, for anguish and for awe,
Like those by doome that are condemnd to dy:
She thinks it best her selfe from hence withdraw,
Else will *Renaldo* take her by and by,
That same *Renaldo* whom she hateth so,
Though loue of her procured all his wo.

12

Vnto the wood she turnes her horse in haste,
Taking a litle narrow path and blind,
Her fearfull locks oftimes she backe doth cast,
Still doubting left *Renaldo* came behind,
And when that she a litle way had past,
Alow the vale a Hermit she did find,
A weake old man, with beard along his brest,
In shew deuout, and holier then the rest.

13

He seemd like one with fasts and age consumed,
He rode vpon a slouthfull going asse,
And by his looke, a man would haue presumed,
That of his conscience scrupulous he was.
Yet her young face, his old sight so illumed,
When as he saw the damsell by to passe.
Though weake and faint, as such an age behoued,
Yet charitie his courage somewhat moued.

An vnchast hermit, or rather hypocrite, in whose person he toucheth the holy Church men that friend much deuotion to such Saints.

14

The damsell of the Hermit askt the way,
That might vnto some hav'n town lead most nere,
That she might part from France without delay,
Where once *Renaldos* name she might not heare,
The frire that could enchaunt, doth all he may,
To comfort her, and make her of good cheare,
Vnto her saftie promising to looke;
Out of his bag forthwith he drew a booke,

15

A booke of skill and learning so profound,
That of a leafe he had not made an end,
But that there rose a sprite from vnder ground,
Whom like a page he doth of arrants send.
This sprite by words of secret vertue bound,
Goes where these knights their combat did intēd.
And while they two were fighting very hard,
He enters them betweene without regard.

16

Good sirs (quoth he) for courtsie sake me show,
When one of you the tother shall haue slaine,
After the trauell you do now bestow,
What guerdon you expect for all your paine,
Behold, *Orlando* striking nere a blow,
Nor breaking staffe, while you striue here in vaine,
To Paris ward the Ladie faire doth carie,
While you on fighting vndiscreetly tarie.

This was slyly deuised by the Hermit to send them a way.

17

I saw from hence a mile, or thereabout,
Orlando with *Angelica* all alone,
And as for you, they iest and make a flout,
That fight where praise and profit can be none,
Twer best you quickly went to seeke them out,
Before that any farder they be gone:
Within the walls of Paris if they get,
Your eye on her againe you shall not set.

18

When as the knights this message had receaued,
They both remaind amazed, dumbe and sad,
To heare *Orlando* had them so deceaued,
Of whom before great iclosie they had;
But good *Renaldo* so great griefe conceaued,
That for the time, like one all raging mad,
He sware without regard of God or man,
That he will kill *Orlando* if he can.

19

And seeing where his horse stood still vntide,
Thither he goes: such hast he makes away,
He offers not the Pagan leaue to ride,
Nor at the parting once adieu doth say,
Bayard that felt his maisters spurres in side,
Gal'ops amaine, ne maketh any stay.
Riuers, nor rocks, hedges, nor ditches wide,
Could stay his course, or make him step aside.

Bayardo is compared with Bucephalus for wit.

20

Nor maruell if *Renaldo* made some hast,
To mount againe vpon his horses backe.
You heard before how manie dayes had past,
That by his absence he had felt great lacke,
The horse (that had of humane wit some tast,)
Ran not away for anie iadish knacke,
His going only was to this intent,
To guide his maister where the ladie went.

21

The horse had spide her when she tooke her flight,
First from the tent, as he thereby did stand,
And followd her, and kept her long in sight,
Being by hap out of his maisters hand.
(His maister did not long before alight,
To combat with a Baron hand to hand)
The horse pursude the damsell all about,
Helping his maister still to find her out,

This Baron was Rogero, as appeareth in Boiardo poeme called Orlando inamorato in which the whole work doth depend.

He

Orlando furioso in English heroical verse, by Iohn Haringto[n], A6ᵛ. ([Imprinted at London, by Richard Field 1591]), HEH62722, STC (2nd ed.), 746. Reproduced by permission of the Huntington Library, San Marino, California.

even Protestant, potential, as it prioritizes active interpretation as a means for cultivating "profit" through a four-level interpretive guide built from scriptural exegesis. Harington tells his readers in his "Apologie" proceeding the text that, "Lastly, at the end of everie booke or Canto, because the reader may take not onely delight, but profit in reading, I have noted in all (as occasion is offred) the Morall, the Historie, the Allegorie, and the Allusion" (Aᵣ).[20]

18 And the womā which thou sawest, is the
great citie, which reigneth ouer ỹ Kings
of the earth.

CHAP. XVIII.

1.9 The louers of the worlde are sorie for the fall of the whore of Babylon. 4 An admonition to the people of God to flee out of her dominion. 10 But they shal be of God, haue cause to reioyce for her destruction.

1 ANd after these things, I sawe another Angel come downe from hea-
uen, hauing great power, so that the earth
was lightened with his glorie.

2 And he cryed out mightely with a loude
voyce, saying, a It is fallen, it is fallen, Babylon ỹ great citie, & is become the habita
tion of b deuils, and the holde of all fowle
spirits, and a cage of euerie vncleane and
hateful byrde.

3 For c all nations haue drōken of the wine
of the wrath of her fornication, and the
Kings of the earth haue committed fornication with her, and the marchits of the
earth are waxed riche of the abundance of
her pleasures.

4 And I heard another voyce frō heauen
say, d Go out of her, my people, that ye be
not parteakers in her sinnes, and that ye
receiue not of her plagues.

5 For her sinnes are e come vp vnto heauen, and God hathe remembred her ini-
quities.

6 f Rewarde her, euē as she hathe rewarded
you, and giue her double according to her
workes: & in the cup that she hathe filled
to you, fil her the double.

7 In asmuche as she glorified her self, and
liued in pleasure, so muche giue ye to her
torment and sorowe: for she saith in her
heart, g I sit being a quene, and am no
h widowe, and shal se no mourning.

8 Therefore shal her plagues come at one
day, death, and sorowe, and famine, & she
shalbe burnt with fyre: for strong is the
Lord God which wil condemne her.

9 And the Kings of the earth shal bewaile
her, & lament for her, which haue cōmit-
ted fornication, & liued in pleasure with
her, when they shal se the smoke of her
burning,

10 And shal stande a farre of for feare of
her torment, saying, Alas, alas, the great
citie Babylon, the mightie citie: for in one
houre is thy iudgement come.

11 And the i marchats of the earth shal we-
pe and waile ouer her: for no man byeth
their ware any more.

12 The ware of golde and siluer, and of
precious stone, and of pearles, and of fine
linen, and of purple, and of silke, and of
skarlet, & of all maner of Thyne k wood,
and of all vessels of yuorie, and of all vessels of moste precious wood, & of bras-
se, and of yron, and of marble,

13 And of synamon, and odours, and oint-
ments, and frankinsence, and wine, and
oile, and fine floure, and wheat, & beastes,
and shepe, and horses, and l charets, & seruants, and m soules of men.

14 (And the n apples that thy soule lusted
after, are departed from thee, & all things
which were fat and excellent, are departed
from thee, and thou shalt finde them no
more)

15 The marchants of these things which
were waxed riche, shal stand a farre of frō
her, for feare of her torment, weping and
wailing,

16 And saying, Alas, alas, the great citie,
that was clothed in fine linen and purple,
and skarlet, and guilded with golde, and
precious stone, and pearles.

17 For in one houre so great riches are come to desolation. And euerie shippe master, and all the people that occupie shippes, and shipmen, and whosoeuer trauail
on the sea, shal stand a farre of,

18 And crye, when they se the smoke of her
burning, saying, What citie was like vnto
this great citie?

19 And they shal cast o dust on their heads,
and crye weping, and wailing, & say, Alas,
alas, the great citie, wherein were made
riche all that had shippes on the sea by
her costlines: for in one houre she is ma
de desolate.

20 O heauen, reioyce of her, and ye holie
Apostles and Prophetes: for God hathe
pgiuen your iudgement on her.

21 Then a mightie Angel toke vp a stone like a great millstone, & cast it into the sea,
saying, With suche violēce shal the great
citie Babylon be cast, and shalbe q founde
no more.

22 And the voyce of harpers, & musicians,
and of pipers, & trumpetters shalbe heard
no more in thee, and no crastes man, of
whatsoeuer crafte hr be, shalbe founde a-
ny more in thee: and the founde of a mil-
stone shalbe heard no more in thee.

23 And the light of a candle shal shine no
more in thee: and the voyce of the bride-
grome and of the bride shalbe heard no
more in thee: for thy r marchants were the
great men of the earth: and with thine in-
chantements were deceiued all nations.

24 And in her was founde the blood of the
Prophetes, and of the Saintes, and of all
that were slaine vpon the earth.

CHAP. XIX.

1 Praises are giuen vnto God for iudging the whore, & for auenging the blood of his seruants. 10 The An-gel wil not be worshipped. 17 The foules and birdes are called to the slaughter.

1 And

Swaddled by such profitable homily, the interpretive frame discourages mimetic reading by disrupting "onely delight" or passionate reader engagement. The glosses help remind a wayward reader to read beyond the hermit's seemingly holy habit—for as astute readers knew a hermit is seldom just a hermit.

Just as the 1560 Geneva Bible glosses, according to its translators, sought to "explicat[e] suche [dark] places" to profit its readers, Harington's heavily annotated translation explicates "dark," often potentially Catholic or "fabulous," passages.[21] The gloss to Revelation 18 of the Geneva Bible, for instance, reads Babylon for Rome: "He describeth Rome to be the sincke of all abomination and devilishnes, and a kind of hel."[22] Just as the Geneva gloss interprets Babylon to be Rome, the seat of Catholic power and "sincke," so is Harington's reader to see the hermit as symbolic of a monk who thinks too much on the saints. The gloss, as it illuminates the "dark places," simultaneously advances a doctrinal position. It extends interpretive license to the reader to construe similar passages in like manner.

Visually and textually, Harington's readerly guide thus daringly proposes that Biblical hermeneutical skills of Catholic origin might be applied to a Protestant reading of the contested form of romance sprung from "dark," "fabulous" origins. The Protestant suspicion of the fabulous, especially what I have called the supernatural marvelous, likely explains why Harington devotes so much energy to explaining how "some things" that appear "meerely fabulous" have, in fact, "an allegoricall sence, which every bodie at the first shew cannot perceive" (A^r).[23] His attention to the marvelous episodes as those most likely to "dazzle" the reader's senses articulates the problem with romance that I trace in part I. Harington's glosses uncover a link between fabulous moments and reader response. The arousal of wonder prompts an arousal of passions more likely to produce careless reading. Here, however, we see another solution to the problem being explored: rather than dismiss the fabulous as a dangerous perversion, one that must be stripped from the story, Harington demonstrates how such motifs might be read for instruction. In doing so, he generates an interpretive methodology that applies Genevan glossing practices to secular romance texts.

In her discussion of how medieval *allegoresis* changes following the Reformation, Jennifer Summit traces how in Augustine's model, *fabula*, or poetic fiction, is the husk to be penetrated through attentive reading. Here, the "fabulous" represents a covering for hidden truth, preserving texts that might not outwardly conform to orthodoxy.[24] When, however, the skepticism toward the fabulous by William Tyndale and other Protestants reduces allegory to the status of fable, insisting instead on one literal sense for truth, as found in scripture, it becomes difficult to believe that truth might be ferreted out from multiple levels of meaning or that glossing might be anything other than "sophistical" or "disingenuous." Yet the same problem confronted post-Reformation approaches as had dogged early Catholic ones: amid the textual remains of an older literary culture: what was worth preserving, and how was it to be remembered? More troubling, how was the gap between an author's words on the page and the reader's understanding of its meaning to be safely bridged? What from Ariosto's very popular tale merited memory for a reader, likely to be Protestant, in Queen Elizabeth's court? Harington accepts that his gloss may appear as Catholic and disingenuous as his translated romance, yet he works to align it with a Protestant repurposing. He advocates a reading process that distills important moral truth from seemingly superstitious or "fabulous" matter through a rigorous gloss that appeals to reason and judgment. In this way, he resembles the middle sage of Alma's castle, who sobered the chimeric imaginings of Phantastes.

Systematically, at three different paratextual levels, Harington models how to read Ariosto's "inchantments": in the reader's preface, again in the allegorical gloss to each canto, and also directly in the margins. Often, his glosses reflect a distinctly Protestant sensibility, as when he reminds his readers in his preface, that the church did teach that prophets performed miracles.[25] Thus, he goes on to claim, Ariosto's Saint John did not overstep the bounds of a Christian credibility of supernatural events: "And sure *Ariosto* neither in his inchantments exceedth credit (for who knoes not how strong the illusions of the devill are?) neither in the miracles that *Ariosto* by the power of *S. John* is fayned to do, since the Church holdeth that Prophetes both alive and dead, have done mightie great miracles" (vii[v]). By equating enchantment with the devil's illusions, Harington neatly Christianizes the pagan, magical aspects and simultaneously suggests that the enchantments represent allegorical temptations of the devil; in doing so, he appeals to the wariness of post-Reformation culture for these narrative devices.[26] The marginal gloss I noted earlier drives home the point: his implication, that the adept friar pejoratively resembles "holy" churchmen overly devoted to "Saints," subscribes to a Protestant sensibility suspicious of saints and their miracle-working capabilities. His allegorical gloss thus enables him keep the "meerely fabulous" episodes of the poem and simultaneously claim that they are there not merely to excite or amuse readers but to edify them. Like the hermit, they might even unveil the fraud underlying Catholic figures and practices.

The substantial challenge to the text itself that this kind of reading poses, however, threatens to topple his carefully stacked interpretive schema. Just as the Geneva Bible, with its extensive annotations, provoked unease among ecclesiastical authorities for the way its marginalia served to create a contested space that opened up indeterminacy in interpretation, the task of glossing at times stretched Harington's hermeneutical ingenuity.[27] His interpretive gymnastics show the difficulty of bridling the Italian poem so that it might readily function as the didactic work he claims it to be. One striking example of this occurs in an allegorical rendering of a magic shield:

> In the shield whose light amazed the lookers on, and made them fall downe astonied, may be Allegorically ment, the great pompes of the world, that make shining showes in the bleared eyes of vaine people, and blynd them, and make them to admire and fall downe before them, having in deed nothing but shining titles without vertue, like painted sheathes with leaden weapons, or like straw without the graine; either else may be meant, the staring beauties of some gorgeous women, that astonish the eyes of weake minded men apt to receave such loving impressions, as Atlantas shield did amaze their sences that beheld it. (B3ʳ)

Providing not just one but two possible allegorical readings for the shield's blinding properties, the gloss diminishes its magic, deflecting attention away from its magical properties and toward its symbolic—and moral—significance. Furthermore, by drawing classical parallels (the "shield it selfe seemes to allude to the fable of *Medusas* head that turned men into stone"), he awards his romance readers the same license that they might exercise when reading classical texts (B3ʳ). His ongoing labor to reenvision such marvelous devices within Ariosto's romance models how a translated story resplendent with fantastic events might be framed by allegorical interpretation, if "weake minded men" but guard against naive astonishment to look beyond magic's marvelous glare. Yet, troublingly, the association between the magic of the shield and the reader's wonder is presented as an axiomatic response; it requires a muscular intervention on the part of the translator to divert the wonder from the magic to the moral lesson. The lesson continually risks being overwhelmed by the story. The difficulty of the task begins to make itself felt in the sententious tonal authority pervading the gloss: the "shining" motifs that "astonish" its readers may captivate more fully than the leaden assertion of a moral that brings little astonishment.

Despite its limitations and potential sophistical reasoning, glossing advocates a process of reading that self-consciously reforms the "fabulous" impulses of romance—and its readers. The extent and depth of Harington's efforts contrast sharply with the unabashed enthusiasm of just such impulses in one of the most popular romances printed during the same decade, Richard Johnson's *Seven Champions of Christendom* (1596). Johnson sells his story by promising an astonishing tale replete with the supernatural marvelous:

> Such Ladies sav'd, such monsters made to fall,
> Such Gyants slaine, such hellish Furies queld:
> That Humane forces few or none at all,
> In such exploits, their lives could safely shield.[28]

Keeping the title page's promise, the story itself teems with more than "Humane forces." A "fell Inchantresse Kalyb," a strangely monstrous birth, a foundling child, and a spell-sealed cave appear in the first few pages with no pedantic gloss, commentary, or paratextual authorial interruption. Johnson illustrates just how popular were the motifs that drew Protestant suspicion. The marvelous motifs so carefully framed by Harington provide the bedrock of heroic status in *The Seven Champions*. They also likely had a hand in making it a best seller. Johnson's popular romance thus highlights the generic tendencies that Harington and Spenser faced. Although more subtle than Harington, whose labor was to translate or "English" Ariosto, Spenser, through his enfolding "in couert vele" and wrapping "in shadowes light," also insists that *The Faerie Queene* be glossed, read with a similarly active, interpretive care, lest the reader be "dazled with exceeding light" (2.0.5).

"THE GOOD SIR GUYON" AS REFORMED READER

Desirous of being disciple to the "unnamed reason" in Alma's turret, Guyon exemplifies the struggles of the post-Reformation reader of romance. The fashioning of "the good Sir Guyon" into the Knight of Temperance shows Spenser rewriting the conduct of a medieval knight, and in so doing, I argue, enfolds within his adventures a hermeneutical gloss that, while less explicit, performs a similar function to Harington's external commentary. Book 2 follows Sir Guyon's training to become a "godly" reader, one who reads the adventures before him with "goodly reason," even when the fabulous and the erotic threaten to overwhelm or distract him from his quest. Through him, Spenser models a reading habit that advocates the use of reason and sober judgment to cull instruction from fabulation.

The notion of an "active," reasoned reader, while not unique to post-Reformation England, gets an increasing amount of attention from writers, who, it seems, were expecting more from their readers. For instance, Lisa Jardine and Anthony Grafton document the "goal-oriented" "strenuous attentiveness" of scholarly reading that was active as opposed to passive; Lorna Hutson chronicles how even romances and novellas were "studied for action"; William Sherman concludes that a range of contemporary reading habits saw the text as a "site of active and biased appropriation"; and Eugene Kintgen reconstructs how the kind of interpretation fostered by education and church services emphasized a radical analytic practice.[29] Stephen Dobranski refers to this as "the reader's changing function," which stemmed from the combined influence of the methods and traditions of allegorical, humanist, and reformist practices that provided lay readers with an opportunity for "interpretive interventions."[30] This newly collaborative function measures a new authority and responsibility for the early modern reader, which Spenser will exploit.

With Sir Guyon—whose literary pedigree invokes an earlier champion, Guy of Warwick—Spenser once again draws from the native medieval romance reservoir, as he had in book 1 with the Redcrosse (Saint George) and Arthur.[31] More than etymology links Guyon to Guy, as shown when Spenser's knight, accompanied by a palmer, recalls the medieval hero, whose story flourished in the sixteenth-century editions of de Worde, Pynson, and Robert Copland.[32] Equally famous as a knight who slew a monstrous dun cow, who bested the pagan giant Colbrond and who battled fierce lion-dragons, and as a pilgrim who journeyed to the Holy Land, Guy is a natural—if complex—predecessor for Spenser's hero. As a medieval knight and pilgrim, Guy fulfilled expectation: he battled monsters and then went on pilgrimage to Jerusalem, his transformation exemplifying the troubling hybrid knight/saint figure that I trace in part I. Like Guy of Warwick, Sir Guyon will eschew chivalric victories and harken to his palmer. Spenser's challenge, when he converts Guy to Guyon, will be to surpass the virtues of this Catholic romance hero and to supplant him with a hero whose vigilance roots out what the reformer John Bale categorized as "the most frivolous fables and lies" from the "truth," in the adventures before him.[33]

An early stanza in book 2 foreshadows the radically different nature of Sir Guyon's quest—and his triumphs—from those of his medieval predecessor.

Seeing a knight from afar "so fierce to pricke," Guyon in "warlike armes" prepares to "rencounter him in equall race" (2.1.26). The two knights are "ready to affrap" when, suddenly in line 7, Guyon reins in his horse, avoiding the impending clash. Guyon's decision to rein in Brigadore, his goodly steed—the following rhymes show us—was a sage one, for "affrap" leads to "mishap" and "entrap" (2.1.26). Avoiding "mishap" by checking his horse's pace, Guyon is rewarded in the next stanza for his sober restraint: he recognizes the other knight to be a fellow Christian and thus avoids "his ready speare" to "sticke" in the knight who, it turns out, is none other than Redcrosse. From this first encounter, self-restraint and a clear-headed "reading" of adventures will be Guyon's trademark, a quality that reverses the heedless, passionate Redcrosse Knight, who it appears in this stanza, still has not learned to rein in his passions and "knew / His errour" only after Guyon stays his "hastie hand," which had from "reason strayd" (2.1.28).[34] Guyon here, unlike Redcrosse, reads the scene of combat carefully and soberly, recognizing "the sacred badge" on Redcrosse's shield even amid the heat of a "fierce" "race" (2.1.26). Guyon rewrites the chivalric victory in this early battle as one of reading rather than of arms.

The pattern continues in another scene of reading when, in his first adventure, Sir Guyon happens upon a *tableau vivant* deep in the forest. Rushing to the source of a woman's shrieks, Guyon discovers the grisly spectacle of a baby contentedly playing in his dying mother's "streaming blood" with "his litle hand" (2.1.40). Nearby on the "soild gras" lies the "dead corse of an armed knight" (2.1.41). As she dies, the lady Amavia tells Guyon how the "vile Acrasia," a "false enchaunteresse," deceived and ruined her knight, Sir Mordant, in that "cursed land" "hight the Bowre of Blis" (2.1.51). A moral object lesson writ large, Sir Mordant's ruination from his reckless passion paints the fate for knights—and readers—who succumb to the erotic enticement of romance as embodied in the arch-temptress Acrasia, a character modeled after similarly devastating Italian seductresses. Guyon's adventure, we learn, will be to correct Sir Mordant's error by capturing rather than capitulating to the enchanting Acrasia. More is at stake than simple revenge. By resisting Acrasia's temptations, Guyon models how romance seductions might be combated, how erotic narratives might be netted for profit.

Guyon, these early adventures suggest, will model how to parse a scene and thus avoid the passionate lures all commentators suggest romance strews in the path of its readers, who are likely to be hapless Sir Mordants led, as Ascham so feared, from "wanton living" to "false doctrine."[35] In keeping with his sober mission, Guyon, unlike book 1's hero, does not enter book 2 "pricking" or spurring his horse across the narrative plain (1.1.1). Rather, his "trampling steed" must tread "with equall steps," checked by the "sage" accompanying Palmer, who inflicts a "sober" pace (2.1.7). Guyon's pace will become a critical index to his temperate reading. Once he quickens into "zealous haste," he mistakes and misreads the situation confronting him (2.1.13). Initially, he too falls for Archimago's tricks. When his "fierce yre" at seeing what he believes to be a wronged maiden (really Duessa) leads us to the stanza mentioned above, when his "affrap" nearly ends in "mishap," a misprision narrowly avoided by his midstanza pause to read the Christian emblem on his opponent's shield.

Guyon's education in "right" reading as one divorced from overly zealous passion becomes more explicit when, a few stanzas later, his horse, a "loftie steed with golden sell" and "goodly gorgeous barbes," is stolen (2.2.11). The horseless Guyon, forced to go on foot all the way into book 5, emblematizes Spenser's repurposing of chivalric romance convention. For "what is a knight but whan he is on horsebak?" Malory wrote. "I sett not by a knight whanne he is one fote, for all batails on fote ar but pelowres batails; for there shold no kinyghte fyghte on foote but yf hit were for treason."[36] A knight without his horse, Malory suggests, loses not only his transportation but with it his virtues. Guyon in this respect is in the position of one of Ariosto's knights, the pagan Sacripante, who too loses his horse, but Spenser puts the unhorsed figure of the knight to vastly different ends.[37] When compared to Ariosto's Sacripante, or closer to home, to Richard Johnson's knightly champions, Spenser's titular knight left horseless looks curiously pointed. The comparison usefully suggests the normative conventions for a romance hero, even in late sixteenth-century England, an England that saw far fewer knights on horseback than had medieval England. The title page of Johnson's *Seven Champions of Christendom* describes how the book will entertain its readers by

> Shewing their Honorable battailes by Sea and Land: their Tilts, Jousts, and Turnaments for Ladies: their Combats with *Giants, Monsters, and Dragons:* their adventures in forraine Nations: their *Inchauntments in the holie Land:* their Knighthoods, Prowesse, and Chivalrie . . . with their victories against the enemies of Christ.[38]

Defined through their triumphs while on horse—battles, tilts, jousts, "turnaments for ladies"—Johnson's knights are "chivalric" heroes, unimaginable *sans chevaux.* Even the woodcut image from book 1 of *The Faerie Queene,* located on the verso to the concluding stanzas, shows a knight (presumably the

Redcrosse) resplendent on his prancing palfrey. The image's placement in the 1590 edition, just opposite book 2's proem—unintentional though it may be—visually emphasizes the difference between Sir Guyon and his dragon-slaying predecessor, the Redcrosse Knight.

The loss of Brigadore so early in his quest symbolically foreshadows Sir Guyon's disciplining to be "temperate," for horses were often used metaphorically, to figure the struggle to conquer the passions.[39] Aptly enough, Stephen Bateman, for instance, names his pilgrim's horse "Will" and a figure called Reason guides him.[40] In A Choice of Emblemes (1586), Geffrey Whitney includes an emblem for temeritas that visually illustrates the link. The galloping horses symbolize, the text below informs us, "That man, whoe hath affections fowle untam'de." The emblem's moral is that he who "runnes neglecting reasons race" must learn to "bridle will, and reason make thy guide."[41] Thus, while most unchivalric, Guyon's pedestrian progress aptly signals his training toward being a knight in control of his passions who must travel to his adventures at the steady pace dictated by his own two feet. Further guided by the slow steps of his "comely Palmer," clad in sober black, Guyon walks with "equall steps," a calculated metaphor for the romance reader, who, like the knight, must study to avoid Sir Mordant's tragic misreading of erotic temptation and to eschew a winged flight that like Ruggiero's lands him at Alcyna's isle (2.1.7). Rather than the horse—and his symbolic passions—showing a loss of knightly virtues, Spenser will use Brigadore's absence as an occasion to make Guyon a better, more tempered knight.

By definition, "Temperance," in its primary sense, means a careful modulation of passions, "a race with reason," self-control, and restraint. The Latin temperare, as Leo Spitzer's classic study shows, also etymologically links with tempus, or timeliness. Guyon's virtue thus encompasses ideals of health, harmony, and balance as well as timeliness: "Accordingly temperare would mean an intervention at the right time and in the right measure by a wise 'moderator' whose purposeful activity proceeds with a view to correcting excesses."[42] A "wise 'moderator,'" for "correcting excesses" seems just the kind of guide that a reformer such as Roger Ascham might wish for a reader who persists in reading romance. When put into the context of post-Reformation polemic, Guyon's horseless temperance quite deliberately counters the experience of readers like the infamous Paolo and Francesca, who are undone by reading a romance and who want to blame the author for their sinful act.[43]

Guyon, who goes on his two feet, tempers "the passion with aduizement

Emblem for *Temeritas*. Geoffrey Whitney, *A Choice of Emblemes*, A3ᵛ. (Imprinted at Leyden: In the house of Christopher Plantyn, by Francis Raphelengius, M.D.LXXXVI. [1586]), HEH79714, STC (2nd ed.), 25438. Reproduced by permission of the Huntington Library, San Marino, California.

slow" (2.5.13) and thus anticipates "goodly reason," the integral mediating sage of the middle chamber of Alma's tower, whose disciple Guyon aspires to be. Moreover, the unhorsing of Guyon serves to make him even more human by de-supernaturalizing him. On horseback a knight becomes a hybrid, centaur-like creature with marvelous powers, one capable, like Redcrosse, of battling monstrous dragons. Without the horse, the knight is just a man: he is human, as Oedipus would say to the sphinx, because a "man" is one who walks on two feet.[44] Guyon, of all Spenser's knights, most resembles Sidney's Pyrocles and Musidorus because he never battles a monster. He looks like Sidney's knights precisely because the Palmer will do for Guyon what Sidney had done to his text: conjure away the monsters. Malaeger, the creature closest to a monster in book 2, has to be killed by Arthur (who still has his horse), and the fearful sea monsters guarding Acrasia's bowers dissipate into mist before the Palmer's mighty staff. Guyon, thus, with his very human "equall steps" and self-determined reading, arguably pedestrianizes romance's "Phantastic" erotic dimensions—the very effects of romance held to be its cloistered, and therefore damning, qualities.

MERRY TALES AND THE IDLE READER

"The lazie Monkes, & fat-headed Friers, in whom was noght but sloath & idlenes," wrote the puritan divine Henry Crosse in 1603, "for living in pleasure & ease, and not interrupted with cares" had time "to vomit out their doltish & rediculous fables."[45] Referring to the by now familiar index of romance titles, Crosse's invective reinforces the long-standing accusation that romance sprang from idleness and encouraged the same quality in its readers. Idleness, or *otium*, as Brian Vickers has observed, held especially pejorative connotations during the Renaissance, even more so within romance epic literary forms such as those of Ariosto, Tasso, and Spenser: "The invitation to rest, indulge the sense, is tantamount to suicide, as Spenser emphasized, and the *locus amoenus* is the scene for the most dangerous degradations of human potential, unless and until some paragon of virtue, divine or human, performs a rescue."[46] Sir Mordant's flirtation "in pleasure and delight" well illustrates Vickers's point, as his indulgence in Acrasia's notoriously idle bower seals his damnable death (2.1.52). The proem too is at pains to distance itself from this term of opprobrium, denying its own birth in "th'aboundance of an ydle braine." Even the fecund Phantastes's "idle thoughtes and fantasies" represent "fained," in other words pleasant, but false "lies," diversions that potentially herald grave peril and are best mediated through reason (2.9.51).

While Vickers does not engage with the religious aspect to the problem of *otium*, I want to call attention to how Roger Ascham's associative link between Arthur's tales and "idle monks" established a popular Protestant slur.[47] During the Reformation, idleness was a quality often aligned with the "false and fabulous"—and potentially popish. To be an idle reader implied being a superstitious one, one who neglected to practice a discerning, interpretive process that winnowed truth from "fabulous" matter. Belphoebe defines the knightly ethos as one of labor and sweat, by which one "who seekes with painfull toile, shall honor soonest find" (2.3.40), whether "abroad in armes" as is Guyon, or "at home in studious kynd" as is the reader (2.3.40). It is the sirens, after all, who urge Guyon to forsake "wearisome turmoyle" (2.12.32). Guyon's adventure across the Idle Lake showcases the great peril romance posed to the Protestant knight and reader. Phaedria urges Guyon to take his hand off his heart, to rest, and to delight only in her "merry tales" (2.6.6). Separated from his palmer, his heretofore reasonable guide, Guyon will prove his sagacity at parsing a scene as he resists giving in to the vagaries or pleasures of the moment. Instead, Guyon "was wise" and "ever held his hand upon his hart" (2.6.26), a supplementary posture that substitutes his own palm to play the role of the now absent Palmer. Guyon's gesture declares his self-control over the fount of his affections.

The Idle Lake, with its merry sailor Phaedria (who fritters away time in "immodest mirth"), figures forth romance's penchant for keeping its heroes—or its readers—from the labors they should be pursuing, whether slaying a dragon or pursuing more just reading matter such as scripture (2.6, headnote). Phaedria, a veritable "store-house" of "merry tales" that she "greatly joyed . . . to faine" joins Cecropia as a duplicitous figure aligned explicitly with Catholicism; Phaedria recalls the legendary "Pope Ione" (2.6.6, 3).[48] Her idly Catholic tales, full of "vaine jolliment," make her a most "merry mariner," and her boat, magically guided by a pin "from rocks and flats," contrasts with the Palmer's well-rigged boat that will later purposefully steer Guyon to Acrasia's lair (2.6.3, 4, 5). Yet here Guyon willfully reverses a hallmark motif of romance. A "rudderless boat," as Helen Cooper shows, typically forces the captive knight into passivity, reversing the forward thrust of a quest.[49] As Tasso had shown, Rinaldo lay at Armida's mercy once he entered the little frigate by the riverbank. And, indeed, Cymochles's fate shadows that of Rinaldo. Quickly succumbing to Phaedria's "light behaviour, and loose dalliaunce," which "gave wondrous great contentment to the knight," he "had no souenaunce, / Nor care of vow'd revenge, and cruell fight" (2.6.8). Sinking happily into an oblivious, amorous "ydle dreme," Cymochles laid aside his arms, looking very much like the naive knight or reader who, as feared by Spenser, Harington, and the reformers, forgets to keep watch for the wolf (2.6.27). By metaphorical extension, the readers of romance, once aboard the bark of romance, allegedly became as hapless as the floating knight who no longer could—or cared—to steer his boat.

Guyon, however, does not fall prey to the "ydle dreme." Phaedria, whisking him away from his palmer, does her prettiest to "drowen [him] in dissolute delights," but he only temperately "ever held his hand upon his hart," and her "dalliaunce he despisd" (2.6.25, 26, 21). As the verb "despised" reveals,

Guyon looks at and reads her, and as he does so, he recognizes her false or "vaine" nature, which pierces through her "merry" outward show. Guyon does not succumb. The extended analogy opening the next canto, canto 7, compares Guyon to a pilot "well expert in perilous wave" (2.7.1). It draws an explicit contrast between the pilot, who "upon his card and compas firmes his eye" "and to them does the steddy helme apply" to Phaedria's magical, but idle, seamanship (2.7.1). Guyon's steadfast denial of Phaedria's beckoning him toward an "ydle dreme," as well as the more Protestant emphasis placed on his strenuous work and labor (his "firme" eye that steers the "helme"), overturns the hallmark "rudderless boat" motif, guided by miracle or magic alone, to suggest that "true" guidance comes through careful, arduous steering—and reading. Approached this way, the Idle Lake and its vain tales pose no threat. Guyon's attentive seamanship represents an important moment of resistance to, and triumph over, idle, superstitious reading.

Here Guyon mimes the habits of an active reader, one who might read as arduously as Guyon sails, extracting from Phaedria's story a warning against the perils of idle reading and neutralizing its threat.[50] Guyon's piercing eye and guarded heart reads truth, even from vain tales told by a figure much like the "merry Pope Ione" (2.6.3). In her analysis of reading after the Reformation, Jennifer Summit notes the practices of Stephen Bateman, who counsels that, through the application of "reason" and labor, even seemingly superstitious, vain texts might yield worthy matter to discerning readers.[51] I am suggesting that Spenser portrays his Guyon reading in a manner similar to that proposed by Bateman, thus showing how even condemned stories might yield a moral harvest. By refusing to indulge Phaedria in this episode, Guyon seemingly has internalized his need for his palmer (or his "glozing"). He returns to the shore no worse for sailing the Idle Lake nor for having listened to vain tales.

Guyon's success models how a reader with arduous "steering" might avoid the alleged idle-inducing, soporific qualities of romance. It proves more difficult, however, to master romance's effects on the hotter passions. Throughout his adventures, from that early near "mishap" with Redcrosse, Guyon encounters multiple figures who misread things to tragic effect, picturing the deleterious consequence of a passionate, as opposed to rational, reading. Spenser, as Christopher Tilmouth argues, inherited a dualistic opposition from classical philosophy reinforced by Erasmus's oft-reprinted *Enchiridion Militis Christiani*. In this familiar dualism, fallen man was constantly striving against his passions toward reason; passions were disruptive forces that needed to be suppressed or eradicated. Passion and reason, consequently, were imagined dueling for the soul.[52] As Guyon leaves behind the Idle Lake to continue his journey, more insistent demands and an increasingly lush romance landscape agitate his passions. Guyon may not be an idle reader, but he is a perilously mimetic one.

THE "GLOZING" PALMER

Guyon's "despising" reading of Phaedria occurs midway on his journey (in canto 6); it represents a performance that he seemingly cannot sustain. Immediately after, his mastery of his passions falters. Instead of keeping his hand on his heart as he does while he listens to Phaedria's merry tales, he relies increasingly on the Palmer's extractive mediation. Bereft of his palmer in Mammon's Cave, Guyon again relies on his own resources, and though while in the cave his passions are rightly ordered, he "Did feed his eyes" with "wonder all the way" (2.7.24). Such a greedy seeing—and reading—of all that Mammon shows him results in his infamous faint. Upon leaving he has to be resuscitated by a triplicate force of the angel, the Palmer, and Arthur. Such a heavenly rescue leaves little doubt that Guyon requires divine intervention in his fluctuating efforts to achieve temperate reading.[53] As book 2 proceeds, rather than growing in skill, Gower looks to the Palmer, who takes on a more anxiously interventionist role, miming as he does so the proliferating glosses of the Geneva Bible, or Harington's triplicate glosses, in an attempt to guide a "correct" interpretation of the "dark" passages for the reader. Like those biblical glosses, the Palmer's mediation proves double-edged.

The Palmer's relationship to Guyon has troubled generations of critics.[54] As a pilgrim figure, he harkens back to his medieval predecessor, Guy, who became a Catholic penitent. In this dimension, his "glossing" recalls the spiritual practice of Catholic commentary. He is also a disciplinarian, associated with the schoolmaster, for as the OED records, a "palmer" was a stick to punish schoolboys.[55] In J. Daus's translation of Henry Bullinger's Hundred Sermons on Apocalips (tr. 1561), for instance, "least they forget them selves," children "are kept in awe with the Palmer."[56] The suggestion that the "palmer" ensures that pupils do not "forget" themselves raises unease as to whether the pupil might "remember himself" on his own. In this aspect, the Palmer begins to look and sound like a personified Genevan gloss, a recruited guide adopted from old practices made to serve a new end. As a pilgrim-tutor, he provides the doctrinal and homiletic advice that we saw printed in Harington's translated marginalia.

In practice, the Palmer aids Guyon, lest he "forget himself."[57] For instance, he immediately recognizes the Redcrosse Knight, confirming Guyon's nearly belated recognition of him (2.1.31). His presence, and Guyon's continued reliance on him, reveals the more general concern within the text over a multiplicity or indeterminacy of meaning that required guidance to distill truth from falsehood, a real damsel in distress from Duessa. The Palmer's presence raises the dilemma whether Guyon might be fashioned to read *without* the careful mediation of his priestly guide. The Palmer, in other words, underscores an uncertainty about readerly license.

The danger posed by forgetting oneself and reading too mimetically, of becoming emotionally credulous, like the superstitious fisherman in Sidney's *Arcadia*, emerges in Phaon's cautionary example. Like the warning tableau of Sir Mordant, lured into error by lust, Phaon falls into tragedy because of his overhasty "read" of a scenario he does not stop or bother to distill. The story, perhaps more familiar to us from Shakespeare's *Much Ado about Nothing*, recounts how Phaon's best friend, Philemon, tells him his wife has taken a paramour. In Spenser's telling, one night, in the "darksome shade," Philemon brings Phaon to where he sees his beloved Claribell amorously dallying with a base groom. "With wrathfull hand I slew her innocent," Phaon regretfully admits (2.4.29). When the dying Pyrene confesses that Philemon made her wear Claribell's clothes, Phaon poisons Philemon. "Thus heaping crime on crime," he next bends his "murderous blade" toward Pyrene, but she flees, and he chases after her until Furor catches and binds him (2.4.31). The Palmer supplies the gloss to the tale: if "affections" bend "gainst fort of Reason," the squire will be "laide thus low" (2.4.34). The homiletic provided by the Palmer leaves little doubt that Phaon's tragedy stands as a warning to the impulsive reader to bridle affection. Guyon chimes in that the squire may ease his "hurts" through "temperance" (2.4.33). Yet, although Guyon can judge Phaon's error, his ability to apply that lesson to his own experience appears frustratingly limited, a worry that Spenser seems also to feel for his reader.

The Palmer's advice directly conflicts with an integral aspect of romance: the efficacious arousal of passion in its knights and ladies as well as its reader. It was this quality, after all, that made Arthur such a compelling figure to medieval monks. Romance appears to be inseparable from what Webster identified, in his dedicatory poem to Anthony Munday's translation of the romance *Palmerin*, as a core virtue: "the sighs of ladies and the spleen of knights."[58] Malory's quip about a knight being inseparable from his horse goes beyond the literal horse: for what is a knight separated from his "spleen" or passion, a lady from her "sighs"? Even Spenser acknowledges that he chooses Arthur, in part, because "men delight to read" about him, and it is this quality that renders him—and romance—fit "for profite of the ensample."[59]

An example of a pilgrim knight more fully divested from his passion illustrates Spenser's conundrum. The steadfast pilgrim of Stephen Bateman, who, as I have just argued, advocates a "reasonable" reading practice, models a more idealized but ultimately much less engaging temperate restraint.[60] Building Pilgrim's journey around the metaphors of the chivalric quest and spiritual struggle, Bateman's free translation of Olivier de la Marche's Burgundian chivalric allegory emphasizes a specifically post-Reformation conception of the Christian life, strongly shaped by English Protestantism. When tempted by Dolor and Debilitie to indulge in idleness and lechery, Pilgrim remembers himself within the space of a few lines.[61] Pilgrim avoids excess of various kinds, helped in part to restraint through the lengthy instruction administered to him by allegorical figures like Thought and Memory and, later, Age.[62] Pilgrim faces temptation, at least in the abstract, similar to Guyon's: idleness on the one hand and lust on the other. Because Bateman's text lacks the rhetorical dilation, however, given these dangers in The Faerie Queene, the reader, like Pilgrim, will likely find their enticement less compelling. The single edition of this text, even with its numerous and beautiful woodcuts, suggests it never quite captured its English audience; there was little market for a reprint. Batemen's text offers a testament to the kind of reading practice advocated by Protestants; it appropriately dwells more on the homiletic than the temptation and consequently makes the lesson more prominent than its cause. Yet it is Spenser, not Bateman, whom John Milton in Areopagitica will later praise, claiming Spenser's Sir Guyon for a "better teacher than Scotus or Aquinas" because Spenser brings him in "with his palmer through the cave of Mammon and the blower of earthly bliss, that he might see and know, and yet abstain."[63]

What Spenser understands is that outright homiletics, sutured onto a romance narrative "or sermoned at large," do not quite get the job done of rousing a drowsy reader.[64] The sober Palmer is hardly anyone's favorite character. For Spenser, like Sidney, realizes that affective identification are necessary to move and instruct a reader. A participatory reading works only if the reader sympathizes with the knight's struggles and, through him, learns to cull "matter of just memory" from Phantastes. Much rides, then, on Guyon's successful parrying of romance's distractions. Book 2 attempts to walk the mean, a kind of literary via media, between the strident, plainly realized precepts of a text like Bateman's and the indulged passions condemned by Ascham in much medieval as well as contemporary romance. Guyon's challenge will be to see, read, and, as he does with Phaedria, sail on with his "hand on his heart." This difficult balancing act, like Harington's reaching glosses, threatens to topple the text. The Palmer, as I shall show, complicates rather than simplifies the interpretive task.

THE BOWER OF BLISS, A CRISIS OF THE MIDDLE WAY

Milton provides an example of at least one disciplined reader who follows Guyon to an understanding of temperance and lays to rest the anxieties voiced in the proem over reader reception. Milton, however, seems more confident of the benefits of tried virtue than do the final cantos of book 2. Although Guyon sails the Idle Lake "of none accompanyde" immediately after, in canto 7, he does not recognize Mammon as so obvious an evil figure as he is and enters his cave. It is hard to imagine the Palmer, were he present, endorsing such action. Guyon resists Mammon, but his greedy gazing while underground exhausts him and leaves him in a faint at the cave's entrance, which Spenser likens to a "slumbring fast" in a "senceles dreame," language that recalls Cymochles's idle sleep on Phaedria's island (2.4.4). Weakened, Guyon is claimed by the intemperate figures of Pyrochles and Cymochles and has to be rescued, as had been Redcrosse, by the deus ex machina of an angel and Arthur, who makes a timely arrival (2.7.2). Guyon will not again be left unaccompanied. Either Arthur or the Palmer shadows him until he rushes off after Florimell in book 3. Even when the angel discharges his care to the Palmer, he proclaims, "Yet will I not forgoe, ne yet forget / The care therof my self unto the end / But euermore him succour, and defend" (2.8.8). Instead of decreasing his reliance on his "faithful guyde," as a quick study might be expected to do, when Guyon approaches his ultimate battle against Acrasia, the Palmer seems more inseparable from Guyon than he was at the outset (2.2.1). The reader's experience, and hence sympathy, furthermore, has been sutured onto Guyon's, since it is through his voyeuristic eye that we see Phaedria, Mammon's cave, Alma's castle, and, most important, Acrasia's bower. The reader sees as Guyon does. The Palmer hovers like a persistent marginal gloss, constantly calling Guyon and his surrogate reader back to the lesson with ever more frequent homiletic interruptions as the story heats up in the bower.

After Guyon swoons at the mouth of Mammon's cave, for instance, an angel summons the Palmer back to Guyon's rescue (2.8.3–9); the Palmer then defends him against Pyrochles and a very angry Cymochles (2.8.12–16); steers

the boat to Acrasia's Bower (2.12.3); moralizes on its dangers (2.12.9); re-
bukes Phaedria and disperses the sea monsters with his staff (2.12.16, 26);
warns Guyon against pity for the wailing maiden and subdues the monsters
guarding the bower's entrance (2.12.28–29, 40); chastens Guyon for gazing over-
long at the two naked damsels wrestling in the fountain (2.12.69); aids Guyon
to capture Acrasia and Verdant with a net he made, pacifies Acrasia's beasts,
and transforms them back to their rightful shape (2.12.81, 84–87); and finally,
in a later book, convinces Guyon not to seek revenge against Britomart after
Guyon has been most unceremoniously knocked off the horse he is riding by
Britomart's power, a final gesture that suggests Guyon needs further chastisement and is not yet ready to remount his own Brigadore (3.1.9–11). The active
verbs here are revealing. Most of the labor of steering, reading, warning, chas-
tising, subduing, and counseling in these final cantos falls not to the hero
but to the glossing Palmer, which makes him an indispensable party to Acrasia's overthrow. The verbs raise the provocative question, would Guyon, without his Palmer, have been able to complete his quest? Spenser makes Guyon
trade in his horse, symbolic of his "passions," for the Palmer, who becomes
a Protestant prosthetic or supplement for active, reasoned reading. He is the
palmer that keeps in awe the pupil. Would Guyon, or the reformed reader,
without the "glozing" Palmer, find his way out of the dark conceits of the
text into the light? Or would he, like Francesca, be "defeated" by the story,
finding himself sojourning in the outer circles of hell rather than the fields of
paradise?[65]

Sans Palmer, Guyon would have "relent[ed] his earnest pace," lost to the
vision of naked damsels disporting in the jasper fountain (2.12.65). The "secret
pleasaunce" that creeps over him, when their "lilly paps aloft displayd," provokes him to gaze but not to "read" them in the same way that he was able to
"despise" Phaedria (2.12.66). The Palmer's rebuke at such a crucial narrative
moment throws into relief the difficulty of successfully checking romance's seductions over the mind and will, for along with Guyon, readers likely relish and
remember the lush verbal imagery pervading the bower more than they do the
Palmer's stern counsel (2.12.65). The sensual, ekphrastic language beguiles the
reader along with Guyon, as both "gaze" on the bower's delights. Guyon "much
wondred" after the bower's "fayre aspect," and only when chastened by the
Palmer does he remember to put his hand on his heart and to suffer "no delight / To sincke into his sence, nor mind affect" (2.12.53). His "wandring eyes"
suggest the reader's continual peril as he succumbs to the bower's charms, reminded of his mission only by the Palmer's quick intervention (2.12.69). Guyon,

only with a little help from his friend, "forward thence" curbs his wandering (2.12.69).

The Bower of Bliss represents, among other things, the figurative heart of romance, a distillation of the form's most alluring and deadly tendencies. Like the wandering wood of book 1, the bower powerfully symbolizes a *locus amoenus* of erotic dalliance, idle dreams, slumbering knights, and sensual indulgence that graphically pictures the very dangers that polemicists thundered against.[66] As Guyon creeps toward the epicenter of Acrasia's lair, he spies a chilling parody of the pietà as the enchantress Acrasia cradles her complicit, inert lover. Verdant's fate fictionally renders the deepest fears of reformers regarding romance's power over its reader. Having abandoned his "warlike Armes" and given up on honor, and spending his days in "wastfull luxuree," he lies blissfully ignorant of his fate under a "horrible enchantment" (2.12.80). While he slumbers, Acrasia "through his humid eyes did sucke his spright" (2.12.73). His utter passivity before her intensifies a sense of the moral failure of romance and the unwary reader's risk as, unbeknownst to him, the book he holds, like a textual Acrasia, steals forth his spirit through his idle eyes.

Confronted by this horrific tableau, Guyon energetically destroys the bower in one blistering stanza of wrath. His passionate violence looks iconoclastic in its fury, but Jennifer Summit argues that Guyon's enacts, through his "rigour pitiless," a post-Reformation ethic preoccupied with chastisement and correction rather than destruction (2.12.83). He seeks, she suggests, to purify "those monuments of the corrosive accretions of monastic influence" in order to preserve the "true history" from "frivolous fables and lyes."[67] In her reading, Guyon does not fail but employs the "fetters of reason" to bind Acrasia, thus successfully reforming a "fabulous" seduction.[68] If we concur with Summit's convincing reading of the bower, and if we then construe Guyon's actions as modeling a Protestant "correction," we are left with a daunting question: what does the "corrected" tale look like? Are its ruins as evocative as were the choirs of Shakespeare's memorable sonnet 73?

When Guyon destroys the bower, as it seems he must, he effectively obliterates romance. For what remains, once romance has been "corrected," of its most alluring and efficacious motifs? His Josiah-like fury may be the only response to the bower's excess, idle dalliance, and siren-like imagery—and, by analogy, to romance's latent potentialities.[69] Yet Guyon's violence, marked by verbs like "broke," "deface," "suppresse," and especially "burne" (2.12.83), calls to mind the zealotry of reformers like Edward Dering, who saw the conflagration, rather than the correction, of romance as the only solution to its seduction. In the bower, Guyon performs the act of judgment that the proem fears, judging the bower to be a "painted forgery" built by "th'aboundance of an ydle braine" (2.0.1). In the wake of the bower's razing, the proem's promise, to turn idle tales into just matter fit for memory or the prospect of disciplining "temperate" readers, looks itself more fabulous then true.[70] Once the enchantment has been broken, what stands beyond the felled arbors of Acrasia's garden? Crucially, what happens to those who have witnessed both their beauty and their destruction? Are they, as Milton will suggest, granted a deeper understanding of virtue?

Conceptually more challenging than the triumphant end to book 1, book 2's metaphoric conflagration raises questions about the potential for reforming romance or training its readers. While Guyon can sometimes exude self-mastery and can "well manège" his horse's passion, as he proves in book 5, when he alone can calm Brigadore at Florimell's wedding (5.3.34), more commonly we see his ineptitude at curbing the passions all too often unleashed within the world of *The Faerie Queene*. Later, in book 3, when Britomart surprises Busirane deep in his spells, she forces him to reverse his charms, and his halls melt away like the monsters before the Palmer's staff. His decayed halls, like the blackened bower, prove unsettling. Britomart, "dismayd" by "their glory quite decayd," suggests that even when overcome, the glories of the fabulous might prove more compelling than their extracted lesson (3.12.42). Likewise, Calidore's vision on Mount Acidale of the dancing graces outshines the homily offered by a grumpy Colin Clout, who has broken his pipe in pique (6.10.10–29). Book 2's ending proves prophetic. When the Palmer frees the men whom Acrasia has perverted through their intemperance into "figures hideous," "they comely men became" in outward appearance. Their minds, however, remain tainted. Gryll most blatantly figures how, once man "delightes in filth and fowle incontinence," he risks forever keeping that "hoggish forme" (2.12.87, 86). He cannot remember "the excellence / Of his creation" (2.12.87). The Palmer's last words haunt the poem: "Let *Gryll* be *Gryll*," he declares; for him there can be no recuperation. His utter forgetfulness of his origins leaves him worse than a beast, a condition that provocatively and dispiritingly recalls polemicists' belief in romance's deleterious effect on readers. Gryll, irrevocably lost by his sojourn in the Bower of Bliss, troubles the notion that a reader might ever be disciplined enough to journey safely through romance's narratives. The denizens who dwell too long under the spell of romance never quite recover their original shape.

In Alma's castle, "goodly reason" shadows the idealized poet who might write "memorable gestes" that balance the fantasies of romance with the imperative of historical veracity and religious belief (2.9.54). Guyon's razing of the Bower, however, dispels the delicate and idealized harmony envisioned by the middle sage. His actions question the very idea that excess might be moderately mediated. When we later meet Guyon in books 3 and 5, his actions further reveal the chastened expectations that pervade book 2's end. Guyon's "disdainefull wrath" and "revenging rage" at being unseated from Arthur's horse by a stranger knight (who turns out to be Britomart) uncomfortably recall his actions in the bower (3.1.9, 11). His anger is cooled not by his temperance but, once again, by the interventionist gloss and better reading of the trusty Palmer, who persuades him that he faces an enchanted spear. A few short stanzas later, after this further lapse of "goodly temperaunce," Guyon charges off in pursuit of Florimell with motives better suited to a knight of Ariosto than to a disciple of Alma; the Palmer, rather pointedly, remains behind, excluded from such emotional tumult and erotic rush (3.1.12, 18). Spenser's leaving the Palmer behind may hint that he's realized that the Palmer is useless in this world at teaching Guyon, the reader. When we last glimpse Guyon, in book 5, he is restrained from "open manslaughter" only by the hand of Artegall. In every subsequent incident, Guyon fails to keep his hand on his heart, a poor student to the lesson of Phaon.

The smoking landscape that closes book 2 foreshadows growing difficulties later in the poem with the Protestant reorientation of romance, even as the text itself digresses further into romance-like dilation: the failure to ever contain the blatant beast; the increasingly severe divisions in book 5 between allegory and romance, between Faerie land and the political entity of England; the less conclusive adventures of the later heroes. Redcrosse recovers Eden in book 1 and appears as an ambitiously and prophetically reformist saintly knight. But book 2 heralds what is to come. In book 6, one doubts whether Arcadia is saved or destroyed by Calidore. In my reading of book 2, a self-neutralizing doubt clouds the Reformation of romance's readers just as the reformation of its narrative strategies halted in unfinished narratives.

The proem to book 4 indicates that, from Spenser's perspective at least, even despite the Palmer's salutary efforts, readers continued to misconstrue and misunderstand, buying into the "false allurement," the "pleasing baite," that "their fancies fed" and were not in "virtues discipled" (4.0.2). Guyon, in other words, turns out to be a typical reader, one presumably too open to passion and, consequently, to misunderstanding. By the final stanza of book 6, the narrational voice of Spenser has even further diminished the idea that his readers might be educated by his poem, concluding rather lamely that his "rimes" only "seeke to please" (6.12.41).

To put all this another way, the romance characteristics threaded throughout *The Faerie Queene* may have been part of a strategy for inculcating a reading process that reflected Protestant practice and appropriated an old vessel for new use, but its increasing defensiveness about that project reflects a growing cultural uneasiness that the failure to reform romance signaled a broader difficulty of reforming a culture. The tensions and strain apparent within Spenser's hybrid literary work open a more sustained argument regarding the ambivalent nature of the English Reformation and its ramifications for a history of reading practices. Guyon triumphs in attaining the rigor and discipline necessary to purify romance's dangerous arousal of ungrounded passions, and in this, he looks like a model post-Reformation reader. Yet this triumph fades against what he leaves behind: a ruined, burned, and "surpressed" landscape with neither fabulousness nor truth, a dispiriting legacy to a post-Reformation act of salvage.

CHAPTER FOUR

"Soundly washed" or Interpretively Redeemed?

Labor and Reading in Lady Mary Wroth's Urania

The shibboleths directed against English romance after the Reformation held it as a malign, dangerous, but seductively powerful hybrid, or "in-between," genre, associated with Roman Catholicism and a pejorative femininity; this comes into sharp focus in the final text I consider: Lady Mary Wroth's *Urania*. I have argued that romance sometimes stood for all that was taken to be wrong with Catholic beliefs and reading practices and that its repurposing stood as a hypothesis for England's Reformation. The romance that is the centerpiece of this chapter takes up Spenser's earlier struggle to discipline, and thereby to define, that newly "middle" reformed reader, and disciple of Alma, who is passionately engaged but who, in Wroth's phrase, refuses "to turne blabb" (1.318).[1] The *Urania* further explores how even the most porous reader might acquire interpretative sagacity within texts believed to incite misprision. Focusing on the implications of Wroth's hermeneutical "middles," and her hybrid or "in-between" reader, this chapter focalizes the ongoing anxiety about romance, gender, its religious dimension, and the act of reading that I have so far traced across male romance writers. As I situate Wroth within this history of reforming the romance, I highlight how challenges of genre and gender produce a series of encounters that shape the written text but that also connect to concerns that range beyond the romance.[2]

The intellectual affinities between Lady Mary Wroth and earlier male Protestant romance writers extend from the forms of their efforts to the broader aims that governed the Reformation. In this chapter, I argue that Wroth's project responds to but also goes beyond that imagined by her all male predecessors.[3] Like them, she envisions a reformation of the romance reader as one that entails less reliance on supernatural incidents and more on rigorous interpretive labor. Just as Sir Guyon had to learn to be a better reader by controlling his passions, Wroth's central female characters undergo adventures that challenge their capabilities, akin to perspicacious readers who are not led astray by superstitious, mimetic, erotic, or overly passionate responses. But Wroth differs in important ways when she proposes that, more than an individual duty, there exists the necessity of building a readerly community that might check and balance individual interpretation. Her romance thus constitutes further engagement with a discussion of how literature might be an important space where religious practice undergoes revision, and pious instruction might be demonstrated within multiple textual locales and not only within the confines of a doctrinal and theological polemic.

In imagining the romance as a place dedicated to the active investigation and production of good interpretive habits, Lady Mary Wroth followed in the path of her uncle Philip Sidney, for whom the romance offered a landscape within which to rethink the supernatural marvelous, and Edmund Spenser, whose text was ordered to fashion a "noble" reader in "vertuous and gentle discipline."[4] A seemingly digressive incident early in the *First Part* articulates the *Urania*'s wider concerns for misprision that is played out in the conflicts of three of Wroth's central heroines, Antissia, Urania, and Pamphilia, whose struggles structure this chapter. Alanius, a forlorn knight driven mad by the loss of his beloved Liana, encounters Nereana, a woman wandering the forests alone who is bewailing her own unrequited love. In a comic but willful example of misprision, Alanius reads her as the forest's resident nymph and goddess. After forcefully redressing her to make her look like the goddess he believes her to be, he begs her for a miracle: to "turne this sweet water into a spring of love" (1.200). "Blesse, and inrich this water," he implores, so that "when my cruell (but still beloved) Liana, shall drinke of it, the vertue of it may turne her heart to sweetest pitty" (1.200). Alanius's desired blessing—that springwater might magically transform his lover's affection—should raise no eyebrows among romance readers. His request draws from a rich reservoir of stories in which a goddess or virgin's blessing (or bathing) transforms water (whether a spring, fountain, or well) into a holy, curative, or otherwise transformative site.[5]

Trussed up even as she is in nymph attire, however, Nereana remains a "distressed woman" whose impotence to perform the desired miracle explicitly parodies the romance trope whereby magical or miraculous interventions— such as blessed water—wash away narrative complications (1.200). In *The*

English Romance in Time, Helen Cooper argues that high-culture romances frequently stage unsuccessful examples of magic in order to meet an audience's pleasurable expectations of magic, all the while instead directing attention toward the character's power and virtue.[6] Cooper does not stress, however, how failed magic might call attention to other more effective modes of transformation or reformation. By revealing the failure—or sheer silliness—of ritually "blessed," enhanced water, *Urania* indulges a reader's expectation of magical, supernatural incidents. Simultaneously, it undermines that desire and thus reconciles the "blessed" water against a Protestant wariness for any Christianized magic that smacked too much of a Catholic penchant for miracles.

In this moment, Wroth looks very much like the niece to Philip Sidney, who in his own romance had worked assiduously to deflate supernaturally generated wonder. Nereana's inability to transform the spring heralds what will be a larger pattern within the text. Her failure to magically resolve Alanius's problem shadows the later ambiguous efficacy of Melissea's water cures to transform Antissia and Urania. It thus directs our attention to the ways that the characters cannot rely on supernatural remedies alone but must instead develop other strategies for coping with their extravagant passion. This tale captures Wroth's subtle practice of dismantling magic's efficacy to alter or educate her characters.

If, as I have argued, one of the key anxieties about romance entailed the act of reading, specifically how the supernatural encouraged "superstitious" habits of reading, then women, whose polemical status painted them to be those readers with the greatest proclivity to error, were the readers most in need of reformation. Through her sustained interest in female interpretive perspicacity, Wroth engages, through the fiction of romance, the critical debates raging during the first quarter of the seventeenth century regarding women's habits of reading, religiosity, and their capabilities as able interpreters. Her emphasis on the process of reading and its potential to temper emotional engagements correlates reading romance with positive affect and potential spiritual discipline in the most unlikely of places. By making women's emotional experience central to her narrative, Wroth uses a literary form maligned for its seductive effects on women, proposing that, if rightly crafted and rightly read, romance might train the passions and solicit interpretive carefulness.

Wroth uses her *Urania* to counter contemporary discourses that continued to reinforce prevalent stereotypes about romance and female reading.[7] She does so, first, by (seemingly counterintuitively) presenting a central female character, Antissia, who is incapable of disciplined reading and whose overly passionate, mimetic engagement with romance texts and conventions confirms antiromance clichés. Wroth then complicates any emblematizing of Antissia with the counterexample of the romance's titular character, Urania. Antissia and Urania, across nearly a thousand folios, present opposite responses to engaging with romance. One becomes increasingly passive and error-prone, while the other hones her critical skills through more engaged and critical reading. Both sides of this tension, finally, emerge most spectacularly in the romance's conflicting portrayal of Pamphilia, who signals resistance to the value system that dictates a gendered capacity for managing the passions as well as a sensitivity to the struggle required to reach interpretive sagacity. She exemplifies the precarious in-between place of romance and its readers post-Reformation. Wroth's pivotal characters thus institute an active, affective, and participatory process of reading that uses emotional investment to integrate rather than excise the passions in the creation of a balanced, astute reader. The *Urania*, then, might be read as a lesson in productive, passionate reading that aligns romance reading with rather than against Protestant reading practice.

ANTISSIA, ERRING, SUPERSTITIOUS READER

In contrast to most earlier romances, Wroth's *Urania* centralizes emotions, shifting, as Paul Salzman points out, the generic emphasis of romance from heroic and courtly exploits (the bedrock of much chivalric and pastoral romance) to the passions and their management.[8] Two capstone episodes in the *First Part*—the ladies' adventures at the Throne of Love and the enchanted theater—imprison characters, literally, for indulging their passions. Wroth's defense of the romance will build from these passionate exemplars and failures. Her text unfolds a double vision, showing the aftereffects of romance's seduction—both as an experience of love from which the characters suffer (and which frequently leads them astray or lands them in prison) and as a story that captivates and often misleads its audience to misprision.[9] In this way she anticipates the modern conflation between the literary sense of "romance," an extravagant story filled with amorous tales, and errancy. Wroth plays these two senses of "romance" to mount a metafictional mirroring that offers a split perspective: passion might be a powerful stimulus for error, or it might spur interpretive perspicuity or savvy.

Not only those opposed to romance viewed it as an effective method for arousing the passions. Published the same year as Wroth's *Urania*, Robert Burton's exhaustive work *The Anatomy of Melancholy* treats amorous tales as being among the most efficacious artificial allurements to love-melancholy. Burton analyzes how readers "incensed by reading amorous toys, *Amadis de Gaule, Palmerin de Oliva, the Knight of the Sun*" are set "on fire."[10] Bolstering his observation with classical precedent, he asserts "no stronger engine" exists "than to hear or read of love-toys."[11]

For the more polemically minded, such affective power should not be courted, especially not by those with a predisposed delicate emotional balance. In *A Mirrhor Mete for all Mothers, Matrones, and Maidens, Intituled the Mirrhor of Modestie* (1574), reformer and schoolmaster Thomas Salter advises matrons (and fathers) to keep their girls away from the "pestilent infection" of such amorous reading material "as maie make her moude (beyng of it self verie delicate) more feble and effeminate."[12] "So soone as they have any understandying in readyng, or spellyng, to cone and lerne by hart bookes," he warns, women turn to "ditties of dalliance," which overexcite "their memories."[13] Reading "ditties of dalliance," Salter writes, enflames the wrong kind of affect, which subsequently produces through its stimulation of memory the wrong kind of knowledge. Salter's trajectory, which targets women's "effeminate" and "delicate" affective balance, sums up a prevailing stereotype about early modern women readers. Riding on this stereotype was an understanding of reading, Helen Smith argues, as "both a bodily and embodied practice."[14] Textual engagement was a somatic process to which women were especially porous, and therefore, susceptible.

As the character studies drawn by the translator and poet Wye Saltonstall in *Picturae Loquentes, Or Pictures Drawne forth in Characters* illustrates, the hapless female romance reader was a convention: the maid who "loves histories as *Amadis de Gaule* and the *Arcadia*" will from them court the "shaddow of love till she know the substance."[15] In brief, romance's "mirror" fostered corruption, not benefit. Wroth seems to have known the stereotype, for she parodies Salstonall's maid in her Antissia, a character who continually confounds shadow and substance to the shame of herself and those who love her. Antissia is the erring reader so feared by Protestant polemicists.[16]

At first glance, Antissia validates Richard Baxter's judgment in the *Christian Directory* that "women are commonly of potent fantasies, and tender, passionate, impatient spirits easily cast into anger or jealousy or discontent, and of weak understandings and therefore unable to reform themselves."[17] Like the proverbial foolish chambermaid, whose readings of the *Mirrour of Knighthood* "so carried" her away that "many times [she] resolv'd to run out of her selfe, and become a Ladie Errant," Antissia embodies the credulous, error-prone, overexcited reader.[18] She calls to mind the contemporary romance heroine Oriana (who shares the heroine's name from the *Amadis*) in John Fletcher's *The Wild Goose Chase* (1621), who, although she scorns those who take *Amadis* and *Palmerin* as "modest and true stories," cannot herself always keep those romances securely in the realm of fiction.[19] Three acts later, Oriana confuses her "real" love life with the stories of love that she reads, accidently—and revealingly—calling her lover "Amadis."[20] Antissia's character invokes this familiar character type but, as the narrative unfolds, interrogates it. Her error is not simply an ipso facto result of her being a woman reader ensnared within a romance; rather, error creeps up as a result of her interpretive naïveté, a naïveté that leads to misprision, attempted murder, and finally madness. She becomes a negative exemplum of a passive, passionate reader who, in Baxter's terms, is "unable to reform" herself.[21]

A royal-born princess to the throne of Romania, Antissia fits the romance heroine archetype: her story includes pirates; her beauty provokes near-ravishment; and her distress necessitates heroic rescue by an unknown, handsome, and gallant knight. This knight turns out to be the romance's ambivalent hero, Amphilanthus, the king of Naples, and noticing his "love-linesse, sweetnes, braverie, and strength," Antissia falls in love with him, and thereby, loses her "libertie" (1.60, 61). Wroth simultaneously establishes Antissia as a quintessential romance heroine (fair, noble, surprised by pirates, betrayed and nearly raped, passionate for her rescuing knight), and a quintessential romance reader. Antissia mimics a rote emotional and interpretive trajectory—seeing the heroic qualities of the famed Amphilanthus "made her like, [and] that made her love" (1.61). Syntactically mirroring the slide from "this" to "that," so common in antiromance discourse, Antissia slips into passion and error.

The romance's early summation of Antissia's fall illustrates how Wroth's omniscient narrator, when read carefully, reveals that Antissia's habitual misreading is brought on by her overly passionate response to what she sees. She looks like the female counterpart to Spenser's Phaon, an object lesson for more sober readers. When Antissia arrives at the court of Morea (where Pamphilia resides) with her beloved Amphilanthus, "shee perplexed with love, jealousie, and losse," becomes consumed by the suspicion that Pamphilia harbors romantic feelings for Amphilanthus (1.114). To express her "restless affliction," she composes a prescient sonnet whose language foretells how she will be "undone, ruind, destroyed" by her passion (1.114). Antissia's poetic compositions indeed predict her behavior, writing shadow into substance. Spying on Pamphilia, she sees her imagined rival embracing a knight in a solitary arbor. With "[t]hat imagination growing to beliefe," Antissia leaps to assumptions and reads the stranger knight to be her own Amphilanthus: "beliefe brought feare, feare doubt, and doubt the restlesse affliction, suspition" (1.93). Using anadiplosis to syntactically underscore Antissia's growing passion, Wroth rhetorically shows how quickly imagination flares into concrete "suspition." Like the naive maid of Saltonstall's portrait, Antissia's overexcited imagination dictates her interpretation and then her actions. Never pausing to consider that all may not be as she thinks, "griefe increased to Antissia, which griefe at last to rage, and leaving sorrow fell to spite, vowing revenge," wherefore shortly "madness grew so upon this" that she "burst out into strange passions" (1.111). Filled with these "strange passions," she accosts the knight whom she believes to be Amphilanthus as a "monster of thy sexe" (1.115). Too late, she realizes her mistake, for the knight in the arbor is Rosindy, Pamphilia's brother. Seduced by her own "inward suspition" (2.33), Antissia lacks judgment that "should have showed her her error" (2.33). She fails, in other words, to correctly "read" the scenario before her.

Throughout the two-volume *Urania*, Antissia steadfastly refuses to correct her initial errors, and they blossom into a willful misprision. Antissia's interpretive problem, Wroth shows, stems from her refusal to maintain boundaries between fantasy and reality. Antissia's misreading of the knight in the arbor presages her ineptitude as a reader and writer. Later, she tells a story to Amphilanthus and Pamphilia about her acquaintance with a "Lady from Brittany" (1.322–24). This lady often walked by the sea, loved, wrote verses, but failed to achieve her beloved because she was ultimately too forward in her affections. As Antissia concludes the story, she confuses her pronouns and "she" becomes "I." Her slip reveals of course that the story she tells is her own story, and not that of some "Lady." The slippage from third to first person mimics the identification that polemicists imagined happened to a woman reader who became what she read: the "she" of the story becoming the "I" of the reader's own experience.

The danger posed by mirroring the passions of romance becomes even more starkly realized as Antissia's adventures unfold. Languishing over a picture Amphilanthus had given her, she "wept on, kiss'd it, wip't it, wept, and wip't, and kiss'd againe" before returning it to her bosom (1.328). She carves her passions into a tree trunk until she had "imbroidered it all over with the characters of her sorrow" (1.328). Through the chiasmic play on "wept," "wip't " and "kiss'd," Antissia's carving on the tree trunk serves to, in the words of Thomas Cooper, "fuell" her desires, acting as a "bellowes there unto" until she should enact the "desires of the mind, in the outward [wo]man."[22] Antissia's writing about romance only intensifies her passion, "like a Nettle, hardly scaping the weeders hand, but growing on, turnes to seede, and from thence springs hundreds as stinging" (1.362). Looking more and more like a moral exemplum, Antissia nourishes the seeds of unruly passion until she loses control of herself and attempts the murder of her scornful but beloved Amphilanthus. Throughout the *First Part*, we watch as Antissia's programmatic misreading allows her passions to seduce her will, vividly illustrating the slide from potent fantasies to misprision and into the overmastering passions of jealousy, anger, and, at last, in almost a parody of the dangers of identificatory reading, attempted murder.

The *Second Part* escalates her abjection. Pamphilia's brother, Rosindy, tells Amphilanthus that he had lately been to Negroponte, where a chastened Antissia had gone to live with her husband, Dolorindus. Rosindy describes his fears that Antissia "can nott cure the smarts" for she "hath sum craks still of her braine-sick fury unstopt" (2.33). Her "braine-sick fury," we learn, grew metastatic as "she fell to study and gott a tuter" who might teach her "to make a peece of poetrie to excel Ovid" (2.40). Antissia's "raging, raving, extravagant discoursive language" sprouts from her study of Ovid's love stories, a study that assures her utter "loss of libertie." Rosindy suggests the fault is hers, "being a dangerous thing att any time for a weake woeman to study higher matters then their cappasitie can reach to" (2.41). Rosindy's words repeat, almost verbatim, ad feminam discourse of the kind instituted with Vives, blaming Antissia's sex and her determined reading—and writing—of amorous literature for her subsequent moral fall.

Antissia's susceptibility to such amorous tales as Ovid's might be explained by considering early modern belief about the passions' origins. Robert Burton, as we have seen, believed reading to be a strong engine to passion. Philip Sidney's *Defence of Poesy*, to take another example, argues that ideally the reader should be moved to act in imitation of what he reads: for "who readeth Aeneas carrying old Anchises on his back, that wisheth not it were his fortune to perform so excellent an act?"[23] Images from reading, then, might generate "excellent" acts by example. Thomas Wright's famous rhetorical treatise *Passions of the Minde in Generall* (1601), a source from which Burton's *Anatomy of Melancholy* draws heavily, influentially describes what happened to readers as they read (or listened to an excellent orator). Wright dwells extensively on "How the Passions Seduce the Will."[24] In Wright's view, the passions are less reflective of an individual quality emerging from an interior self than a result of a migratory process, a transfer from one host to another. As he describes it,

> The wind a trumpeter bloweth in at one end of the trumpet, & in what maner it proceedeth from him, so it issueth forth at the other end, & commeth to our eares; even so the passion proceedeth from the heart, & is blowne about the bodie, face, eies, hands, voice & so, by gestures passeth into our eies, & by sounds into our eares: & as it is qualified so it worketh in us.[25]

Wright's metaphor of the trumpeter's wind that blows through the instrument from the player into the hearer illustrates how polemicists believed readers absorbed the passions they read on the page. The page, like the trumpet, became the conduit through which passions could be passed from writer to reader, from page to soul, literally migrating like a disease from host to host. The new host, the imagined reader or listener, would then experience a similarly aroused passion.[26] Sidney had tapped into this power of textual example to excite knights toward right actions; the obverse was seen as the more likely outcome for maids who read romance.

Antissia, indeed, amplifies what she encounters in the text. Her husband condemns how her "expressions to immodestie" produce but "vaine phantesies" (2.51). Rebuking her, he reiterates the advice of generations of reformers: "Fy, fy Antissia, if you will write, write sence and modestie, nott this stuff that maides will blush to heere" (2.51). Antissia's engagement with amorous reading and writing serves only to confirm her erring, passionate, female nature. But Wroth frames Antissia's naïveté, her raving compositions, and her ineptitude as a perspicacious interpreter. She shows these errors to grow out of Antissia's bad reading habits coupled with a willful obliviousness to social convention rather than out of any innate quality of the woman reader or her romance.

When Antissia takes on Ovid, she does so naively. When Margaret Tyler translated the first part of Ortuñez de Calahorra's *Mirrour of Princely Deedes and Knighthood* (1578), her prefatory epistle self-consciously constructs her capability to handle the text she translates even though it might be judged as "more manlike than becometh my sexe."[27] Tyler's consistent, careful framing of her work as one for "profit & delight," reckons with the cultural biases regarding women's susceptibility to romance's delight—whether as readers or translators. Importantly, she shows her awareness of convention in order to supersede it, legitimating her bold choice to translate a text doubly problematic because it is both Spanish and a romance. Antissia, it seems, never develops this ability to frame her reading or writing practice. Being "willing for the most part to heere her self speake," she demonstrates little self-awareness (2.250). Her programmatic and un-self-reflexive habits in the *First Part* produce her full-fledged "braine-sick fury," in the *Second Part*, a "deliration," Baxter might say, of character. Her "deliration" requires miraculous intervention because Antissia can no longer reform herself. Melissea, the enchantress, chastises Antissia's extreme lack of self-possession, "nott usually found in Ladys, especially of your fashion," and undertakes to cure her that she might "wash away" her "follies" (2.52, 241). What follows is a dense, symbolic moment within the text with important ramifications for Wroth's advocacy of interpretive labor as the "cure" for naive, overly passionate habits of reading. Melissea's magical powers to cure the passions of foiled, disappointed lovers seemingly works wonders in the earlier Saint Maura episode, wiping emotive memory clean by a quasi-miraculous, almost sacramental procedure designed to correct debilitating passions.[28] In a richly associative episode, Melissea places Antissia abed in "extreame darck," then immerses her in a "deepe Lake of water, luke warme" for "four and twenty howers" (2.52). When Antissia awakes, lest her "ancient woemanish thoughts" return, Melissea administers a further nostrum, a "rich cup of Gold" that dissolves her "vaine phantesies" (2.53, 51).

Wroth experiments here with a core romance motif.[29] Miraculous water cures of various kinds dot the romance tradition: Bevis of Hampton's miraculous cure from the dragon's poisonous slime, to cite one example, occurs when he falls into a well made holy by a virgin's bathing; Spenser's Redcrosse Knight too finds revival in a well during his culminating dragon battle.[30] The fantasy of healing offered by these water cures looks like the ways that baptism, in Christian belief, washed away sin. Wroth, however, employs this old motif to a very different end. Instead of confirming the efficacy of such a ritual motif or action, Wroth's narrative exposes its limitations and questions its efficacy for transforming character. The "artifissialy" induced cure works superficially to reform Antissia but ultimately fails (2.252).

Antissia's baptism in miraculous water never fully vanquishes her dragon; she neither masters her passions nor becomes a better reader. In her final appearances in the romance, we see her slip into her old habits of reading and naive narration, particularly when she later recounts her story to the queen of Bulgaria. Her "strange narration, especially of her self" makes the queen smile secretly to herself, and as Antissia prattles blithely away, she admits that she might be "nott soe perfectly recovered in my owne opinion," fearing she will lapse into her "olde whimsies againe" (2.253, 255). Antissia's "strange narration" shows that although the magical water cure might have temporarily washed away her vain fantasies, her failure to gain interpretive perspicuity leaves her at risks of a relapse. She embodies the resistance to reformation that recalls Gryll and, for polemicists, romance itself. Full transformation, Wroth will show, entails a more laborious process, one that Antissia never engages. The cure produces a magical oblivion, but it does not transform Antissia into a wiser lover or a more careful interpreter; for that, we must turn to the example of Urania, whose experience parallels in important ways that of Antissia.

URANIA, GODLY READER

In chapter 1, I argue that Sidney adapted and instituted Urania as a figural muse for English Protestant romance. Wroth, by naming her titular character "Urania," pointedly aligns her romance not only with her family but also with a Protestant literary heritage. Much more than an "absent presence" or a mere heavenly beauty who inspires men to sing her praises, Wroth's Urania institutes a figural godly reader of romance. She models an alternative strategy whereby active participatory listening, reading, and talking within a community offers a long-lasting way to gain critical distance from the passions that romance elicits.[31] She succeeds where Guyon failed. In crucial aspects, her narrative parallels Antissia: both love fickle knights who betray them; both undergo a magically induced water cure; and in each case, the magic fails to produce a thoroughly transformative cure.[32] Yet while Antissia remains ever error-prone, Urania flourishes as a voice of reason who, like Spenser's middle sage in Alma's brain turret, mediates for and wisely counsels many who wish to be her disciples.

Spenser's fashioning of Guyon, my previous chapter argues, shows *The Faerie Queene* paying attention to how readers engage romance as part of the broader concerns within the poem, to recuperate the genre for a Protestant audience. Wroth, too, fashions her Urania with a self-conscious eye to reformed polemic with all its complaints regarding romance's deleterious effect on readers, especially the weak and vulnerable or female ones. Urania will come to represent salutary reading practices, accessible to male and female readers alike, that dismantle the negative stereotype Antissia embodies. The reading practice Wroth represents through Urania is informed by the principles of reading and interpretation espoused by Richard Hooker's *Laws of*

Ecclesiastical Polity (books 1–4, 1593) and thus offers a fictional model of "right reading" drawn from a Protestant template. According to Deborah Shuger, Hooker's position on what should form the grounds for sound hermeneutical practices derived from the polemical context of Puritan claims that interpretation stemmed from divine inspiration. Hooker asserted, "Most sure it is, that when men's affections do frame their opinions, they are in defence of error more earnest a great deal, than (for the most part) sound believers in the maintenance of truth apprehended according to the nature of that evidence."[33] As Shuger argues, Hooker's thought opposes reason built on evidence as opposed to "emotional delusion."[34] What matters for our understanding of Urania is how Hooker establishes a binary of interpretation that privileges the role of reason and evidence over the passions in the interpretive process. He devalues the role of "men's affections" in order to suggest that "the maintenance of truth" relies more on reason and less on emotion. Although the debates over interpretation are too involved to discuss in detail here, it is important to register the centrality such debates held across the spectrum of early modern religion from the more orthodox Anglican to the heterodox positions of Puritans, Calvinists, and others. The reformed standpoint insisted that all spiritual guidance could be found in the scriptures, *sola scriptura*. Yet, as Hooker's concerns show, it became an ongoing problem to ensure that the scriptures were being read "aright."

Crucial to right reading, the passions needed to be invoked, but controlled. The Reformation did not entirely banish the passions, but rather, as Richard Strier has demonstrated, made it more imperative that they be correctly directed. A discourse about how to foster "sanctified" affections, or a better kind of passion, grew in the early 1600s just prior to Wroth's publication. As Christopher Tilmouth has shown, a growing recognition for the complex forces of corporeal passion and its role in determining man's actions fractured older philosophical and theological constructions of what self-control entailed.[35] In short, as Spenser's book 2 predicted, the training of emotion was a critical component to training godly minds armed with interpretive acumen.[36]

The centrality of reading, and the role affect was to play in that reading, remained a hot issue well into the early seventeenth century. The ongoing publication of guides to instruct lay people in their reading of the Bible evidences this concern. The following list of titles aptly sketches the preoccupation: *A Methode or Brief Instruction Very Profitable for the Reading and Understanding of the Old and New Testament* (Edward Vaughan, 1590), *Directions for the Private Reading of the Scriptures* (Nicholas Byfield, 1618, 1626), and *The*

Practise of Pietie Directing the Christian How to Walke that he may Please God (Lewis Bayly, 1612, forty editions published by 1640).[37] This general concern for teaching sound interpretation became even more pointed when it came to women's interpretive skills.

In her evocative reading of the title page image of John Foxe's *Acts and Monuments*, Edith Snook shows how visually the image typifies "not only the association between Protestantism and reading" but also illustrates the "unmistakable involvement of the female reader in signaling the practices of the 'true' faith."[38] While Snook's argument concerns the symbolic representation of the female reader of vernacular scripture, her insights suggest why the religious conflict around romance became especially heated in regard to women readers. The debates over women's capability as interpreters of the Bible come to bear on their reading practice more generally. In his *The English Housewife* (1625), Gervase Markham expresses distrust of women's judgment when it comes to matters of religious instruction, arguing that they should not usurp "to themselves a power of preaching and interpreting the holy word," a standard critique instituted with Saint Paul.[39] Richard Brathwaite similarly inveighed against women commenting on scripture, or "the strange opinions of Shee-clarkes, which as they understand them not themselves, so they labour to intangle others of equall understanding to themselves."[40] Not everyone shared such views, but Brathwait's extremity does describe a persistent cultural bias against women learning and employing interpretive strategies. "The underlying thinking determining what women should read," writes Danielle Clarke, "was that they lacked the interpretive skills to make distinctions and discriminations."[41] If a female reader lacks the interpretive skills, she likely will be the excessively literal reader who excels at "translating" the substance of texts directly into life. Because of this fear, English Protestant educators poured especial energy into teaching women how to read properly so that, under their guidance, the woman reader might not err and lead her family to follow suit as had Eve with Adam.

Wroth's aunt, Mary Sidney Herbert, was a woman reader and writer who showcased how a Protestant woman might use her skills as an interpreter to the benefit of the larger religious community. Mary Sidney's work in translating the Psalms, Beth Wynne-Fisken argues, reflects her "intense commitment" to an "introspective Protestant tradition which stressed the role of the psalms as meditative paradigms"; yet it also shows her "shrewd understanding" that religious translations "were a sanctioned form of intellectual exercise for a noblewomen."[42] Wroth invokes her as a kind of interpretive paragon within *Urania* as the queen of Naples (and mother to Urania), "perfect in Poetry, and all other Princely virtues as any woman that ever liv'd," and a woman who actively engages in storytelling and exchanging poetry (1.371).[43] Wroth boldly puts to use that heritage of active, Protestant women and applies it to romance as another space where women might learn how to become better readers to benefit their community. By making such a claim, Lady Mary Wroth exploits her family heritage of capable women interpreters to make an even bolder claim that reconfigures a prevailing religious stereotype about women and reading.[44] She further refits this stereotype for a genre that is not explicitly religious and, indeed, for a romance that avoids, almost entirely, direct religious commentary.

In contrast to Antissia, Urania's agency, within the material world of her own romance, models how the passions enflamed by reading romance might be channeled into beneficial interpretive acts for the individual and her community. Urania, from the first episode, mobilizes reason to train passion toward the kind of noble action that Sidney advocated. Discovering the melancholy knight Perissus languishing in a cave, she asks to hear his story because "it may be I shall give you some counsel, and comfort in your sorrow" (1.4). Perissus's story, framed within the larger context of *Urania*, establishes Wroth's technique of using embedded storytelling as a model for readers' responses to overly passionate outbreaks in the text. Chiding Perissus for indulging an "idle, and unprofitable" passion of lament, Urania urges him to leave "these teares, and woman-like complaints" to go forth and to "revenge [Limena's] death" (1.14–15). Perissus heeds her counsel, declaring that he "must obey that reason which abounds in you," and vows to leave his "melancholy abiding" and don his armor (1.15, 16). Wroth distinctly deploys Urania as the figure who can turn a knight's emotional paralysis into active resolve through her participatory engagement with his tale of lost romance. She, rather than he, becomes the sagacious interpreter.

Urania, moreover, will be no fugitive cloistered in virtue, unfamiliar with the seductions of love's overmastering passions. Shortly after proving herself a kind of "unnamed reason" within the text, she meets and falls for Parselius (prince of Morea and brother to Pamphilia), who is searching for his lost partner Amphilanthus. A scant few pages after Urania chastens Perissus's "woman-like complaints," she utters her own: "I have heard my imagined Father, and many more, talke of a thing called *Love*, and describe it to be a delightfull paine, a sought, and cherish'd torment, yet I hope this is not that," only to concede a few pages later, "Passion, O Passion! Yet thou rulest Me"

(1.15, 25). Cast as the woman ruled by passion, the reader's experience becomes sutured to hers as she learns to regain her initial equanimity and to master the "cherish'd torment" and "Passion" that threatens to rule her.

The dangers of succumbing to "Passion" are writ large during the Throne of Love adventure in the *First Part*. On the journey toward Morea (where she seeks to learn her identity), Urania, Parselius, and her company of travelers land at the Throne of Love, an enchanted series of three towers—those of Cupid (Desire), Love, and Constancy—situated atop a little hill on the island of Cyprus. The night before hazarding the towers, the company camps by a river whose waters turn out to be treacherous. When the thirsty travelers drink, each becomes inflamed by various passions, and Urania rushes off to conquer the first tower, Desire (1.49). Fuelled by her overpowering passion for Parselius, she enters the tower's "Inchantment" (1.49). As the walls close around her, she experiences Desire's destructive power, its isolating torment, and her own vulnerability. Parselius journeys on to betray her love by dallying with Dalinea, who connives him into marriage. Urania, meanwhile, languishes in Desire's tower for hundreds of pages until rescued by Amphilanthus and Pamphilia.

Her error of succumbing to Passion's rule bears lasting consequences that haunt her to the narrative end, yet she, unlike Antissia, will model the response Wroth invites of her readers. Her implicit contrast to Antissia begins shortly after she too experiences a miraculous water cure. Melissea tells her that "death in apparance must possesse your dainty bodie" in order that "when you shall revive," affections "with him you now love" (Parselius) would turn "to another love, and yet as good, and great as hee" (1.190). Urania places faith in Melissea's instructions and allows herself to be thrown from the Rock of Santa Maura into the sea. Santa Maura, situated on an Ionian island known as Leucas, was a fort famous for its high promontory and a place rife with romance allusiveness; in some accounts, sacrificial victims were hurled down from its heights to appease the gods' fury. Sir John Harington describes it in a gloss to his translation of *Orlando Furioso*: "The rocke of Lewcade, where men that were mad for love leapt into the water, and washed away (as they thought) that fancie."[45] In *Arcadia, & Piscatorial Eclogues*, Jacopo Sannazaro wrote that whoever leaped from it into the sea and did not suffer injury would be free from sorrow.[46] All of these legends point to Santa Maura's overtones of magic, as well as of religious sacrifice and healing, a place of a watery, ritual expiation and cleansing that baptized all who leapt of their crippling passions.

Like Antissia's later cure, the results are immediate and seemingly complete. Amphilanthus throws her down into the sea, his own heart "drownd in as deepe an Ocean of despaire" (1.230). Before the sentence even ends, however, Wroth reveals, "he call'd to wonder" (1.230). For no sooner has Urania "suncke into the water," but the "waves did beare her up againe" (1.230). Parselius, meanwhile, lurking nearby in a craggy nook, seeing Urania fall, determines himself to drown, for he wishes to "never outlive Urania"—despite his recent amorous diversion (1.230). Buoyed up by the waves and rescued by two men in a boat, Parselius and Urania arrive safely on shore, "soundly washed" (1.230). There on shore, all those present witness "the operation of that water": Urania and Parselius, in an early modern instance of *The Eternal Sunshine of the Spotless Mind*, find their former passions forgotten (1.230). Parselius "knew nothing of his former love" (1.230). Urania, without "jealousie, or anger," wishes Parselius happiness with his new bride, Dalinea (1.231). Seemingly, this watery immersion, an almost baptismal moment, miraculously resolves the misdirected passions, mistakes, and debilitating guilt that dogged both characters. Here in its immediate execution, the Santa Maura episode resembles the magical oblivion found by the lovers in Jorge de Montemayor's *Diana*, one of the many sources influential to the *Urania*.

As the story unfolds, however, Wroth departs from her model to reveal that Santa Maura's curative effects are not long term. A lingering sense of betrayal haunts all the characters. Sad dreams disturb Parselius, wherein Urania appears and "furiously revild me for my change" (1.243). Urania, despite her acceptance of Steriamus's love and their happy marriage and children, reminisces along with her friends in the *Second Part* of "olde passions," in a discourse mixed "with hunny, with Gall, with pleasure, with torture, with injoying, with flatt laments for never obtaining" (2.32). Perhaps most tellingly, one of the final portrayals of Urania occurs when she hears of Parselius's death. In a dramatic reversal of roles, we learn that Pamphilia must offer Urania some comfort, "for still she cowld nott butt love Parselius Vertuously" (2.403). In this last poignant picture of Urania weeping for the dead Parselius, we glimpse how the promised magical oblivion of Santa Maura failed to fully erase Urania's memory and her early passion. The magic cure fails to procure lasting forgetfulness, just as we have seen its failure to fully cure Antissia of her brainsick fury and vain fantasies. This subtle change is crucial to my reading of Wroth's project of reform: because she ends up in a very different place than Antissia, Urania points the reader toward strategies beyond a magical water bath to govern the passions.

To fully grasp Wroth's strikingly different attitude toward the virtues of water cures as a magic resolution to problematic passions, it is useful to compare it with Jorge de Montemayor's *Diana*. Much of *Diana*'s trajectory reaches toward the promised release from unrequited love that drives the main characters Sylvanus, Syrenus, and Selvagia to despair.[47] The sage enchantress Felicia, "whose course of life, and onely exercise, is to cure and remedie the passions of love," offers the desired balm—a magical release—for the unhappy lovers.[48] A nymph, Cynthia, advises the afflicted shepherds and shepherdesses to seek Felicia, because time is too "slowe and tedious a phisition" to cure love's pain and "though one departs from the presence of her lover, yet the remembrance of him afterwards remaines in her eies . . . wherof she still sees the Idea of the thing that she desireth."[49] The root fault here lies in the overly strong affect or passion, love, which rouses desire, and invades memory, a problem with romance that we witnessed Sidney address in his revised *Arcadia*. In *Diana*, the cure, administered by Felicia in "two cruets of fine cristall," transfixes the afflicted lovers into a sleepy oblivion. Intriguingly, Bartholomew Yong's translation uses the word "cruet" to describe the cups that hold the magic water, a word with specific connotations to Catholic practice. The *OED* records that it was often a small container specifically for the water or wine used in the Eucharistic service.[50] The language in this scene thus enhances a sense that we witness a miraculous transformation that, like transubstantiation, utterly transforms its material subject: "Thou shalt marvell yet more, after they awake," Felicia promises the anxiously waiting friends, "because the water hath by this time wrought those operations it should do."[51] True to her pronouncement, the former lovers soon wake with "perfect wits and judgement."[52] Its effects, furthermore, seem to be long-lasting, as they sustain Syrenus when later he comes across his former beloved, the titular Diana: "It was so forcible a motion in his minde, that if the vertue of the water, which sage Felicia had given him, had not made him forget his olde love: it might well have beene, that there was nothing else in the worlde that coulde have let him from renewing it againe."[53] In brief, the magical cure does its work, fully cleansing the couples of their unruly passions and leaving them with clear judgment—even when confronted by their former passion.

Wroth, by contrast, does not show magic cures as the answer to educating, or indeed saving, her characters. Urania's "baptism" in the waters of Santa Maura, which fail to fully transform her, is suggestive of a symbolic status where ritual or magic alone cannot transform the inner being; true transformation requires understanding and training. After the Santa Maura purge,

Urania engages herself in a network of counsel and carefully avoids her earlier mistake of adventuring Desire alone. She accepts Melissea's advice that
"just change" is inevitable—even in love (1.190). Steriamus (future king of
Albania) soon thereafter woos her, and they exchange love tokens and vows
that "never truer shall any love be" (1.265). Although the narrative describes
how Urania and Steriamus "lived the rest of their dayes in all happinesse
and joy," this happiness exists alongside their memory of former loves that
shadow both of them (1.512). Urania, however, unlike Antissia, never succumbs
again to her former passions. While Antissia remains a hopelessly naive storyteller and listener, Urania hones her skills of narrative and interpretive ability
through continual practice. She builds community by means of an active network of storytelling, in which her "devine" council moves characters—even
males ones—from their "extravogante passions" (2.173). As a guide, not so unlike Guyon's palmer in book 2 of Spenser's *The Faerie Queene*, who glosses romance, Urania glosses the romances of those about her and models to them a
process of salvation where true transformation of the inner being occurs
through a process of telling stories, listening, offering advice, and interpreting aright.

Like Arthur in Spenser's *Faerie Queene*, who intervenes when the heroes
cannot conquer the monsters they face, Urania rescues others. When she
hears the tale of a lady twice jilted by a knight, she listens to her story and advises her that she must leave her anger (1.509–12). As with Perissus, Urania's
counsel refuses to indulge the passions and instead urges reason and action,
as opposed to emotional volatility or paralysis. She tells the lady that if she
wishes to continue to love the knight, she will simply have to accept that, to
him, she will never be more than "mistress." When Pamphilia finds herself
wretchedly tormented by love, Urania strives "to discover her melancholy"
(1.458). Pamphilia, Urania reminds her, must place her duties as a queen above
her impassioned melancholy. By listening to friends' stories (as well as the
stories of those she meets) and providing advice, Urania remains active: listening, judging, and advising.

Urania becomes increasingly self-confident as a counselor in the *Second
Part*, where she occupies a central place in a storytelling coterie. Her advice to
a young shepherdess shows her authority: "Itt may bee some of us may give
you such counsel as may stand you in good stead if you hearken to us"
(2.37). Most importantly, she becomes the key mediator to, and counselor of,
Amphilanthus and Pamphilia, whose fraught relationship drives both to
despair. As one of their closest friends, she witnesses their *de praesenti* mar-

riage (2.45). When those vows are broken, she counsels both. In essence, she becomes the voice of reason amid all the stories of uncontrolled passion.

Significantly, it is not only women who listen to her. Urania takes advantage of the authority that comes from her own experience and is instrumental in saving Amphilanthus twice from suicide. Overwhelmed by his own error in believing Pamphilia to have married another, and himself having consequently married the princess of Slavonia, his passions overmaster him, and twice he tries to leap overboard in his own attempt at a watery cure (2.171–72). Respectful yet confident, Urania invokes her past success to win his confidence: "You shall see," she promises, that "my fortune wilbee to serve you to all blessednes againe. Did nott I say thus much to Perissus, and did itt nott fall out soe? Did nott I for my everlasting blis redeeme and save my deerest Lord Steriamus, and his brave brother, and most worthy sister Selarina?" (2.139). Reminding him (and the reader) of her successful mediation of her own passions, she urges him to leave his "bootles complaints," confront Pamphilia, and beg her pardon for his foolish rashness. In effect, she becomes his glossing palmer, guide, and interpreter. Through Urania, Wroth insists a woman might offer counsel to a man on how to control his passions, for Amphilanthus harkens to the "all discreet and devine counsel of Urania . . . and now saw with the cleere eyes of understanding, of true understanding. Soe as, like a free man from his late extravogante passions," he resumes his kingly duties (2.173). Urania's "devine" counsel capably transforms characters— even males—out of their "extravogante passions."

Importantly, Urania accomplishes this transformation through her capacity to listen to and to tell stories and not through a magic cure. The stories that Urania interprets—stories that Edward Denny might well lambaste as "lascivious tales"—are the same kind of stories that constitute Wroth's romance.[54] Wroth's *Urania* offers an extraordinary range of interpretive freedom for her titular female narrator. In the midst of numerous vignettes of women caught up in impassioned stories and experiences of love that reveal romance's powerful and often seductive and destructive emotional force, Urania's counsel models interpretive carefulness and urges action instead of "idle" rumination. Through her example, Wroth portrays how a woman might hear and even read "lascivious tales" yet emerge with "the cleere eyes of understanding, true understanding" (2.173).

Melissea's ultimately failed cures interrogate one tenet of romance's troubling penchant for the marvelous and supplement it instead with a cure grown out of a diligent reading practice. Urania, like Guyon with his hand over his heart in Phaedria's "gondolay," monitors her own response and conveys the message that she does not need a male guide to do this work for her. My reading of Urania's interpretive skills suggests a parallel method at work, within a romance that draws on Protestant hermeneutic practice for training vernacular readers of the Bible. The *Urania* emerges from a culture in which the scriptural basis for religion emphasized the importance of careful reading and interpretation on an individual level and warily regarded ritual and popish miracles. Wroth takes up a promising motif of magic and diverts its expected quality of marvel in front of our eyes, displaying a high degree of literary self-awareness as she complicates the role of magic and Catholic-like miracle within her romance. Moreover, Urania's interpretive agency includes female readership in hermeneutical exercises usually denied them, making women readers more than passive recipients of a magic process. Active engagement, debate, discussion, reading within social contexts—the very stories that make up romance—supplant the supernatural properties of the magic water cure. As Urania constructs reading as a form of labor and proposes a method of reading that relies on participation as a hermeneutic tool, she creates a practical model for embodying the difference of Protestant reading from Catholic practice. She legitimates, moreover, the shift in women's interpretive agency as one grown out of an active vernacular reading of, surprisingly— that once most Catholic tainted of all genres—the romance.

PAMPHILIA, THE "IN-BETWEEN" READER

Antissia and Urania provide contrasting templates for how readers might respond to romance. Together they realize a polarity of misprision and perspicacity, through which Wroth confirms and challenges the long-standing reformist position. But Wroth, unlike Roger Ascham and other male commentators, goes beyond a binary proposition. She grays such neat distinctions by including a third figure, one whose struggles illuminate a complex middle ground where impassioned response confronts marked restraint, a refusal to "turne blabb"—that is, to turn indiscreet, as had Antissia (1.318).

Pamphilia, often read as the character who most fully figures Lady Mary Wroth herself, attempts to curb her passions, mapping out a territory of volatile emotions, heroic battles, and mediating acts of reading and writing, which render visible the strain and emotional cost facing any writer or reader, male or female, of potently affective, often profligate forms.[55] Through Pamphilia, Wroth turns a self-conscious eye to what it meant to be a woman who read and wrote romance within a culture steeped in the belief that romance and women were equally prone to error. In an allusive textual mise en abyme, the reader happens upon Pamphilia reading a romance. She wanders throughout a park, carrying in her hand a book whose "subject was Love, and the story she then was reading, the affection of a Lady to a brave Gentleman, who equally loved, but being a man, it was necessary for him to exceede a woman in all things, so much as inconstancie was found fit for him to excell her in, hee left for a new" (1.317). The story Pamphilia reads might as well be her own story, for at this point in the *Urania*, she too has been abandoned by her most "inconstant Gentleman," Amphilanthus. Pamphilia responds to the narrative, however, not with sympathetic identification but with outrage.

Throwing down the book, she launches a tirade against romance writers who fashion love "according to their various fancies" (1.317). She wishes to "punish such Traytors" and begs that Love might instead "cherish mee thy loyall subject" (1.317). Pamphilia's disgust for the common romance motif, where a feckless knight might pursue and rescue any number of distressed damsels, inaugurates her determination to overturn romance clichés and to fashion love by different rules. She resists the reading offered by the story within a story and insists on correcting it. In her frustration with conventional romance's descriptions of axiomatic male and female desire, Pamphilia blames such limited accounts on the writers. Her comment seems a pointed indictment of male romance writers and polemicists who, like Alanius, can only read Nereana as the goddess or nymph he wants her to be. Pamphilia's comment on the romance she reads reveals the gap between the story and her own desires, or romance's failure to represent female desire and will, beyond stock categories of the kind we saw represented in Antissia.

Pamphilia's subsequent struggles (and failures) complicate the more tidy binary I have thus far traced between Antissia's interpretive naïveté and Urania's perspicuity. Starting the *First Part* with promise, Pamphilia conquers the first great enchantment, the Throne of Love, thus winning the title of Constancy. Her victory, however, proves short lived. "Destiny that governes all our lives," Melissea forewarns, "hath thus ordain'd, you might be happy, had you power to wedd, but daintinesse and feare will hinder you: I cannot finde that you shall marry yet, nor him you most affect, many afflictions you must undergoe" (1.190). Unlike Edmund Spenser's heroine Britomart, who pines for her knight Artegall but holds Merlin's promise of future dynastic marriage, Pamphilia's quest receives no such assurance and has no prophetic end. She must persevere knowing she will fail at what she most ardently wants—the love of Amphilanthus. Knowing her failure, she nonetheless persists to "be ordaind, or licensed to be the true patterne of true constancy," thus elevating constancy to a noble virtue equal to that of knights' bravery in attacking dragons and monsters far beyond their strength (1.244).[56] Her constancy will entail, among other things, including loyalty, a determination to rewrite the rules for how romance might be written and read.

Pamphilia soon finds herself in a double bind. Committed to writing and reading as a method to manage her passions, she finds herself accused of engaging in an idle labor. Like Wroth herself, Pamphilia does not turn to translating psalms. As Pamphilia strives to use the reading and writing of romance-like vignettes to achieve critical judgment over her passions, she continually confronts the cultural stigma of romance. From the rumpled sheets of a sleepless night, wherein she is tormented by Amphilanthus's attentions toward Antissia, she takes to writing about her passion, aware as she does so that her "owne hands" do "witnesse against me, unblushingly showing my idelnesses to mee" (1.63). Her fear that her writing testifies to her "idelnesses" invokes the same anxiety as Spenser's proem to book 2, which worries over being judged the stuff of an idle brain. Pamphilia courts and then engages the terms of abuse. She does so, I argue, in order to preempt their accusation.

In a typical attempt to rout her "disorderly passions," in one episode she turns to the trees with her carving knife, inscribing therein her "heart-blood" (1.92). She hopes to transfer her passions to the trees' skin, thereby absolving herself of some of their torment. Just as Urania uses her experience of love to boost her own authority and control, Pamphilia tries to imagine that her "disorderly passions" might be exorcised through reading and writing. So, for instance, when Pamphilia and Orileana together "made verses," they direct their passion through metaphor, a process that, Pamphilia explains, allows her to "wring" her passions from her breast onto the page (1.364, 2.279). Pamphilia thus locates *writing*, as well as reading, romance narratives as a means to mediate, squeeze, and extract something from her passion.

This episode vindicates a woman's writing of romance, but it will also reckon with what polemicists argued was its intrinsic hazard. When Pamphilia reads and writes of passion, she often inflames what she means to control. Cognizant of this danger in others, Pamphilia warns Antissia against writing: "Leave these dolorous complaints," she advises, for they only encourage "melancholy, the nurse of such passions" (1.147). "Truly that is enough to spoile any," she muses, for "so strangely it growes upone one, and so pleasing is the snare, as till it hath ruind one, no fault is found with it, but like death, embraced by the ancient brave men, like honour and delight. This I have found and smarted with it; leave it then, and nip it in the bud, lest it blow to overthrow your life and happinesse" (1.147). Pamphilia's snarled syntax, a grammatical rendering of her own confusion, makes her analogy difficult to follow, but the core comparison she makes aligns a woman's writing of "dolorous complaints" with the equally pleasurable diversion the pursuit of honor might be for brave men; yet, tellingly, both pursuits, while seemingly noble, "spoile," "snare," and ruin.

Pamphilia's wariness proves prophetic. After one of Amphilanthus's rejections, she falls into a deadly melancholy, obsessively reading and reciting stories of neglected love, thus courting the shadows of love and transforming into "the shadow of her self" (1.457). Although Urania's experience of love's pain makes her a stronger, more authoritative voice, Pamphilia slides into despair, neglecting her appearance and imagining her "poore body a loyall sacrifice to love" (1.465). She becomes the passive subject to romance's mastery; she makes her passion an idol unto which she "sacrifices" herself. Urania, intervening like a female Arthur, urges her friend to recognize how she has collapsed the necessary distinctions between her reading and writing. She reprimands Pamphilia for allowing disorderly passions to rule, and even more troublingly, for reading and writing about her experience in an idolatrous manner. "I love Love, as he should be loved," Urania chides Pamphilia. "He is not such a Deity, as your Idolatry makes him" (1.469). Implicit in Urania's trajectory is the fear that overwrought passions will produce idolatry, displacing reason with passion. Although etymologically distant, the homonyms *idle* and *idol* create a resonant signifying pair in Pamphilia's experience of love—the Scylla and Charybdis of romance through which the savvy woman reader must navigate. Both represent a real and symbolic danger of romance.

The various meanings of *idol* instructively outline how this term came to represent what was wrong with romance and why Pamphilia should maintain a critical distance. Beyond its primary sense of a simulacrum of a deity that, in Christian parlance, equaled a false god, *idol* could figuratively refer to anything that became the object of supreme devotion and that usurped human affections from God.[57] The word *idol* also might signify a person who lacked the proper energy, who neglected duties, or who was "idle." In his *Lectures Upon Jonas*, the chaplain John King exploits the homophones when he complains how romance encourages its readers "to commit idolatry with such books (both men and women in this idle learning)."[58] Finally, *idol* might further suggest a fantasy, a false or misleading fallacy. A loaded word, Urania's "idol" thus conjures the specter of error and misplaced passion. A story, if it encouraged its audience to neglect duties, usurp the affections, and arouse passions without a proper end, could incite idolatry with all of its post-Reformation Catholic taint (to paraphrase Thomas Cooper). All these various permutations of *idol* garnered narrative vehemence within different strands of Reformation thought that clung persuasively to romance.

Pamphilia's battle against romance's seductive "idelness" and "idolatry" occupies much of the *Second Part*. When Urania's exhortations fail, a stronger intervention becomes necessary. Not surprisingly given her role in instructing and "curing" both Antissia and Urania, Melissea appears as the one to administer a powerful rebuke: arriving as a deus ex machina complete with a "strange darknes" and "fearfull fire," drawn in a chariot with "four firy dragons," she holds "privatt conference" with Pamphilia (2.112–13). Significantly Melissea never offers Pamphilia a magical water cure for her suffering. She may arrive on a dragon, but she engages in "privatt conference," invoking Urania-like skills of female mediation through verbal counsel language rather than magic (2.113). Although we the readers are not privy to that private conference, we witness a "verie pretty show" put on "indeed onely to please the Queene" that is suggestive of Melissea's message to Pamphilia (2.113).

An old shepherd and an "extreamly amourous" youth engage in a singing match in which the youth praises the "Goddesse sole of Love," while the old shepherd scorns love as "butt a phantesie light, and Vaine, / Fluttering butt in poorest braine" (2.114). Although their debate touches upon conventional matter, the concluding off-rhyme couplet, sung in several parts by the lad, the shepherd, and a nymph (to whom the lad addresses his love), raises some provocative questions. Their concluding lines, "Noe saints by imprications move / To bace idolatrie of love," broach the controversial key words we have seen Wroth cultivating in regard to Pamphilia's experience of romance (2.115). The final lines link "love" and the woes of romance to "saints" and "idolatrie" in a familiar trope of false worship. Read literally, the concluding lines simply acknowledge that saints refuse to intercede with heaven on behalf of love because they (the saints) know well love's "forgeries." Read symbolically, the language overgoes literal translation to engage a specific set of generic controversies and fears.

This song warns against a growing fear that Pamphilia will unwittingly commit idolatry through her stubborn veneration of the passions solicited by love. She makes of her passions a God. At one remove, the reader, whose experience is sutured onto Pamphilia's, also runs the risk of being led to commit the kind of textual idolatry warned against by John King, focusing on the passions rather than extracting the lesson. Pamphilia makes her reading and writing of romance into a shrine to her passion rather than using the process as a corrective or purgative. Many critics, Clare Kinney among them, argue that while in the *First Part* Pamphilia legitimates the experience of a female romance reader and writer, the *Second Part* portrays a fading optimism.[59] This argument grows from Pamphilia's cessation of writing, a move often read as mimicking Wroth's own retreat from the world of print after the *First Part*'s publication, which incited at least one male courtier to label her a "Hermophradite in show, in deed a monster."[60] This critical reading argues that Pamphilia's failures serve as a kind of harbinger for the fate of Jacobean women who were so foolish as to write or read romance. My reading strenuously disagrees with this, suggesting instead that Wroth remained deeply engaged with the difficulties and necessities of retooling romance to the very end.

The *Second Part* does unravel many constituent romance motifs, including, as Mary Ellen Lamb notes, a sense of wonder; knights age and suffer deaths from unchivalric causes such as obesity.[61] Pamphilia becomes a bedridden heroine, spending much of the *Second Part* suffering from a leg injury sustained while hawking. Yet the text's dismantling of so many romance motifs deliberately validates Pamphilia's promise to transform the expected tropes of romance against which she rages in that early metanarrative moment in the *First Part*. By the conclusion of the *Second Part*, Pamphilia has cast down her idol to become self-possessed and entirely self-conscious. In the process, her dramatic experiences figure how a romance might end without a miraculous deus ex machina or other magical intervention. Although she remains a desirable woman (the king of Tartaria woos her to marriage, Lenulphus falls in love with her picture, and the usurping Sophy of Persia invades her country when she refuses his offer of matrimony), she subdues her passions for Amphilanthus and insists on the autonomy of her own active desire and self-possession without the need for the mastery of a different, magical force.

While we no longer see her actively writing, she increases her engagement within an active coterie of writers, acting as an advisor to others, as when she asks to hear Philarchos's poetry and thanks him for sharing it with her (2.122). Such engagement reflects recent critical argument that Wroth's decision not to publish the *Second Part* does not necessarily signal failure but rather reflects a conscious decision to control the circulation of the manuscript.[62] By self-selecting a coterie audience, Wroth gains more control over how her romance circulates. By reading Pamphilia's cessation of writing in the *Second Part* as an autobiographical comment on what we as modern critics perceive to be Wroth's failure to continue publishing, we risk the mistake of reading too mimetically, like Antissia, who always misses the bigger picture.[63] Rather, we might instead ask how it is that Wroth portrays Pamphilia conquering her idolatrous passion for love while maintaining a central place within her coterie of friends, who write, read, and exchange poetry. Romance will not possess her passions or her will.

Pamphilia is the crucial figure in Wroth's reformation of romance stereotypes perpetrated by male polemicists. She refuses to end her story in either marriage to her beloved or wanton lust. She models, instead, a middle way: chaste yet intimate friendship with Amphilanthus. Despite, or perhaps because of, all her struggle and effort, Pamphilia never endures a miraculous erasure of memory to resolve her passion (as do Urania and Antissia), yet neither does she achieve the long-awaited marriage to Amphilanthus. Instead, Wroth offers a surprising solution that says much about her sense of feminine agency. Pamphilia's experience shows that romance reading might be a preventative occupation, integrating female desire into reading and knowing, that flouts limiting constructions of the female mind as one prone to disorderly passion or one for which the only story that matters for women is a marital one.

In a pivotal scene near the story's end, Pamphilia hears a voice in a fountain and discovers there a nymph who urges her to an unconventional solution to her affection for Amphilanthus. "Pull up your spirits; injoye one an other hapily, and the more hapily in chaste loves," the nymph advises, for "what a fruictles business is this (your wailings, your sufferings to death) when as itt is butt fond, Vaine folly of mistaken sence" (2.379). Pamphilia listens and vows, "All is forgot, I wilbee an new woeman, yet the same constant lover still; and you shall for youre deere advise have the honor of procuring our Chastest and renewed loves" (2.380).

One might be tempted to read the nymph's appearance from inside a fountain as a version of the miraculous water cures administered by Melissea. But it differs significantly. Although the nymph lives in the fountain, it is her speech and counsel, not the waters, that penetrate Pamphilia's consciousness. Rather than being immersed and "soundly washed," as are Urania and Antissia, Pamphilia learns at last to listen to reason and to heed counsel. Pamphilia's long, difficult struggle to master her passions is consciously undertaken and won only with great labor. In these three women, whose stories occupy a central place throughout *Urania*, Wroth incorporates different trajectories of romance seduction, suggesting that the outcome depends on how each figure or reader reads, writes, and interprets.

The fountain nymph's "deere advise" facilitates Pamphilia's reconciliation to Amphilanthus. Once the two vow chaste friendship, they learn of the treacherous role Amphilanthus's old tutor played by deceiving him into believing that Pamphilia had married when she had not. The narrative breaks off abruptly with Amphilanthus and Pamphilia strolling about the woods on the Island of Love as Amphilanthus recites verses to her.[64] By rewriting the expected end to Pamphilia's story, suggesting that the conclusion of romance for a reader or a writer might be chaste love instead of "wanton luste" or marriage, Wroth derails the rote emotional trajectory portrayed in Antissia's fall. Pamphilia's failure to wed Amphilanthus facilitates Wroth's rewriting the expected end of romance. The conclusion of Pamphilia's and Amphilanthus's transformation of desire into friendship overturns normative conceptions of female desire as resulting only in disruptive and threatening behavior. *Urania*'s end, that is, thus dismantles one of the core objections against romance.

Although the *Urania*'s engagement with religious polemic is more subtle than that of her earlier male counterparts, its attention to the problematic figure of the female reader of romance places it squarely within Protestant concerns.[65] The text's continued insistence on the importance of right interpretation resonates with debates current in Protestant thought. Through her narrative, Wroth makes the romance into an experimental site in which analytical processes of reading sponsor an active investigation into properly managed passions. Her insistence that women readers can develop effective interpretative practice by reading romance includes female readership in a hermeneutical exercise usually denied them.[66] Wroth endorses Pamphilia, a "constant" reader who, despite the most bitter disappointment, temptations, and emotional torments, constitutes a virtuous model for women. Simultaneously, by resisting male commentators' accusation that romance corrupts its most vulnerable readers, Wroth critiques the religious polemic that painted romance as a genre whose proclivity toward superstitious motifs made it a perpetrator of popish errors. The romance, instead of being a repository for the cloistered past, becomes the locus for generating interpretive savvy. Imagined as a textual site for the performance of exegetical skills—paying attention to who tells the story, to whom, and how characters variously respond to the telling—Wroth's romance disrupts the rhetorical triumvirate of Rome, its Babylonian whores, and their fabulous stories.

If women, those readers deemed highly susceptible, can wring from romance good interpretive habits befitting a Protestant practice, then in Pamphilia we glimpse an in-between figure whose hybridity produces strength rather than heralding ruin. Far from Guyon's felled arbors, we leave the *Urania*'s bower of bliss, the woods on the Island of Love, with the echo of Amphilanthus's recited verses provocatively ringing through the air, dangling on an incomplete sentence. Far too from retiring into a nunnery, as had the medieval Guinevere, Pamphilia remains a respected sovereign in her own country. Urania and Pamphilia persevere, we realize, in part because they actively participate in a community of readers who help to puzzle out and determine what constitutes good behavior. Wroth thus alleviates the burden for the lone individual wrestling for correct reading; instead of relying on glosses, or a palmer, *Urania*'s characters assert a different model of Protestant virtue, which gives the community a central role in determining proper behavior and reading. The reader, who is shaped by her encounters with the text, in turn works upon her environment, participating in a constitutive relationship that changes text, reader, and community. It institutes a new habit of thought and a new way of seeing romance and disciplining the self. It offers an important, startling vision for, and a new way of reading, a popular reservoir of stories.

Romance would continue to be abused and would sometimes even be aligned with later Royalist and Catholic constituents, but the repurposing shouldered by Sidney, Spenser, Shakespeare, and Wroth lessened the pejorative hegemony. Romance was proved a genre capacious enough to be both continuity for and catalyst to English culture after the Reformation.

Exceptional Romance

If we compare the romance world of Sir Thomas Malory with that of Sir Philip Sidney or Lady Mary Wroth, we can catch a glimpse of some of the Reformation's impact on England. Simultaneously, we can witness between them the continuities that tell a different story than that told by many reformers. I have addressed in the preceding chapters what I see as a particular moment in England, in the late sixteenth and early seventeenth centuries, when authors strove to reformulate romance; yet the authors under consideration represent an anomalous effort, a small sampling in a large corpus of romance texts. Works like Richard Johnson's *Seven Champions of Christendom* or the serial translations by Anthony Munday of the *Palmerin*, for instance, piled on assorted monsters, enchantments, and the adventures of seven leading saints at the same time as Sidney, Spenser, Shakespeare, and Wroth worked to restrain and reform such elements in their own romances. The aspects of romance from which some post-Reformation authors had been so keen to distinguish themselves remained by and large the most compelling strand of stories. The texts I have studied represent the exception to the ongoing legacy of romance rather than the rule. Their reformations were bafflingly piecemeal and strangely abortive.

Their anomalousness, however, should not discredit them as evidence for cultural change across three or four generations. Rather, as exceptional evidence, their stories present us with a set of texts that unsettle easy oppositions in this early modern moment. They remain stubbornly transitional narratives in between medieval and Renaissance; saints' lives and romances; Catholic and Protestant; dramatic and nondramatic; poetry and prose. With their intercultural and hybrid narratives, they both challenge the boundaries of discourse and subtly change its terms by establishing an "in-between" space for the negotiations of cultural and religious authority. They thus change the conditions for recognition while maintaining their visibility. Pamela and Philoclea, Marina, Guyon, and Pamphilia find their places in the English canon of literary memory, in part perhaps because their stories are literary emblems of a religious, cultural, and generic schism. Their stories chart how women, and men, might be emboldened to find the meaning of their lives by relying less on supernatural intervention and more on greater interpretive savvy. Because they are ambiguous heroic figures in exceptional texts, they bring the paradigms into an arena of discussion as well as contention, shedding light on these larger logics through their particular manifestations.[1]

Their "in-between" status gives us a glimpse into the confused traditional divide that brought both the "hotter sort" of godly Protestants who condemned romance and those of a more cosmopolitan outlook who sought to reform it to a similar conundrum. Their stories produce new uncertainties, challenges to religious authorities anxious to establish allegiance. Romance's solicitation of wonder awakens a readerly faith that, to some extent, both parallels and challenges one structured by scriptural narratives. A gloss from John Harington's *Orlando Furioso* illustrates their proximity: "The fatall heare of Orillus, though it be merely fabulous yet hath it allusion to some truth" because Orillus's "fabulous," "fatall heare" can be likened to the biblical Samson: "the scripture testifies the vertue of Samson's strength to have bene in his heare, which is as straunge for reason as any of the rest."[2] In sum, if some of the more fabulous elements of scripture might be true, so might fabulous things in a romance. But the logic also works in the reverse. Banishing the "fabulous" risks a concomitant undermining of the "strange" truths in scripture. Samson's hair may be as legendary as Orillus's.

Sidney recognizes this danger in unmasking all supernatural marvels as false. Cecropia's practice of "subtile slightes" brings her to the brink of atheism when she denies all superstitious belief in providential intervention. A fine line exists between banishing superstitious wonder and banishing *all* wonder, including wonder at the working of providence. Spenser's adaptation of romance as a mirror for providential English history in book 2 ends in a complicated way when Guyon must destroy the *locus amoenus* of romance and raze the Bower of Bliss, suggesting that using romance to articulate a Protestant, temperate version of history can only fail. *Pericles* likewise shows how the miraculous, supernatural pull of a romance narrative is not easily relegated to an irretrievable past, as the play concludes with Pericles hailing "Dian" (whom the puritan William Perkins called the "Romanish-Catholics Sweet-Heart") and making oblations to her in the final lines. Even Wroth's suggestion that romance narratives might teach women to be able interpreters of their own passions subtly undermines the need for scripture to do so. All of these works, in their different ways, reveal that it may only be partially possible—or desirable—to strip romance of its bewitching, fabulous elements or to claim it for absolute sectarian and generic divisions.

As early modern English polemicists and writers alike recognized, romance, with its efficacious power to arouse the passions, could be a powerful ally to inspire religious and, by extension, political loyalty. Later romances and romance writers again embroil the literary form with confessional and political allegiances. The tensions I have traced throughout this story erupt in the mid-seventeenth century when anonymous printed romances such as *Cloria: Or, the Royal Romance* (1653–61), the unfinished *Theophania* (1655), or Richard Brathwaite's *Panthalia* (1659) articulate a royalist and disgruntled Catholic critique of contemporary politics, suggesting anew how romance might galvanize religiously motivated banners.[3] We might also glimpse in John Milton's *Paradise Lost* or John Bunyan's *Pilgrim's Progress* a trace of the struggles to reconcile romance materials and biblical stories with a particular religious loyalty.[4] Although these texts are beyond the horizon of this study, they suggest how Protestant and Catholic tensions continued to animate romance narratives and how those narratives continued to trouble the boundaries of Catholic and reformed belief.

All four of the now-canonical texts I read throughout this book present challenges to the binary optimism of reform. Spenser, Sidney, and Wroth stop their romances before they are completed. Sidney's revised text breaks off in midfight with Zelmane's shame, and we never know how Amphilanthus will respond to Faire Design's unfinished search for him; Spenser's mutability cantos too are problematic, enigmatic thoughts that fragment rather than conclude. Only *Pericles*, which returns to the ember eves of Gower and the Ephesian, Catholic realm of miracle, offers narrative closure. But the play itself incurred generations of criticism for its inchoate, uneven materials. Each of these romances, then, in various ways, defers not just ending, but completion. Their incomplete, unfinished reformed romances evocatively gesture toward the impossibility of reforming the romance tout court in print. Rather, their structural incompleteness takes us back to the "ruined choirs" of Shakespeare's sonnet that enshrine, rather than a triumph, a process of change, generating a yellow, "golden" memory as they do so.

This failure may be their victory. For these texts—*Arcadia*, *The Faerie Queene*, *Pericles*, and *Urania*—now form what we might call a "white list" or index of canonical romances. They are frequently taught as representative texts within an early modern curriculum, when in fact they are texts estranged from their contemporary native and continental counterparts, a contradictory hybrid literary kind. In-between narratives inspired by the religious crisis of their culture, they dissolve convention to produce something familiar yet unrecognizable; they exude the contradictions, as well as the distinctions, of England after the Reformation. Like the Church of England, they remain evocative reminders of the religious turmoil of the post-Reformation era. Paradoxically, their strange, abortive achievement overcomes the parameters of their culture to become the defining elements of it. By going against the most deeply engrained piety of their age, they shatter their own expectation to create a kind of "endless moniment" to their struggle.[5] They are what we remember: read, puzzle over, and interpret.

Notes

Introduction

1. Shakespeare, *Sonnets*, 64.

2. For a description of these abbeys, see Phillips, *The Reformation of Images*, 83–100. Iconoclasm was but one cultural factor that drove the dismantling of local abbeys. See Jones, *The English Reformation*, 58–94; and Shagan, *Popular Politics and the English Reformation* (Cambridge: Cambridge University Press, 2003), 162–96.

3. Marshall, "(Re)Defining the English Reformation," 564–86, discusses how Protestant polemics favored the term "popish" as a means to establish an identity in opposition to a competing religio-political "other," often Catholicism or, more pejoratively, "popery." "Protestant," as I use the term throughout this book, then, refers not to an homogeneous label or set of beliefs but rather to an oppositional stance that defined itself as against what it saw as "popery."

4. Phillips, *Reformation of Images*, 28–29, 38, 204–5. See image at fig. 24b.

5. Ibid., fig. 16. For the practice of "blotting" stained glass, particularly the heads of saints or popes, see Aston, *England's Iconoclasts*, 260n19.

6. Phillips, *The Reformation of Images*, fig. 28. The contentious issue of rood screens would return under Queen Elizabeth, provoking a royal order in 1561 that sought to minimize iconoclasm by ordering the rood lofts to be taken down to the beam and "some convenient crest" to be placed on top of them—in many cases the royal arms. Similar mandates were issued in 1565 and 1571, suggesting the ongoing nature of the problem. See Aston, *England's Iconoclasts*, 306–14. In addition to these physical changes, the Reformation greatly affected the administration of local abbeys and their role within the local community. A spectacular example of these changes is traced in the Westminster Abbey records by Knighton and Mortimer, *Westminster Abbey Reformed*.

7. In the sonnet, "nature" and its seasonal cycle is at fault. The metaphor thus could be read as naturalizing the destruction of Catholicism as part of a larger cyclical pattern. Yet the architectural metaphor raises the question of human agency in this cycle.

8. The intermittent and sporadic nature of iconoclasm during the English Reformation is traced by Aston, *Faith and Fire*, 261–89; and K. Thomas, "Art and Iconoclasm," 16–40.

9. Dering, *A Briefe and Necessarie Catachisme*, A3^v–A4^r.

10. Bhabha, *The Location of Culture*. While Bhabha's theories describe a postcolonial

context, the relevance for his hybridity theory to an understanding of premodern cultures is evident in the work of scholars such as J. Cohen, *Hybridity, Identity, and Monstrosity*. Although I do not address questions of ethnicity or race, my argument positions religion as a crucial category of identity within the culture of post-Reformation England.

11. "Post-revisionist" Reformation scholarship proposes that England's long Reformation was a matter of myriad, contested allegiances that resulted in a provisional and partial redefinition of terms. For an overview, see Marshall, "(Re)Defining the English Reformation," 564–86; and Shagan, *Catholics and the "Protestant Nation,"* 8–18.

12. Notable works in this vein that assess the provisional nature of religious reform within literary contexts are Diehl, *Staging Reform, Reforming the Stage*; and Murray, *The Poetics of Conversion*.

13. S. Cohen, *Shakespeare and Historical Formalism*. See also Rasmussen, *Renaissance Literature and Its Formal Engagements*.

14. Jameson, "Magical Narratives," 129–63.

15. Spenser, *The Faerie Queene*, 2.0.1.

16. The English taste for Spanish texts, despite their Catholic heritage can be glimpsed in, for instance, Professor Alexander Samson's database of Spanish-English translations, as seen on the King's College London's Early Modern Spain website. Samson, "Bibliography of Spanish-English Translations."

17. The lack of official censorship may account for the tendency among modern critics to downplay the significance of sectarian opposition to romance's development. Lewis, *English Literature in the Sixteenth Century*, 316, influentially declared that "the only difference between a Roman and a Protestant humanist was that the former had to be content with calling the romances barbarous and silly while the latter could add 'and popish too.'" See also Adams, "Bold Bawdry and Open Manslaughter," 33–49, esp. 42. H. Cooper, *Romance in Time*, 6, 38, acknowledges romance to be "ideologically Catholic" but does not read it as a serious consideration within romance's transformation, a position followed by A. Davis, *Chivalry and Romance*, 1–39.

18. For a survey of Catholic literature in England, see Shell, *Catholicism, Controversy*. Other notable studies of Catholic writing include Marotti, *Religious Ideology and Cultural Fantasy*; and C. Sullivan, *Dismembered Rhetoric*.

19. The "marvelous," according to Greenblatt, *Marvelous Possessions*, 76, is a "departure, displacement or surpassing of the normal or probable." It held conflicting, overlapping meanings with "magic" and "miracle" in early modern culture, as illustrated in Daston and Park, *Wonders and the Order of Nature*, esp. 14, 122–24. For the often contradictory relationship of Protestantism to the marvelous in general, see Crawford, *Marvelous Protestantism*; and Parish, *Monks, Miracles and Magic*. For Protestant identification as one of *sole fide*, see Cummings, *The Literary Culture of the Reformation*.

20. I take up these issues in part II and engage the relevant scholarship as it pertains to my argument. My study differs from recent work on the textuality and materiality of reading in early modern England undertaken by scholars such as Hackel, *Reading Material in Early Modern England*; Sherman, *Used Books*; and Andersen and Sauer, *Books and Readers*. My focus is on the imagined or "implied" reader, a fickle entity, but one whose status

can reveal much about the negotiation, essential to Christian notions of identity, over the proper reading of scripture and the world. In this way, I hope to suggest how an imagined reader might draw our attention to the concerns of real historical readers. For reader response critics, see Iser, *The Implied Reader*; Iser, *The Act of Reading*; and Jauss, *Toward an Aesthetic*.

21. My understanding of romance's sympathetic appeal to a spectrum of early modern English readers, from the chambermaid to the nobleman and gentleman scholar, stems from Lori Humphrey Newcomb in *Reading Popular Romance*. She usefully reconstructs how pervasively romance was published and read through a case study of the wide-ranging influence of Robert Greene's *Pandosto*.

22. In *Scenes of Instruction*, Jeff Dolven has made a persuasive case for just how complicated romance's pedagogical, or educative, function becomes in sixteenth-century English romance. His understanding of how the pleasures of the genre conflict with its need to teach informs my reading of the great difficulty faced by writers who sought to reform the genre for an altered religious context.

23. Spenser, *The Faerie Queene*, 2.0.1.

24. Benedict Robinson in *Islam and Early Modern English Literature* has already pointed to one aspect of English identity facilitated by romance narratives which explore "difference" in its most radical forms: Englishness versus the overdetermined "Saracen," "Moor," and "Turk." His study of Islamic, "theologized difference" argues that because romance "thinks intensely about difference" it thus provides a "cultural space" where "competing forms of identity can be imagined" (1–26 at 4); I build from his insights about romance's centrality to developing English identities by arguing that representation of difference mattered to a local, as well as global, understanding of Christian, confessional, and, therefore, distinctly English identity.

25. Reference to Sidney's *Arcadia* is often confusing. I use *The Countesse of Pembrokes Arcadia*, as it is the title form used in manuscript and print; it appears in the Huntington Library catalog for the 1590 edition, which I reference throughout this book (RB 69442/ STC [2nd ed.], 22539). I also follow scholarly tradition in designating as the *Old Arcadia* Sidney's earlier manuscript-only version. On occasion for distinction from the *Old*, I use the *New Arcadia* to refer to the revised version published by Fulke Greville in 1590 after Sidney's death.

26. Scholars have become increasingly attuned to the continuity between medieval and early modern England; see, for example, the influential collection of McMullan and Matthews, *Reading the Medieval*.

27. Jonson, *Works of Ben Jonson*, 1.6.123–28. Jonson provides a similar list in several contexts. See also *Every Man Out of His Humor* (2.3.67–68) and *Eastward Ho*. In the latter, Gertrude complains, "Would the Knight o'the Sunne, Palmerin of England, have used their Ladies so, Syn? Or Sir Lancelot? Of sir Tristram?" (5.1.32–34). In "An Execration Upon Vulcan," from *Underwoods*, the narrator describes the "whole sum/Of errant knighthood" as compiled from "Amadis de Gaule/The Esplandians, Arthurs, Palmerins, and all/The learned Librarie of Don Quixote" (*Works of Ben Jonson*, ed. Gifford, p. 830, lxi.29–31).

28. G. Fletcher, *Of the Russe Common Wealth*, N^v.

29. Metaphors that equate the wickedness of the popish past with one of "darkness" contrasted against the "light" of the Protestant present were frequent from John Bale onward. See Simpson, *Reform and Cultural Revolution*, esp. 12–22.

30. Ben Jonson's conflicted religious allegiance is receiving new critical scrutiny, as indicated by Martin Butler, "Ben Jonson and Other Catholic Dramatists," unpublished paper delivered at "Representing Politics on the Shakespearean Stage," Huntington Library seminar, September 2009.

31. Jameson, "Magical Narratives," 129–63.

32. Whether romance is best identified as a "genre" or a "mode" remains under debate. I follow Colie, *The Resources of Kind*, in understanding "genre" to be a repertory of frames for viewing the world, or what H. Cooper, *Romance in Time*, terms "memes," reiterative story patterns or "narrative strategies" in Fuchs, *Romance*. Frye, *Anatomy of Criticism*, describes a difference between a category, or "genre," and a "mode," which indicates participation with a recognizable kind of literature without being classified as such. Fowler, *Kinds of Literature*, 106, clarifies the distinction by considering a genre to be in noun form and a mode to be adjectival. Understanding genre as what Fowler calls "a network of family resemblances," as opposed to serial perspective rules, moves closer to the elusive early modern romance by eliminating the endless task of winnowing the essential and accidental features that determines a generic kind.

33. Frye, *The Secular Scripture*, 35–61, writes that the purest form of romance qua romance was the medieval. Furrow, *Expectations of Romance*, 43–94, traces how medieval readers expected to encounter romance and thus expands the distinctions enumerated by Strohm, "The Origin and Meaning."

34. The Italian *romanzi* came under scrutiny as early as 1525 by Bembo and sparked ongoing critical quarrels over the works of Ariosto and then Tasso. For a classic account, see Weinberg, *A History of Literary Criticism*. For its paradoxical relationship to European humanism and Christian culture more generally, see Everson, *The Italian Romance Epic*; Gregory, *From Many Gods to One*; and Javitch, *Proclaiming a Classic*.

35. Romance is conspicuously absent from the English gallery of kinds in major critical accounts of genre such as Thomas Elyot's *Boke Named the Governour* (1531), Sir Philip Sidney's *Defence of Poesy* (publ. 1595), and Francis Meres's *Palladis Tamia* (1598), which list epic, lyric, tragedy, and comedy, among other forms. According to a study done by Sasha Roberts, presented in an unpublished paper at the Shakespeare Association of America Conference in 2004, between 1580 and 1599 no works are identified as "romance," "antiromance," or "mock-romance" in the British Library public records.

36. Shakespeare, *Hamlet*, 2.2.379–82.

37. Puttenham, *The Arte of English Poesie*, 42. See also Greville, *The Life of the Renowned Sr Philip Sidney*, C3[r]. For notable discussions of the distinction between "romance" and "epic," see Burrow, *Epic Romance*; Quint, "The Boat of Romance"; and Quint, *Epic and Empire*.

38. L. Wright, *Middle-Class Culture*, 382. For the vogue for medieval reprints, see R. Crane, *The Vogue of Medieval Chivalric Romance*; H. Cooper, *Romance in Time*; A. Davis, *Chivalry and Romance*; and A. King, *"The Faerie Queene" and Middle English Romance*. On the resurgent interest in Greek romance, see Doody, *The True Story of the Novel*; Gesner,

Shakespeare and the Greek Romance; Mentz, *Romance for Sale*; Skretkowicz, *European Erotic Romance*; and Wolff, *The Greek Romances*. For the growing market from the 1570s onward for continental and Iberian romance, see Boro, "All for Love"; H. Thomas, *Spanish and Portuguese Romances*; and Patchell, *The Palmerin Romances*. Anthony Munday's central role in this regard has been studied by D. Hamilton, *Anthony Munday and the Catholics*.

39. I adopt the metaphor of the "forest" to describe various senses of romance from Lamb and Wayne, *Staging Early Modern Romance*, introduction, esp. 2. Different metaphors for addressing the crossbred fertile terrain of dramatic and narrative forms of romance include a "sea," as in Womack, "Shakespeare and the Sea of Stories." Another model for conceptualizing the romance is that of the tree, with its loose but connected branches; Moretti, *Graphs, Maps, and Trees*.

40. Shakespeare, *Pericles*, 1.0.12.

41. I borrow the term "negative canon" from Ross, *The Making of the English Literary Canon*, esp. 79, who uses it to account for the practice of blacklisting by Protestant polemicists, a practice, Ross notes, that parallels that of Catholic indexes.

42. Without the teeth of the official Catholic *Index Librorum Prohibitorum* (List of Prohibited Books), the lists I describe chart a cultural rather than legal prohibition. For the political and legal wrangling entailed in the Catholic *Index*, see for example Godman, *The Saint as Censor*.

43. Heliodorus, *An Aethiopian Historie*, A3ʳ.

44. Similar to Fuchs, Helen Cooper defines romance through its recurring literary motifs; see H. Cooper, *Romance in Time*, 1–44. See also Fowler, *Kinds of Literature*.

45. Acts 19:19.

46. Cervantes, *Don-Quixote*, D3ʳ.

47. As M. Patterson, *Domesticating the Reformation*, 267–90, demonstrates, it was a best seller, going through fifteen editions by 1606.

48. Dering, *A Briefe and Necessarie Catachisme*, A4ʳ.

49. Cervantes, *Don-Quixote*, D3ᵛ.

50. Ibid., D2ʳ⁻ᵛ.

51. Hathaway, *Marvels and Commonplaces*. Recently, Moore, "Romance," 240, too notes the centrality of "romance wonder" to early modern writers of the genre. Other studies will be cited as they pertain to my argument. Significant accounts of the various cultural functions of wonder and marvel in early modern England include Biester, *Lyric Wonder*; Crawford, *Marvelous Protestantism*; Daston and Park, *Wonders and the Order of Nature*; Greenblatt, *Marvelous Possessions*; and Platt, *Reason Diminished*.

52. Vives, *A Very Fruteful and Plesant Booke*, E3ᵛ–E4ʳ. Issued in at least thirty-six English and continental editions, Vives's was the most popular conduct book for women in the sixteenth century, argues Wayne, "Some Sad Sentence," 15.

53. A. Davis, *Chivalry and Romance*, 10.

54. See, for instance, the discussion in Hathaway, *Marvels and Commonplaces*; Ife, *Reading and Fiction in Golden-Age Spain*, 1–37; Eisenberg, *Romances of Chivalry*; and Fumaroli, "Jacques Amyot and the Clerical Polemic."

55. Gregory, *From Many Gods to One*, 4.

56. Marshall, "(Re)Defining the English Reformation," 585.

57. For an argument in favor of the term "early modern Christianity," see O'Malley, *Trent and All That*. Early modern uses of oppositional terms are common, as exemplified by those of John Foxe, who begins a section in his *Acts and Monuments*, "Here beginneth the reformation of the church in the tyme of Martin Luther." See Foxe, *Acts and Monuments*, 1576 edition, 803. Likewise, Bishop Lancelot Andrewes hailed the "the Reformation of the Church of England, and the ejection of Popery" in Andrewes, *Of Episcopasy*, 29.

58. Marshall, "(Re)Defining the English Reformation," 585.

59. The relationship of religious history to sixteenth-century English polemic is studied by Felicity Heal in "Appropriating History." She argues that English Protestants worked ingeniously to appropriate historical claims regarding the Christian church. My argument aligns romance as an imaginatively engaged part of this appropriative struggle for identity.

60. I will not be engaging the question of whether Shakespeare personally was or was not a recusant Catholic. For scholarly debate on this issue, see the recent studies by Beauregard, *Catholic Theology in Shakespeare's Plays*, 30–31; Wilson, "Jesuit Drama in Early Modern England"; Richmond, *Shakespeare, Catholicism, and Romance*; and Rist, *Shakespeare's Romances*. More likely is that Shakespeare practiced a hybrid faith (Mayer, *Shakespeare's Hybrid Faith*).

61. The phrase "lying wonders" comes from Perkins, *A Discourse of the Damned Art of Witchcraft*, 238.

62. Crawford, *Marvelous Protestantism*.

63. Dolan, *Whores of Babylon*; and Hackett, *Women and Romance Fiction*.

64. *The Middle English "Mirror,"* 1.

65. Furrow, *Expectations of Romance*.

66. Snook, *Women, Reading, and the Cultural Politics*, esp. chapter 1, "Gendering the English Reformation," which argues that the female reader becomes a central focus within the English Reformation's polemical attempt to distinguish between Catholic and Protestant practice.

67. John Whitgift, a representative voice for the Church of England, calls attention to Foxe's many examples for how many "came to the light of the gospel only by reading" in Whitgift, *Defence*, 30–31.

68. Pioneering scholarship on early modern affect includes Paster, *The Body Embarrassed*; Paster, *Humoring the Body*; Paster, Rowe, and Floyd-Wilson, *Reading the Early Modern Passions*; Schoenfeldt, *Bodies and Selves*; and Tilmouth, *Passion's Triumph over Reason*.

PART I.   Fabulous Texts

1. "Romish" was pejorative shorthand for Catholicism in early Protestant polemic by writers such as John Bale. See Brumbaugh, "Edgar's Wolves"; Ascham, *Toxophilus*, A^r: "These bokes (as I haue heard say) were made the moste parte in Abbayes, and Monasteries, a very lickely and fit fruite of suche an ydle and blynde kinde of lyuynge"; Nashe, *The*

Anatomie of Absurditie, A2^r; Harvey, *A Discursive Probleme Concerninge Prophesies*, K2^v–K3^r; Dering, *A Briefe and Necessarie Catachisme*, A3^v–A4^r; and Jonson, *The New Inn*, 1.6.128.

2. Heisterbach, *Dialogus Miraculorum*, 233.

3. Heng, *Empire of Magic*, 2.

4. S. Crane, *Insular Romance*, uses the term "insular romance" to refer to Anglo-Norman romances with English heroes and national interests that are attuned to realities of English life. Another scholar of late medieval romance concurs that "English romance has in any case tended to be more consistently pious than its French counterpart, in the sense that the ideology it promotes is almost universally compatible with Christian morals"; see H. Cooper, "Romance after 1400," esp. 697.

5. *South English Legendary*. Because of its inclusion of specifically English saints (like Thomas à Becket of Canterbury), the *Legendary* suggests a focus for both national and devotional impulses that readily blurs saints with romance-like behavior, according to Speed, "The Construction of the Nation"; and Wogan-Browne, "'Bet . . . To . . . Rede.'"

6. The relationship of medieval romance to hagiography sparks continued scholarly debate. Notable interventions that argue for overlap include Pearsall, "John Capgrave's *Life of St. Katherine*"; Fewster, *Tradionality and Genre*; and Wogan-Browne, "'Bet . . . To . . . Rede.'" Their overlapping material history further complicates the distinction. Speed, "The Construction of the Nation," 143, discusses how the oldest extant manuscript of the *South English Legendary* was bound with the main text of *Havelok* and *King Horn*, which was not an uncommon practice. A critical conspectus of those who advocate the differences rather than the similarities can be found in Whetter, *Understanding Genre and Medieval Romance*, 35–51.

7. Kaeuper, *Holy Warrior*, argues that the two discourses of knighthood and religion were in tension throughout the flowering of the chivalric code in medieval England.

8. Saunders, *Magic and the Supernatural*, surveys the complex negotiation of magic in medieval romances, drawing distinctions between the Christian supernatural and what she terms the "faery" or more classical and pagan influences. Both, she argues, are omnipresent in medieval romance.

9. Owst, *Literature and Pulpit*, 15, cites the example of Felton from MS. Harl. 4, fol. 31.

10. MS. Bodleian 48, fol. 47, quoted in Halliwell, *The Thornton Romances*, xx. A corresponding citation from MS Royal 17.C.viii is given by Owst, *Literature and Pulpit*, 13.

11. Piramus, *La Vie Seint Edmund Le Rei*, 59. *Partenopeus de Blois*, a thirteenth-century French romance, is largely a variation of the Cupid and Psyche myth. It has been sometimes credited to Denis Piramus based on the ambiguous passage cited above from the prologue to *La Vie Seint Edmund*.

12. Ibid.

13. Critics have argued that condemnation of romance by religious writers stems from professional competition over the same audience. See, for example, Owst, *Literature and Pulpit*, 10–16; and Legge, "Anglo-Norman Hagiography and the Romances."

14. I thank Gambirasi Heathcliff (and James Lo) for helping to produce harmonized translations. Latin Text from Ailred of Rievaulx, *Speculum Caritatis*, 2.17. References to Latin texts of the church fathers are to Abbé Migne *Patrologiae cursus completus series latinus*,

195:565. For a complete English translation, see Aelred of Rievaulx, *The Mirror of Charity: The Speculum Caritatis*. A similar example comes from Peter of Blois (ca. 1135–1212), who in *De confessione sacramentali* confesses: "Recitantur etiam pressurae vel inuriae eidem crudeliter irrogatae, sicut de Arturo et Gangano et Tristanno, fabulosa quaedam referunt histriones, quorum auditu concutiuntur ad compassionem audientium corda, et usque ad lacrymas compunguntur" (Furthermore they tell of pressures and wrongs imposed cruelly on a man, such as in the stories of Arthur and Gawain and Tristan, fabulous tales that the *histriones* repeat, on the hearing of which the listener's hearts are smitten by pity and pricked all the way to tears.) Latin text from Peter of Blois, *De confessione sacramentali*, *Patrologiae cursus completus series latinus*, 207:1088. Andrea Hopkins cites another story: in one sermon on the Gospel given during Holy Week, the writer tells of an audience member who, upon "hearing the deeds of Guy of Warwick read aloud, when he came to the place where it dealt with the gratitude of the lion and how it was cut into three, wept uncontrollably." The writer continues with a certain amount of righteous scorn: "O ungrateful wretch who drops so many tears for such a trifle, yet does not grieve for Christ who was condemned and put to death for your sake"; Hopkins, *The Sinful Knights*, 74–76. Original source BL MS Harley 7322, f. 49.

15. New English editions of *Gesta Romanorum*, often alternatively titled as *A Record of Ancient Histories*, printed by Wynkyn de Worde emerged in 1502 (STC [Addenda] / 21286.2), 1510 (STC [2nd ed.] / 21286.3), 1515 (STC [2nd ed.] / 21286.5), and 1525 (STC [2nd ed.] / 21286.7), as did one credited to J. Kynge in 1557 (STC [2nd ed.] / 21287). There were in addition numerous manuscript copies in both Latin and English.

16. Chambers, *Palestina*, 200.

17. Heng, *Empire of Magic*, 5.

18. H. Cooper, "Romance after 1400," 695.

19. Frye, *The Secular Scripture*.

20. Spenser, *The Faerie Queene*, 4.6.22.

21. Juan Luis Vives, *A Very Fruteful and Plesant Booke*, E4^v.

22. Nashe, *Pierce Penilesse*, B3^v.

23. Another theoretical model for describing this in-between quality of romance is liminality. Anthropological theories of the liminal by Turner, *The Ritual Process*, and Gennep, *The Rites of Passage*, discuss how subjects that dwell in between networks of classification render their identities ambiguous and thus potentially threaten the society's understanding of its own identity.

24. See in this regard Young, *Colonial Desire*, esp. 18.

25. Tom G. Bishop, personal correspondence to the author, April 16, 2007.

26. Parker, *Inescapable Romance*, 4; and Nohrnberg, *The Analogy of "The Faerie Queene."*

27. Robinson, *Islam and Early Modern English Literature*, explores how the romance played a key role in articulating the uncertain allegiances and affiliations in an attempt to establish various kinds of identity, both religious and cultural, in early modern England.

28. Douglas, *Purity and Danger*.

CHAPTER 1:   Fabulous Romance and Abortive
Reform in Philip Sidney and Edmund Spenser

1. My attention was drawn to this volume by Sherman, *Used Books*, 80–83. Davenport, *English Embroidered Bookbindings*, presents evidence that such embroidered covers for religious texts were not uncommon in Tudor and Jacobean England, although this volume represents an especially elaborate specimen. A 1630 *New Testament*, for instance, also contains the figures of Abraham, Isaac, and David; see fig. 22 in G. Barber, *Textile and Embroidered Bindings*.

2. Crosses and the crucifix provided but one ongoing target of iconoclastic debates. See Aston, *Faith and Fire*, 283–89.

3. Spenser, *The Faerie Queene*, 714. All subsequent parenthetical references to *The Faerie Queene* cite the Longman (2001) edition, ed. Hamilton, Yamashita, and Suzuki.

4. All parenthetical citations of Sidney, *The Countesse of Pembrokes Arcadia*, are to signature in the London, 1590, edition.

5. Although Sidney banishes monsters, giants rove the revised *Arcadia*. In a region of "cruell monsters, & monstrous men," for instance, a full description follows for the "monstrous men" but the monsters themselves never appear (T4^v). This may be because, although larger in scale, giants remain human. For the English view on giants, see Prescott, *Imagining Rabelais in Renaissance England*; Scherb, "Assimilating Giants"; and Stephens, "Incredible Sex."

6. H. Cooper, *Romance in Time*, 3, 21.

7. Dering, *A Briefe and Necessarie Catachisme*, A2^r–A3^r.

8. These motifs, or what H. Cooper, *Romance in Time*, calls "memes" and what Fuchs, *Romance*, esp. 3–11, terms "narrative strategies," represent those features commonly identified as constituting recognizable signatures of early modern romance.

9. Both Sidney's *New Arcadia* and Spenser's *The Faerie Queene* have long spawned debates over genre. While both texts undoubtedly mix multiple genres, recent criticism acknowledges their place within and debt to the "romance forest," as does A. King, "Sidney and Spenser."

10. By the "supernatural marvelous," I mean the intrusion of powers or things transcending nature's ordinary course. The border between the preternatural, or marvelous, and the supernatural, or miraculous, was often porous, as well illustrated in Daston and Park, *Wonders and the Order of Nature*, esp. 14, 122–24. On the struggle to redefine supernatural intervention from a polytheistic, classical pagan form to one that was Christian and monotheistic, see Gregory, *From Many Gods to One*, especially the introduction. Post-Reformation writers had to further reform their texts to make Protestant what had been Catholic. Much Protestant polemic, for instance, conflated supernatural marvels with "lying wonders," a phrase often read as shorthand for Catholic practices. One anonymous pamphlet suggests how papists might be identified by their practice of "coniurationes, magicall artes, false miracles, lying wonders, deceiuable signes, malitious deuises": *A Reply with the Occasion Thereof*, A4^r. For the pejorative association of the "superstitious" after

the Reformation with supernatural events, see Clark, *Thinking with Demons*, esp. 489–508; and Thomas, *Religion and the Decline of Magic*; for the problem of the marvelous more generally, see n. 19 to the introduction of the present volume. For motivations other than religious ones to use magic in literary texts, see Friesen, *Supernatural Fiction*.

11. The Protestant polemicist Arthur Dent uses the phrase "fabulous devices"; see below, n. 34.

12. Although earlier studies remark on Sidney's derogation of the marvelous, none have linked it to a genre crisis triggered by religious reform. See Goldman, "Sidney and Harington as Opponents of Superstition." On p. 534, he notes, "Though Sidney borrowed enormously from the *Aethopica* of Heliodorus, *Le Morte Darthur* of Sir Thomas Malory, and the *Amadis of Gaul*, he made no use whatever of the enchantments and other supernatural prodigies with which these works abound." Goldman argues that Sidney downplays astrology and prophecy because such beliefs contradicted his belief in God's providence. Lee, "The English Ariosto," traces a general cultural wariness toward the marvelous but does so in the context of morality rather than specific Reformation controversy. More recent critics recognize Sidney's investment in Reformation debates. See Kingsley-Smith, "Cupid, Idolatry, and Iconoclasm," which traces Sidney's depiction of idolatry and iconoclasm in this context.

13. Ascham, *The Schoolmaster*, 68.

14. Ibid. Ascham's invective against romance is part of a larger pedagogical objection to Italian influence on young men. His attack on pernicious books engages his fear that they represent a covert religious threat designed to lure Englishmen to Catholicism by subtly undermining morals. See Ord, "Classical and Contemporary," 202–16, esp. 210.

15. Ascham, *The Schoolmaster*, 68–69.

16. Late medieval and early modern culture, according to Caroline Walker Bynum, understood wonder to be a "significance-reaction: a flooding with awe, pleasure or dread owing to something deeper lurking in the phenomenon." See Bynum, *Metamorphosis and Identity*, 73. According to Greenblatt, *Marvelous Possessions*, 14, "wonder" as understood by an early modern audience is an instigation to knowledge as "an emotional and intellectual experience in the presence of radical difference." See also n. 19 to the introduction to the present volume.

17. Ascham, *The Schoolmaster*, 67, 64.

18. Dering, *A Sparing Restraint*, B3ᵛ.

19. Memory—how it worked, how it might be trained, and how it might be ruined—fascinated early modern writers. The seminal book in this regard remains F. Yates, *The Art of Memory*. Medieval understandings of memory provide an important historical context for the early modern. See Carruthers, *The Book of Memory*; and Carruthers and Ziolkowski, *The Medieval Craft of Memory*. For its representation in early modern texts, see Stewart and Sullivan, "'Worme-Eaten, and Full of Canker Holes,'" 215–38; G. Sullivan, *Memory and Forgetting*; and Summit, *Memory's Library*, esp. 124–35.

20. All parenthetical citations of Sidney, *Defence of Poesy* are to signature in the London, 1595, edition. Like the *Arcadia*, the nomenclature for Sidney's *Defence* can be confusing. I use here the title and spelling as it appeared in the authorized 1595 printing and subsequent reprints.

21. For further views on attitudes toward romance's useful didactic qualities, see Stani-vukovic, "English Renaissance Romances."

22. Ronald Levao, for instance, provides a sensitive reading of how the *New Arcadia* strives toward didacticism in *Renaissance Minds and Their Fictions*, 183–249, esp. 185. See also Schneider, *Sidney's (Re)Writing of the "Arcadia."*

23. Critics struggle to reconcile the seemingly contradictory impulses within Sidney's political, religious, and literary life. Ultimately, locating Sidney within a particular confessional circle may be less insightful than understanding the fractured, ever-shifting nature of religious allegiance. Some find Sidney's Protestant piety within English Calvinism to be at odds with his literary philosophy; important in this regard are Sinfield, "Protestantism"; Weiner, "Sidney, Protestantism, and Literary Critics"; and Weiner, *Sidney and the Poetics of Protestantism*. By contrast, others locate Sidney within a continental network of "cosmopolitan-minded reformers" whose piety is less at odds with Sidney's poetic philosophy. See Kuin, "Querre-Muhau"; Kuin, "Sir Philip Sidney's Model"; Stillman, *Sidney and the Poetics*; and Skretkowicz, *European Erotic Romance*.

24. Skretkowicz, *European Erotic Romance*, 168–224, argues that Sidney sought to align himself with Philhellene Protestants such as his mentor, Hubert Languet, to represent a continuum of Protestant romance.

25. For Du Bartas's high esteem among English writers, see Prescott, "The Reception of Du Bartas in England," esp. 62. Apparently, Sidney even wrote a version of Du Bartas's *Premiere Sepmaine*, although it has long been lost; see Ringler, *Sidney's Poems*, 339. Although Prescott questions just how much the English were influenced specifically by Du Bartas's Protestant sympathies, she does note that Gabriel Harvey saw him as a "Jeweller of Divinity"; Prescott, *French Poets and the English Renaissance*, 167. On the relationship between Du Bartas and Sidney and the evolution of the goddess Urania into a Christian muse, see Campbell, "The Christian Muse."

26. Sidney, *Old Arcadia*, 4–6.

27. Influential readings that suggest a Neoplatonic schema include W. Davis, *Sidney's Arcadia*, esp. 84–89; and Duncan-Jones, "Sidney's *Urania*." For the *Arcadia*'s political critique, see A. Patterson, "'Under . . . Pretty Tales.'" For its signaling a move toward "heroically ambitious narrative," or epic, see Quilligan, *Incest and Agency*, 192.

28. Montemayor, *Diana*.

29. J. N. King, *Spenser's Poetry and the Reformation*, 37; and Brumbaugh, "Edgar's Wolves." The conceit of the "Romish" wolf infiltrates the polemical language of Reformation controversy from Henry VIII onward. Exemplary in this regard is Turner's *The Hunting of the Fox and the Wolfe*, which features an image of a wolf-headed figure dressed in Catholic robes devouring a sheep. Scribner, *For the Sake of Simple Folk*, discusses its presence in Reformation debates on the Continent.

30. Gratarolo, *The Castel of Memorie*, E3^v–F4^r.

31. Parish, *Monks, Miracles and Magic*, esp. 45–70. See also Collinson, *The Birthpangs of Protestant England*; Collinson, "From Iconoclasm to Iconophobia"; and Collinson, *Godly People*. On the influence of iconoclasm on "biblioclasm" (Brian Cummings's term), see Cummings, "Iconoclasm and Bibliophobia."

32. More, *The Co[n]futacyon of Tyndales Answere*; and Tyndale, *An Answere Vnto Sir Thomas Mores Dialoge*.

33. Parish, *Monks, Miracles and Magic*, 50.

34. Dent, *The Plaine Mans Path-way to Heaven*, Bb2ᵛ.

35. Ibid.

36. The phrase "lying wonders" is from Perkins, *A Discourse of the Damned Art of Witchcraft*, 232–39, at 238. Although not a reformer, John Harvey, in *A Discursive Probleme Concerninge Prophesies*, K2ᵛ-3ʳ, wished to make a distinction between kinds of supernatural practices in order to justify his own astrological dabbling.

37. Dering, *A Briefe and Necessarie Catachisme*, A3ʳ.

38. Prideaux, *An Easy and Compendious Introduction*, xxʳ.

39. Sidney, *The Defence of Poesy*.

40. Frye, *Anatomy of Criticism*, 33.

41. Sannazaro, *Arcadia*, 92.

42. In the 1555 edition of Hawes's text, the woodcut illustrates a three-headed allegorized giant whose heads figure, respectively, falsehood, imagination, and perjury (U1-2ʳ) STC (2nd ed.) / 12952; the image does not appear in the 1554 edition. In the other two stories, it represents an epic battle between a knight and a dragon.

43. H. Cooper, "Magic That Does Not Work," 131.

44. Peter Platt also notes that beauty and love engender the benign forms of wonder in the *New Arcadia*; see Platt, *Reason Diminished*, 79–84.

45. Others have read this "error" of the fishermen as a representation of difference between a class- and gender-bound "geometry of vision and perception" that produces radically different desires and actions. See J. Yates, *Error, Misuse, Failure*, 3–27, at 16.

46. Basilius's unquestioning belief in the oracle's prophecy too looks more like superstition than virtue; the disastrous result for the kingdom of Arcadia, subsequently wrenched apart by popular unrest in his absence, testifies to his error. See Worden, *The Sound of Virtue*, 368n72.

47. Clare Kinney shows how Mopsa's reduction of the Cupid and Psyche myth from Apuleius's *Metamorphoses* emphasizes the "questionable nature" and the interminability of the narrative of desire. See Kinney, "On the Margins of Romance," 143–52, at 50. The tale's resemblance to folklore legends has been commented on by Watson, "Folklore in Arcadia."

48. Sidney, *Old Arcadia*, 42–44.

49. Peter Platt argues that Sidney exposes the "dark and dangerous side" of the marvelous both in the *Old Arcadia* and the *New Arcadia*; see Platt, *Reason Diminished*, esp. 79–84. My argument emphasizes Sidney's mistrust of the marvelous specifically when it engages the supernatural.

50. Adams, "Bold Bawdry and Open Manslaughter."

51. The phrase is from N. Baxter, *The Lectures or Daily Sermons*, B3ʳ⁻ᵛ. I am indebted to Anne Lake Prescott for alerting me to this reference. Prescott, *Imagining Rabelais in Renaissance England*, esp. 21.The ultimate generic category for *The Faerie Queene* continues to spark debate, in part because it has often been conceived in binaristic terms. The poem itself encourages such a split. The proem to book 1, which claims "Fierce warres and faith-

full loues shall moralize my song," plausibly suggests a model of Virgilian epic. The open-ing line to the first canto, " A Gentle Knight was pricking on the plaine," however, locates the reader within a romance framework. Some compromise and claim the poem as a "romantic-epic," modeled after the Italian models of Ariosto and Tasso, perhaps most famously Burrow, *Epic Romance*; P. Cheney, *Spenser's Famous Flight*; and Greene, *The Descent from Heaven*. Like Sidney's *Arcadia*, Spenser's text flirts with a variety of modes; however, recent critical attention has regarded its complex relationship to a na-tive, vernacular romance as crucial to reading the text within its immediate cultural context: see A. King, "Sidney and Spenser"; as well as A. King, *"The Faerie Queene" and Middle English Romance*; A. King, "Lines of Authority"; and A. King, "'Well Grounded, Finely Framed.'" For an overview of the critical conspectus regarding the difference between epic and romance pace Spenser, see Wilson-Okamura, "Errors about Ovid and Romance."

52. J. N. King, *Spenser's Poetry and the Reformation*, 202.

53. Spenser's letter to Ralegh in Spenser, *The Faerie Queene*, 714.

54. Summit, *Memory's Library*, 122.

55. N. Baxter, *The Lectures or Daily Sermons*, A3^r–A3^v. Arthur's contradictory status in British history has engaged much recent critical attention: Dean, *Arthur of England*; Esc-obedo, *Nationalism and Historical Loss*, chapter 2; Hume, *Edmund Spenser: Protestant Poet*, 40–45, 48–49; Ingham, *Sovereign Fantasies*; A. King, *"The Faerie Queene" and Middle English Romance*, 69–77, 173–80; and Summit, *Memory's Library*, 119–21.

56. Spenser, *Shorter Poems*, 82. Much critical energy has been expended to uncover the identity of the mysterious annotator "E.K." See, for instance, Schleiner, "Spenser's 'E.K.'"; Green, "Who Was Spenser's E.K.?"; and Heninger, "The Typographical Layout of Spenser's *Shepheardes Calendar*." Scholars now deem it most safe to conclude that E.K. represents some version of the author, Spenser, himself. See Waldman, "Spenser's Pseudonym 'E.K.'"; and McCarthy, "E.K. Was Only the Postman."

57. Polydore Vergil's *Historia Anglicana* (1534) deals Arthurian history a devastating blow. John Leland and John Prise were among those who sought to defend it, respectively, in *Assertio inclytissimi Arthurii regis britanniae* (1544) and *Historiae Brytannicae defen-sio* (1573). For the chronicle war waged after Polydore Vergil, see Millican, *Spenser and the Table Round*; Hankins, *Source and Meaning in Spenser's Allegory*; and Summers, *Spenser's Arthur*.

58. Malory, *The story of the moste noble and worthy kynge Arthur*, prologus, iii^v and iii^r.

59. Spenser, *The Faerie Queene*.

60. Ibid., 715. *The Faerie Queene*, especially book 2, invokes a combination of epic, ro-mance, fabliau, novella, and chronicle. Critics have rightly noted how Guyon's descent into Mammon's cave, for instance, recalls an epic journey. See, for instance, Bond, "Medieval Harrowings of Hell," which argues for a persistent medievalism. By contrast, I read that persistent medievalism as part of book 2's sustained engagement with romance motifs, particularly as it looks back toward *The Odyssey* and Circe in its culminating cantos.

61. Shakespeare, *Pericles*, 1.0.1.

62. Puttenham, *The Arte of English Poesie*, 83. Puttenham's attitude toward romance, like that of many of his contemporaries, was not consistent. While here he claims they are tales

best told in taverns, elsewhere he seems proud to say that he composed a romance himself; see A. Davis, *Chivalry and Romance*, esp. 30.

63. *Oxford English Dictionary*, adj. and n. "antic." See also "antique" adj. and n.

64. Ibid., s.v. "abbie-lubber." The OED credits Thomas Starkey with the first use of "abbie-lubbers" in 1538. It peaked as a term of abuse, during what Patrick Collinson has identified as a second wave of reform in the 1580s. Collinson, "From Iconoclasm to Iconophobia."

65. Tyndale, *The Pentateuch*, 295.

66. For the medieval views that influenced later early modern understanding of the mind's physiological conceptions of memory, see Carruthers, *The Book of Memory*. For more on the period conception of psychological theory, see Siraisi, *Medieval & Early Renaissance Medicine*, 81–82; and Harvey, *The Inward Wits*, 1–2, 30. See also G. Sullivan, *Memory and Forgetting*.

67. The three rooms with their three sages have long been recognized as a critical locus for Spenser's treatment of Reason and its relationship to the higher faculties of the mind and the sensitive soul; see Anderson, "'Myn Auctour'"; and Reid, "Alma's Castle and the Symbolization of Reason." A. King, *"The Faerie Queene" and Middle English Romance*, esp. chapter 7, discusses them as competing impulses of history and romance. For its reflection of the tensions in the poem's account of memory, history, discipline, and heroic action, see Stewart and Sullivan, "'Worme-Eaten, and Full of Canker Holes.'" Spenser's debt to the selection of library-worthy books by post-Reformation catalogers like John Leland is argued in Summit, "Monuments and Ruins," and expanded in Summit, *Memory's Library*, 106–35.

68. Summit, *Memory's Library*, 120.

69. Ariosto, *Orlando Furioso in English*, 3.26–48.

70. Walsham, *Providence in Early Modern England*, 21.

71. H. Berger, *The Allegorical Temper*, 80n3.

72. Harper, *The Sources of the British Chronicle*. My analysis throughout remains indebted to Harper's careful delineation of differences between source material and Spenser's presentation. Other accounts of his originality in handling sources include Mills, "Spenser and the Numbers of History"; O'Connell, "History and the Poet's Golden World"; and Rathborne, *The Meaning of Spenser's Fairyland*, 65–154.

73. Harper, *The Sources of the British Chronicle*, 80.

74. Holinshed, *Chronicles of England, Scotland, and Ireland*, 1:B4^v.

75. Stow, *The Chronicles of England*, ff. 28–29.

76. *Mirour for Magistrates*, I^r.

77. For the ambiguous resonances that Stonehenge carries in Spenser's account when he associates the most famous national "moniment" with infamy, see McCabe, *The Pillars of Eternity*, 103–9; and Rossi, "Britons Moniments: Spenser's Definition of Temeprance in History."

78. *Mirour for Magistrates*, F2^r.

79. N. Baxter, *The Lectures or Daily Sermons*, A3^r–A3^v.

80. Ibid.

81. According to Mills, the "climacteric" stanzas are the advent of Christianity and the

coming of the House of Arthur. The first is "climacteric" because it is the 49th stanza (stanza 53, but the story begins at 5), a significant number in the numerology of Jean Bodin. See Mills, "Spenser and the Numbers of History," 283.

82. Malory, *Caxton's Malory*, 2.16.

83. A. Hamilton, *The Faerie Queene*, 2.10.53n, draws attention to this reading.

84. Kermode, *Shakespeare, Spenser, Donne*, 40–45, argues for *Acts and Monuments* as a context for Spenser's allegory. See also for its specific relationship to book 1, J. N. King, *Spenser's Poetry and the Reformation*, 190–91.

85. Foxe, *Acts and Monuments*, 1563 edition, B3ᵛ.

86. Ibid., 1576 edition, book 1, p. 96.

87. However, one may be very skeptical about how successfully he did this, as his re-telling of the Agnes legend, for instance, includes nearly as many supernatural elements as the one told by the *Golden Legend*, a point I discuss further in chapter 2. See Foxe, *Acts and Monuments*, 1576 edition, book 1, p. 95.

88. For a fuller account of Spenser's treatment of the discourses of preaching, see Mallette, *Spenser and the Discourses*, esp. chapters 1 and 2.

89. Eumnestes's imperfect library has been linked to a variety of material concerns, including antiquarianism and early modern libraries' cataloging problems, as well as more general anxieties over memory's supposed functions. In addition to Stewart and Sullivan, "'Worme-Eaten, and Full of Canker Holes,'" see, for instance, Rhodes and Sawday, "Paper Worlds"; and Summit, "Monuments and Ruins."

90. Puttenham, *The Arte of English Poesie*, 19.

91. A. King, *"The Faerie Queene" and Middle English Romance*, 180–88. The proximity and radically different narrative modes of Arthur's and Guyon's histories have baffled critics. Most see them as articulating opposing narrative views of "history" and "romance," Protestant and Catholic. Readings that see them as representing opposing narrative modes include O'Connell, *Mirror and Veil*; and H. Berger, *The Allegorical Temper*. History and romance, in Andrew King's reading, remain distinct because the poem seems to question whether the historical world might achieve the desired end of romance. A. King, *"The Faerie Queene" and Middle English Romance*, 187; and A. King, "Lines of Authority." See also Hume, *Edmund Spenser: Protestant Poet*, 156–57, which argues that the poem shows how history and poetry produce different effects.

92. Spenser, *Shorter Poems*, 115.

93. Crawford, *Marvelous Protestantism*.

94. Ford, *Parismenos*; and Ford, *Parismus the Renowned Prince of Bohemia*.

95. While various factors figure in the high esteem awarded the *Arcadia* (see, for instance, Lori Newcomb, who discusses the complexity of social distinction and the divide between literary and popular print in *Reading Popular Romance in Early Modern England*), my argument stresses how religious agendas affect its later reception. For further discussion of its mixed reception, particularly for women readers, see Hackel, *Reading Material in Early Modern England*, 154–55. For a comprehensive account of Sidney's literary reception, see Alexander, *Writing after Sidney*.

96. Meres, *Palladis Tamia*, Nn8ᵛ.

97. Ibid. The *Arcadia* referred to (with the possible exception of Greville's account) was

likely the composite edition published in 1593 that contained the 1590 revisions concluded by the final two books of the *Old Arcadia*.

98. Hakewill, *Apologie of the Power*, 236.

99. J. King, *Lectures Upon Jonas* (Oxford: Joseph Barnes, 1597), Z2^r. Since *Orlando Furioso* figures here, however, this could also be a reference to Sannazaro's text of the same name.

100. See, for instance, Hackel, *Reading Material in Early Modern England*, 154, which cites this as evidence of the *Arcadia*'s perceived danger to female readers.

101. Saltonstall, *Picturae Loquentes*, E6^v.

102. Torshell, *The Woman's Glorie*, G2^v.

103. Ibid., G2^v–G3^r.

104. Prideaux, *An Easy and Compendious Introduction*, title page.

105. Ibid., Xx^{r-v}.

106. Ibid.

107. Ibid., Xx^v.

108. Sidney, *The Countesse of Pembrokes Arcadia*, A3^v.

CHAPTER 2:   Saint or Martyr?

1. Johnson, *The Seven Champions of Christendom*, 168.

2. Lupton, *Afterlives of the Saints*, argues that the "afterlife" of hagiographic motifs infiltrates disparate genres of secular Renaissance literary works. My reading draws from Lupton's understanding of typological transformation.

3. Dering, *A Briefe and Necessarie Catachisme*, A3^v–A4^v.

4. H. Cooper, *Romance in Time*, esp. in her chapter "Women on Trial," 269–323, traces how romance heroines are frequently accused of perfidy in medieval and early modern romance alike. Ascham, *The Schoolmaster*, 68–69, is representative of such complaints as he singles out the licentious behavior of Malory's heroines: "The wife of King Arthur," with Sir Lancelot, "the wife of King Mark" with Sir Tristram, and, even more incestuously, of Sir Lamorak with the wife of King Lot "that was his own aunt." As I argue in my introduction, the negative association between romance and women does not begin with the Reformation but is complicated by it. For medieval anxiety over women and romance, see, for instance, Urban, *Monstrous Women*.

5. This damning rhetorical triangle came into focus in the excellent study by Dolan, *Whores of Babylon*.

6. All subsequent parenthetical references to Spenser, *The Faerie Queene*, cite the Longman (2001) edition, ed. Hamilton, Yamashita, and Suzuki.

7. Recent scholarly interest has sought to bridge the critical divide between prose romances and early modern plays; see the introduction to Lamb and Wayne, *Staging Early Modern Romance*, 1–20.

8. *The hystory of the two valyaunte brethren Valentyne and Orson*, C4^v.

9. Luborsky and Ingram, *A Guide to English Illustrated Books*, 1:722.

10. 1506 (STC 2nd ed. 21259) at A^r, 1508 (STC 20875.5) at A^v, 1519 (STC 21260) title page.

11. Church of England, *Thirty-Nine Articles*, B1^v.

12. Duffy, *The Stripping of the Altars*, 394.

13. Strype, *Annals of the Reformation*, 408–10.

14. Ibid.

15. The last printing during the sixteenth century of Caxton's *Legend* was by Wynkyn de Worde in 1527. For its continued influence, see White, *Tudor Books of Saints and Martyrs*, esp. chapter 3, "The Attack on the Saint's Legend." Summit, *Memory's Library*, 142–74, notes how early modern collectors carefully selected and culled the saints' legends in order to satisfy post-Reformation imperatives.

16. Shakespeare, *King Henry V*, 3.1.34 and 4.3.47.

17. Shakespeare, *Pericles*, 1.0.1.

18. All parenthetical citations of Sidney, *The Countesse of Pembrokes Arcadia*, are to signature in the London, 1590, edition.

19. For Cecropia as figuring Mary Queen of Scotts, see Worden, *The Sound of Virtue*, 172–83. For her parallels to Catherine de Medici, see Greenlaw, "The Captivity Episode in Sidney's *Arcadia*"; and Raitiere, *Faire Bitts*. Her symbolism as the papal church is argued by Brumbaugh, "Cecropia and the Church of Antichrist."

20. Sidney mobilizes in Cecropia a character who pejoratively figures Catholicism and stagecraft. His antitheatricalism toward romance on the stage differs from his practice of reforming romance in his prose. For Sidney's complex attitude in this regard, see Mulready, "'Asia of the One Side.'"

21. Sidney likely draws this image of stage illusion from a fellow Protestant whose treatise took great delight in debunking witchcraft, and magic more generally, Reginald Scot, *The Discoverie of Witchcraft*, Dd7^{r-v}.

22. Dent, *The Plaine Mans Path-way to Heauen*, Bb2^{v}.

23. Perkins, *A Discourse of the Damned Art of Witchcraft*, 238.

24. Ascham, *The Schoolmaster*, 69.

25. For the ways that wonder worked to mobilize the political as opposed to the religious, see Biester, *Lyric Wonder*.

26. Critical tradition has read this speech for its classical precedent rather than for its currency within Catholic and Protestant debate. See, for instance, Syford, "The Direct Source of the Pamela-Cecropia Episode in the Arcadia."

27. Moffet, *Nobilis*, 75.

28. Summit, *Memory's Library*, 155–74, traces the shifting status of the saints and their place within Protestant historiography, noting that Foxe was often more eager to claim the saints as admissible figures in British history than later Protestant collectors such as Cotton and Camden.

29. Mary Ellen Lamb calls attention to how Pamela's debate skills establish her as Protestant heroine in Lamb, *Gender and Authorship*, 103.

30. Helen Hackett traces how medieval saints' lives had established "an iconography of female virtue" on which Pamela and Philoclea appear to be modeled; her argument, however, compares them to Catholic saints to find emergent concepts of female selfhood and protofeminism in book 3. See Hackett, *Women and Romance Fiction*, 123–29, at 124.

31. J. N. King, "The Godly Woman," offers an extended discussion of how the traditional

iconography of various female saints was appropriated as examples for the godly Protestant woman by male reformers.

32. This Eulalia is often confused with Saint Eulalia of Barcelona. The number and method of tortures differs according to source; however, most seem to agree on these details as reported in Butler, *The Lives of the Saints*, 12:120.

33. Foxe, *Acts and Monuments*. 1576 edition, book 1, p. 94.

34. Ibid., 95.

35. Ibid.

36. Ibid.

37. Winstead, *Virgin Martyrs*, 85.

38. Foxe, *Acts and Monuments.*, 1576 Edition, book 1, p. 95.

39. Ibid.

40. Ibid.

41. White, *Tudor Books of Saints and Martyrs*, 56.

42. Hackett, *Women and Romance Fiction*, 127.

43. Foxe, *Acts and Monuments*. 1576 edition, book 1, p. 95.

44. Ibid.

45. Ibid.

46. Ibid.

47. The extended arguments over the nature of the collaboration in *Pericles*, the status of the 1609 quarto, the play's exclusion from the first folio, and related questions over textual origins are beyond the scope of this chapter. For an introduction to textual issues, see Gossett, *Pericles*, esp. 8–70 and 161–63.

48. O'Connell, "Continuities." For the development of dramatic romance in England between 1570 and 1610, see Cobb, *The Staging of Romance*, 60–116.

49. Notable studies of this play's use of motifs drawn from medieval religious theater (miracle plays, saints' plays, and moralities) include Hoeniger, *Pericles*, lxxxviii–xci; Hunter, *Shakespeare and the Comedy of Forgiveness*, 132–41; Felperin, *Shakespearean Romance*, 143–76; and Miola, *Shakespeare and Classical Comedy*, 143.

50. Parenthetical citations of Shakespeare's *Pericles* are to the Arden Shakespeare, 3rd series, ed. Gossett. Gower is central to critical debates about the play. H. Cooper, "'This Worthy Olde Writer,'" examines how Shakespeare's use of Gower signals the high value of native English traditions in poetry. Other studies include Dynmkowski, "'Ancient [and Modern] Gower'"; Hillman, "Shakespeare's Gower and Gower's Shakespeare"; Oesterlen, "Why Bodies Matter"; and Williams, "Papa Don't Preach."

51. Caxton, *The Golden Legend*, 1:63–66. Although the last printing of Caxton's *Legend* was by Wynkyn de Worde in 1527, it remained influential; see n. 15.

52. Each bore close ties to the season it introduced, and some included their own special Mass. Ember eves fell on the Wednesday, Friday, and Saturday following the first Sunday of Lent, Whitsunday (Pentecost), the Feast of the Exaltation of the Holy Cross (14 September), and Saint Lucy's Day (13 December). See Hoeniger, *Pericles*, 5n; and Gossett, *Pericles*, 172n.

53. Bale, *The Pageant of Popes*, b4^r.

54. Duffy, *The Stripping of the Altars*, 394.

55. Womack, "Shakespeare and the Sea of Stories," esp. 72, suggests that romance and

hagiography blur readily into one another because they are part of the same "sea" of stories. Along a similar line, Newcomb, "The Sources of Romance," argues that we must discard the notion of source text in relation to Shakespeare's late plays in favor of an "intertextual matrix."

56. For an account of the problems surrounding the Cholmley players being persecuted for performing *Saint Christopher* at Gowthwaite Hall, see Keenan, *Travelling Players*, 72–73, which describes how they were taken to the Star Chamber in 1609 by Sir Thomas Hoby against Sir Richard Cholmley because of the plays' "Conteyninge in them much poperie."

57. Richmond, *Shakespeare, Catholicism, and Romance*, 17, argues that "the romance was more elusive than plays of legends of the saints," and therefore the romance could be a "cover" for recusant Catholicism. In an attempt to prove Shakespeare a Catholic recusant, Richmond misses many of the nuances within romance's deployment.

58. While O'Connell, *The Idolatrous Eye*, argues that the reformed antitheatrical polemic eventually led to the abolishment of theater, Diehl, *Staging Reform, Reforming the Stage*, argues that reformed religion is not necessarily antitheatrical. According to Diehl, reformers did rely on dramatic genres, but they worked to critique and replace what they considered the idolatrous spectacle of the Catholic Church with their own form of ritual and spectacle.

59. Shakespeare, *The Winter's Tale*. Beckwith, "Shakespeare's Resurrections," argues that Shakespeare's resurrections reveal a deep exploration of memory at both the personal and the communal levels. Benson, *Shakespearean Resurrection*, 122–48, sees *Pericles* as exploring the limits of the stage. Here I argue such resurrections reckon with the memories of a ruptured religious history in order to reinvoke the past.

60. Ephesus has fascinated critics as well as early modern preachers and their audiences. Notable studies are Bicks, "Backsliding at Ephesus"; Hart, "'Great Is Diana'"; and Relihan, "Liminal Geography." See also Dean, "Pericles' Pilgrimage"; Hunt, "Shakespeare's *Pericles*"; and McJannet, "Genre and Geography."

61. The cultural shift from the pagan Diana to the Catholic Mary has been traced by Ramsey, "The Worship of the Virgin Mary," esp. 87; P. Berger, *The Goddess Obscured*; Baring and Cashford, *The Myth of the Goddess*.

62. Another famous medieval story, captured in Giotto de Bondone's fresco (ca. 1370) that depicted scenes from the life of Saint John the Evangelist, told how the saint resurrected a young woman, Drusiana, outside the walls of Ephesus. Caxton's *Golden Legend* records how "all the people of Ephesus came against him singing and saying: Blessed be he that cometh in the name of our Lord. In that way he raised a woman which was named Drusiana. . . . S. John had great pity on her that was dead, and of the people that wept for her, and commanded that they should set down the bier, and unbind and take away the clothes from her. And when they had so done he said, hearing all, with a loud voice, Drusiana, my Lord God Jesu Christ ariseth thee; Drusiana arise, and go into thy house, and make ready for me some refection. Anon she arose and went in to her house for to do the commandment of S. John, and the people made three hours long a great noise and cry." See Caxton, *The Golden Legend*, 2:72–79.

63. Barlow, *A Defence of the Articles*, E2^v.

64. Benson, *A Sermon Preached at Paules Crosse*, D4^r.

65. Vicars, *Babylons Beautie*, B^r.

66. For some Protestants Ephesus could be a spectacular model of reform—as well as an urgent warning against backsliding. Mason, *The Anatomie of Sorcerie*, L3^v–L4^v, praised those who "dwelt at Ephesus, [who] magnified the name of the Lord Iesus, confessing their sinnes. . . . [T]hose that had vsed vaine and curious artes; that is, charmes, inchantments, coniuring, and other magicall deuises . . . brought their vaine books, and burned them in the sight of the people." Mason references the story as told in Acts when God worked "no smale miracles by the hands of Paul" to cure the sick and to expel evil spirits (*The Geneva Bible*, Acts 19:11–12). The exposure and willing capitulation of the Ephesian false miracle-workers acknowledged the superiority of Paul's healing powers and sharply delineated a distinction between true and false miracles, a distinction that Protestants were eager to endorse.

67. Perkins, *A Discourse of the Damned Art of Witchcraft*, 232–39. Mason will later echo Perkins in *The Anatomie of Sorcerie*.

68. Walsham, *Providence in Early Modern England*, especially chapters 3 and 4, shows how sensational news reports of unusual weather patterns, monsters, and the like were dismissed as papistical figments; yet Protestants also set store by their own miraculous portents, which crept into the homiletic discourses. In short, strange weather was ominous to both Catholic and Protestant believers.

69. Garber, "The Healer in Shakespeare."

70. A possibility acknowledged by Gossett, *Pericles*, 293n.

71. Twine, *The Pattern of Painful Adventures*, 448.

72. The *odor sanctorum* was a Catholic motif. John Foxe records no examples of such odors from the bodies of his martyrs that I have found—quite possibly because he seldom leaves any bodies to emit odors. However, he comes close in describing the Marian martyrdom of Joan Hornes as a burnt sacrifice to the Lord, "*in ordorem bonæ fragrantiæ* in the sauour of a sweete and pleasaunt smell." See Foxe, *Acts and Monuments*, 1570 edition, book 11, 2092. I thank Thomas S. Freeman for drawing my attention to this reference.

73. Gossett, *Pericles*, 298n.

74. Bynum, "The Female Body and Religious Practice."

75. Gossett, *Pericles*, 300n.

76. Shakespeare, *Othello*, 2143.

77. Twine, *The Pattern of Painful Adventures*, 449.

78. Hart, "Cerimon's 'Rough' Music."

79. White, *Tudor Books of Saints and Martyrs*, esp. 8, argues that the development of hagiographic narratives called for the authority of the witness.

80. Her invocation of Diana is unique. Hart, "'Great Is Diana,'" argues that it increases the sense that a goddess presides over the play's action. Further, I suggest that it enhances the supernatural effect and in particular the sense that we witness a saintlike miracle, for though it is Diana and not the virgin who presides, her conflation to Catholic narratives, as Vicars's rhetoric reveals, was not uncommon. On Vicars's language, see n. 65.

81. Twine, *The Pattern of Painful Adventures*, 450.

82. For example, *Measure for Measure* (1604) also portrays the bawdy world; Dekker's *The Honest Whore* (1605) offers a moralized position on brothels; *The Dutch Courtesan*

(1605) seems to suggest they are a necessary evil to protect the sanctity of the family; Sharpham's *Cupid's Whirligig* (1606–7) argues that courtesans fulfill the needs of a kingdom's soldiers and young men. For the proliferation of these scenes, see Howard, *Theater of a City*, which argues that these plays map the problems of what she calls the "hybridized city" that cannot keep the boundaries distinct between wife, whore, marketplace, and household.

83. Lorraine Helms describes how the legend of Saint Agnes looms behind Marina. Her argument, however, differs from mine in its emphasis on Marina's story as an example of potential rape and the insistence of patriarchal categories of representation for women's sexuality. Helms, "The Saint in the Brothel."

84. Caxton, *The Golden Legend*, 2:109–12.

85. Ibid.

86. Ibid.

87. Foxe, *Acts and Monuments*, 1576 edition, book 1, p. 96. This quotation prefaces the life of Saint Katherine, which follows right after the life of Agnes.

88. Ibid., p. 95.

89. Ibid.

90. Happé, "The Protestant Adaptation of the Saint Play," esp. 226ff, offers a sustained reading of how Wager rewrites the Digby version of Mary Magdalene's story. See also Badir, *The Maudlin Impression*.

91. Wager, *The Life and Repentaunce of Marie Magdalene*, C1^r.

92. J. N. King, *English Reformation Literature*, esp. 283ff.

93. Ibid., 283.

94. Dekker, *The Whore of Babylon*, 2.1.103ff.

95. Peter Platt argues that the play's emphasis in Marina's story on a kind of wonder predicated on narrative and verbal skill shows an embryonic version of a "wonder shift" that directs attention toward the mechanics of dramatic art. See Platt, *Reason Diminished*, esp. 124–38.

96. In contrast to Miola, *Shakespeare and Classical Comedy*, 143–55, which argues that the play conjoins romance narrative, early religious drama, and New Comedic elements, I suggest this act deliberately rewrites the Christian miracle play. Miola accounts for the play's tonal shift in part by suggesting how Latin new comedic deep structure furnishes the backdrop for what becomes in this act a "miniature Christian miracle play" (149).

97. For more on these lines as representing a central paradox, see C. Barber, "'Thou That Beget'st Him.'"

98. A summary of these debates is offered by Marshall, "(Re)Defining the English Reformation." Haigh, *English Reformations*, launched a full-scale revisionist assault on earlier Reformation historiography by demonstrating England's resistance to the Reformation. His view has been joined by later scholars, including the hugely influential Duffy, *The Stripping of the Altars*. How much of religious change was the result of collaboration at all social levels remains an active topic of debate; see, for instance, Shagan, *Popular Politics and the English Reformation*.

99. The phrase is from Ascham, *The Schoolmaster*.

100. Only recently have critics begun to see this play as being coherent and inno-

vative. Yet debate still surfaces as to whether difficulty with the play stems from an intrinsic problem of the play or with its place in Shakespeare's canon. The controversy still demands that we ask, as does the play's Norton editor, Walter Cohen, "Does the romance pattern fully succeed in mastering the messiness of the play's materials?" See Greenblatt et al., *The Norton Shakespeare* (2008), 2723. For a more critical stance on the play's coherence, see his earlier introduction in *The Norton Shakespeare* (1997), 2709-18, esp. 2709. The sentiments in Walter Cohen's *Norton* introduction follow a critical reading long established by editors. See also, by way of comparison, Maxwell, introduction to *Pericles*.

101. Bishop, *Shakespeare and the Theatre of Wonder*, esp. 93-122.

102. The phrase is from Vicar, *Babylons Beautie*, B^r.

PART II: Superstitious Readers

1. R. Baxter, *A Christian Directory*, 401.

2. Vives, *A Very Fruteful and Plesant Booke*, E3^v. These comments represent the ongoing early modern association between romance and the passions, specifically in the ways that romance affected its female readers.

3. Ibid.

4. See, for instance, Carr, *The Shallows*, which argues that what, and especially how, we read literally rewires brain function. Although Carr writes about the neurological effects of online reading, his cognitive insights suggest that the early modern fear for how reading might affect the mind were not simply alarmist.

5. Vives, *A Very Fruteful and Plesant Booke*, F^v.

6. Ascham, *The Schoolmaster*, 70.

7. See n. 20 of my introduction. I eschew the separation proposed in the introduction by Jennifer Richards and Fred Schurink to the special edition of *The Huntington Library Quarterly* between a textual/materialist approach to reading and theories of reading, Richards and Schurink, "The Textuality and Materiality of Reading." I see the "implied" reader and the historical reader as mutually constitutive to understanding and reconstructing early modern habits of reading.

8. For a Jacobean audience, what might most closely approximate what we call "emotions" were termed "passions" and "affections," terms often used synonymously. See Paster, Rowe, and Floyd-Wilson, *Reading the Early Modern Passions*, esp. introduction. I use the terms "affections" and "passions" interchangeably, following Thomas Cooper's conflation. On occasion, I also use the modern term "emotion."

9. Pendergast, *Religion, Allegory, and Literacy*, esp. chapter 3.

10. A. Davis, *Chivalry and Romance*, 7-8.

11. Kearney, *The Incarnate Text*, 33.

12. Cooper's treatise extends the pivotal debate over "passions" or "affections" described in T. Wright, *The Passions of the Minde in Generall*. Both treatises are exemplary for their vacillation between Stoic and Augustinian poles for interpreting emotion positively or negatively. For further discussion of the relationship of "passions" to "reason," see Cockcroft, *Rhetorical Affect*; Schoenfeldt, *Bodies and Selves*; and Tilmouth, *Passion's Triumph over Reason*.

13. T. Cooper, *The Mysterie of the Holy Government*, B1^v–B2^r.

14. Much recent work on early modern theories of the passions by scholars such as Gail Paster in *The Body Embarrassed*; Paster, Katherine Rowe, and Mary Floyd-Wilson in *Reading the Early Modern Passions*; and Michael Schoenfeldt, *Bodies and Selves*, work with the Galenic theory of the humors and have shown how early modern ideas of selfhood and identity saw them as deeply imbedded in the body. Thomas Cooper, in the passage here cited, however, suggests the opposite: that the process of physiology and psychology in the passions might originate in the soul and migrate into the body. For critical arguments that take up this direction of argument, see J. Miller, "The Passion Signified."

15. T. Cooper, *Mysterie of the Holy Government*, B11^v–B12.

16. Vives, *A Very Fruteful and Plesant Booke*, E3^v.

17. Dante, *The Inferno*, 5.119–23.

18. Cooper writes that two primary passions produce all others: "Love, whereby wee vehemently affect a thing; and Hate, being a vehement affection of disliking" (B2^v–B3^r).

19. Ascham, *The Schoolmaster*, 68.

20. T. Cooper, *The Mysterie of the Holy Government*, D9^r.

21. Vaughan, *Golden Fleece*, C2^r, lists books such as *Mirrour of Knighthood*, *The Knights of the Round Table*, *Palmerin de Oliva*, and "the like rabblement."

22. Strier, "Against the Rule of Reason," argues that Protestantism held a vested interest in the training of the passions. Tilmouth, *Passion's Triumph over Reason*, traces the emergence of a tradition that revalued the affections as morally constructive forces, if controlled.

23. T. Cooper, *The Mysterie of the Holy Government*, E8^v–E9^r.

24. Ibid.

25. Ibid.

26. *The treasurie of Amadis of Fraunce*, A2^v–3^r.

27. Ibid., A2^{r-v}.

28. See, for example, Vaught, *Masculinity and Emotion*.

CHAPTER 3:   Glozing Phantastes in the *Faerie Queene*

1. Ariosto, *Orlando Furioso in English*, A^r.

2. Spenser, *The Faerie Queene*. All parenthetical references to *The Faerie Queene* cite the Longman (2001) edition, ed. Hamilton, Yamashita, and Suzuki.

3. Book 2's specific engagement with epic has been influentially argued by Borris, *Allegory and Epic*; Burrow, *Epic Romance*; Waktins, *The Specter of Dido*; and Wofford, *The Choice of Achilles*, 248–52.

4. Critics disagree about Spenser's portrayal of Temperance, but most read the book's conclusion as Guyon's failure to embody it: Morgan, "The Idea of Temperance"; Silberman, "*The Faerie Queene*, Book II"; Cefalu, *Moral Identity*, 47–76; and Suttie, "Moral Ambivalence." Tilmouth, *Passion's Triumph over Reason*, 37–74, reads Guyon's performance of temperance throughout book 2 as "stumbling."

5. Spenser, *The Faerie Queene*, 714.

6. Ibid.

7. Dolven, *Scenes of Instruction*, 3-8.

8. Spenser, *The Faerie Queene*, 714.

9. Ibid. For Protestant acceptance of allegory as a pleasing vehicle to transmit religious and moral truth, see the following seminal studies: J. N. King, *Spenser's Poetry and the Reformation*, esp. 76-9; H. Berger, *The Allegorical Temper*; and MacCaffrey, *Spenser's Allegory*.

10. Tyndale, *The Pentateuch*, 295.

11. Ariosto, *Orlando Furioso in English*. All citations are to signature. Harington and Spenser moved in similar court circles and likely read each other's work. Harington shows his knowledge of Spenser, for instance, when he refers to the Squire of Dames "in his excellent Poem of the Faery Queen" (Ii4ʳ). Spenser's own complex relationship to Ariosto has been recently reevaluated in D. Cheney, "Spenser's Undergoing of Ariosto."

12. Scott-Warren, *Sir John Harington and the Book as Gift*, 25-55, discusses the ramifications of this apocryphal tale and its implications for Harington's negotiation of patronage relationships at court. See also Gerard Kilroy, "Advertising the Reader," 107-9.

13. Elsewhere, Harington displays a cosmopolitan attitude toward England's religious divisions: "What if I should aunswere againe (as I did once in sporte, though some would have moved his Maᵗⁱᵉ against me in earnest), that I am neither Papist, Protestant, nor Puritan, or a protesting Catholique Puritan, professing good faith, good workes, good wordes, might I not easily make an apollgie for such an aunswere . . . and to justifie the aunswere I did then but jestifye"; Harington, *A Tract on the Succession*, 108-9. For a discussion of Harington's complex religious sympathies, see Scott-Warren, *Sir John Harington and the Book as Gift*, 95, 148, 196, 212, 225.

14. Harington modeled his textual apparatus on Italian commentators but extensively expanded the notes and introduction. For his debt to the Italian critical tradition, including Lionardo Salviati's defense of *Orlando Furioso*, see Javitch, *Proclaiming a Classic*, esp. chapters 6 and 8. Harington's use of Simone Fornari's *Spositione sopra l'Orlando Furioso* as a source for his notes has been traced in McMurphy, *Spenser's Use of Ariosto*; and Townsend, *Harington and Ariosto*, esp. 50-69. For the influence of the commentaries in the Venice 1584 Franceschi edition, see Spevak, "Sir John Harington's Theoretical and Practical Criticism." Harington's departures from Italian sources have been studied in Lee, "The English Ariosto"; Javitch, *Proclaiming a Classic*, esp. 195-96nn16-17; and Nelson, "Sir John Harington and the Renaissance."

15. *Oxford English Dictionary*, s.v. "gloss." Sherman, *Used Books*, 20-24, 83-109, discusses the various nomenclature for commentary and its uneasy place within Protestant discourse.

16. See n. 14.

17. Underdowne's translation of Greek romance provided extensive marginal gloss. See his translation of Heliodorus, *An Aethiopian Historie*, which arguably sets a standard for a Protestant translation of romance. It had accrued Protestant, humanist backing abroad when it was first published in 1534 in Basel, edited by a humanist translator of Luther from German into Latin, *Heliodod ōrou Aithiopi ̃kes Historias Biblia Deka. Heliodori Historiae Aethiopicae libri decem, nunquam antea in lucem editi*, ed. Vincentus Obsopoeus (Basel: ex officina

Hervagiana, 1534). Obsopaeus's connections with the Luther circle may well have influenced its reception and translation in England. For more on its textual history in England, see Doody, *The True Story of the Novel*, 233–46; and Hägg, *The Novel in Antiquity*, 192–201. For an argument on the immense influence of this text on later English romance, see Mentz, *Romance for Sale*, 47–73.

18. Dobranski, *Readers and Authorship*, esp. chapter 1.

19. Ibid., 29.

20. The interpretive categories themselves matter. The inclusion of a "morall" recalls the popular heavily moralized editions of the *Gesta Romanorum*, which began and ended with the story's moral, as in the Huntington library copy of *A Record of Ancient Histories, Entitled in Latine: Gesta Romanorum* (London: printed by Richard Bishop, 1640). The "historie" gloss promotes the romance as more than a fantastic story by providing historical analogues to the cantos' characters and events. The deliberate blending of history with romance suggests the powerful ways that the popularity of romance narratives might be mobilized to create a view of history. The third category, "allegorie," provides the most explicit moral rational for reading a work heavily saturated with romance motifs, both marvelous and supernatural. It is this narrative cloak that most legitimizes Ariosto's depiction of miracles and monsters. Harington's category of "allusion" further justifies romance by showing how it contains numerous allusions to the more acceptable category of classical fiction. Each of these hermeneutical categories reinforces Harington's claims about the moral benefit of his translated Italian romance.

21. The phrase is recorded in Pollard, *Records of the English Bible*, 282–83. For a discussion of the unease provoked by marginalia and glossing in the Bible, see Sherman, *Used Books*, 71–86.

22. *Geneva Bible* (London, 1560), GGg4^v.

23. My analysis draws from Javitch, *Proclaiming a Classic*, esp. 139–44, which argues that Harington's goal was to preempt the "condemnation of [Ariosto's] marvels as sheer lies" (136) but Javitch does not connect this to England's post-Reformation context.

24. Summit, *Memory's Library*, 112.

25. Harington realizes the slipperiness of the ground here, at least rhetorically, for as he notes in another context, the marvelous held a perceived affinity with Catholic belief, because Catholics "ar gernerallie charged to be more superstitious and credulous, and to attribute more to old prophecies and traditions of men then either Protestantes or Puritanes." See Harington, *A Tract on the Succession*, 120.

26. Cagily avoiding the controversy as to whether such beliefs represent truth, Harington, *A Tract on the Succession*, 110, acknowledges that belief in wonders and miracles are, at the very least, unfashionable: "signes and wonders, which wee ar not to lok for now, considering as one of the Fathers said very well, *Quisquis adhuc prodigia ut credat inquirit, magnus est ipse prodigium, qui mundo credente non credit*. He that lookes now for miracles to confirme his faith may be thought a miracle (or monster) him self that beleeves not that the world beleeves."

27. On the debates over annotation for scripture, see Betteridge, "The Bitter Notes"; Slights, *Managing Readers*; and Sherman, *Used Books*, 74.

28. Johnson, *The Most Famous History of the Seven Champions of Christendom*, A4^v.

29. Jardine and Grafton, "'Studied for Action,'" 30; Hutson, "Fortunate Travelers"; Sherman, *John Dee*, 65; and Kintgen, *Reading in Tudor England*. See also Woolf, *Reading History*.

30. Dobranski, *Readers and Authorship*, 23–32.

31. Critics note a multivalent resonance in the name "Guyon." For instance, "Gihon," one of the four rivers of Eden, was traditionally associated with temperance; see Fowler, "Emblems of Temperance." Camden, *Remains Concerning Britain*, 67, records how "Guy" derives from the Latin *guido* and French *guide*; in the *Golden Legend*, "geon" signifies "wrestler," according to Snyder, "Guyon the Wrestler." For more on Spenser's complex appellative associations, see Fowler, "Spenser's Names," esp. 39. The most complete study of the various permutations of the Guy of Warwick legend is Richmond, *The Legend of Guy of Warwick*. Andrew King explicitly connects Guyon to the medieval romance tradition in *"The Faerie Queene" and Middle English Romance*, esp. chapter 7.

32. Guy of Warwick appealed across genres. He starred in newly reprinted chivalric romance (even becoming one of the Nine Worthies in Richard Lloyd's version [1584]), was sung in ballads, appeared on stage, featured in chapbooks, was named in all the major chronicle histories, and was sought after as a genealogical ancestor by various noblemen. For a full account of the *Guy of Warwick* legacy in Renaissance England, see Richmond, *The Legend of Guy of Warwick*, esp. chapter 5. Richard Johnson names the eldest son to Saint George and Sabra as Guy in his *Seven Champions*, an intriguing genealogical link to Spenser's placement of Guyon after the first book; see Johnson, *The Most Famous History of the Seven Champions of Christendom*, Dd3ʳ. More concretely, John Lane, in his unpublished "Corrected Historie of Sir Guy Earle of Warwick" (1621), canto 26, stanza 16, connects Spenser's Guyon and Sir Guy in his marginal notation.

33. This distinction is one that Summit, *Memory's Library*, 106–21, reads as characteristic of much of Bale's efforts in cataloging surviving monastic books.

34. I am indebted for this reading to Erik Gray's introduction to Spenser, *The Faerie Queene, Book Two*, xvi.

35. Ascham, *The Schoolmaster*, 68.

36. Malory, *Caxton's Malory*, 10.48.

37. Ariosto, *Orlando Furioso in English*; the episode occurs in canto 1. While Spenser likely has this episode in mind, he uses it to very different effects. Sacripante doubles up with Angelica, a position that does not hinder his continued plotting to assault her virtue.

38. Johnson, *The Most Famous History of the Seven Champions of Christendom*, title page.

39. Prescott, "Tracing Astrophil's 'Coltish Gyres,'" notes that in moral discourse during the Renaissance, the allegory of the horse drawn from Plato's *Phaedrus* could take on specifically Pauline associations for subduing temptations. For more on the culture of horses generally, see Raber and Tucker, *The Culture of the Horse*.

40. Bateman, *Travyled Pylgryme*.

41. Whitney, *A Choice of Emblemes*, A3ᵛ. I thank Anne Lake Prescott for reminding me of this image.

42. Spitzer, *Classical and Christian Ideas*, 320.

43. Dante, *The Inferno*, 5.133–37.

44. E. Hamilton, *Mythology*, 257.

45. Crosse, *Vertues Common-Vvealth*, N4^r.

46. Vickers, "Leisure and Idleness in the Renaissance," 149.

47. Ascham, *The Schoolmaster*, 68–69.

48. For the uneasy fascination with this figure after the Reformation, see Craig Rustici, *The Afterlife of Pope Joan*.

49. H. Cooper, *Romance in Time*, 106–36.

50. Although, of course, not all readers read alike, the increasing stress placed on individual interpretation by humanist and Protestant models led to a greater attention to contemporary strategies for reading. On how contingent factors such as readers' ability, background, and inclination affect reading habits, see Darnton, "First Steps." Other critics have attempted to present a more unified overview of reading processes drawn from individual case studies, such as Kintgen, *Reading in Tudor England*; and Woolf, *Reading History*. The materiality and physiology of individual and cultural reading practice continues to be reexamined in early modern scholarship, as evidenced by the fall 2010 special edition of the *Huntington Library Quarterly*. See Richards and Schurink, "The Textuality and Materiality of Reading."

51. Summit, *Memory's Library*, 117–19.

52. Tilmouth, *Passion's Triumph over Reason*, esp. 15–74, demonstrates how this *psychomachia* is instantiated in Spenser's *Faerie Queene*. Spenser's use reflects the prevailing philosophical model that gradually fractured in the early 1600s with the growing recognition that reason was weak and that a better kind of passion, or affections, might be an integral component to moral regeneration.

53. In contrast to Dolven, *Scenes of Instruction*, 147–71, who sees Guyon personifying a steady development of skill at reading.

54. The palmer, as a character, has troubled many critics, including James Nohrnberg, *The Analogy of "The Faerie Queene,"* 290, who recognizes him as a teacher. Hoopes, *Right Reason in the English Renaissance*, esp. 150, 154, and Sirluck, "*The Faerie Queene*, Book II," proceed on the assumption that the Palmer is an allegory of the faculty of reason within Guyon. Cefalu, *Moral Identity*, 56–64, reads him as a "mis-educator"; and Dolven, *Scenes of Instruction*, 156–58, dubs him a troubling pilgrim-tutor often taken as a figure of Reason.

55. *Oxford English Dictionary*, s.v. "palmer."

56. Daus, *Bullinger's Hundred Sermons*, 61.

57. Kaske, *Spenser and Biblical Poetics*, and Silberman, "*The Faerie Queene*, Book II" discuss the Palmer's role in helping—or not helping—Guyon and the reader understand the allegorical moments they encounter.

58. Munday, *The Third and Last Part of Palmerin of England*, A4^r.

59. Spenser, *The Faerie Queene*, 715.

60. Prescott, "Spenser's Chivalric Restoration," illuminates the parallel to Redcrosse Knight as well as Guyon and the Palmer.

61. Bateman, *Travyled Pylgryme*, G2^r.

62. Ibid., C3^v–E2^r.

63. John Milton, *Complete Poems and Major Prose*, 729.

64. Spenser, *The Faerie Queene*, 716.

65. The phrase here, as translated by Pinsky, blames one particular moment in the reading that "defeated" the lovers, leading to the fatal kiss. Dante, *The Inferno*, 5.119.

66. Parker, *Inescapable Romance*, 64–65, discusses how the "wandring wood" operates as an "archetypal locus of romance, the *selva obscura*" that invites allusion to other romances. I read the Bower of Bliss to be a similar romance locus for book 2.

67. Summit, *Memory's Library*, 134–35.

68. The phrase is Maurice Evans's, cited in A. Hamilton, *The Faerie Queene*, 297n.

69. As at least one commentator has noted, the bower must be destroyed for its temptation to knights such as Mordant and Guyon; see Strauss, "Allegory and the Bower of Bliss." For iconoclastic readings, see Greenblatt, *Renaissance Self-Fashioning*, 189; Sinfield, *Literature of Protestant England*, 37; and H. Berger, *The Allegorical Temper*, 218. For an extended treatment of Spenser's iconoclastic impulse, see Gilman, *Iconoclasm and Poetry*.

70. The optimism of the proem's latter stanzas is discussed in Platt, *Reason Diminished*, 69–72, which argues that "Spenser makes a surprisingly confident leap . . . and does so by invoking the power of the marvelous. . . . [H]e asserts that wonder has the potential to stretch the frontiers of human imagination and intellectual possibility." (69).

CHAPTER 4:   "Soundly Washed" or Interpretively Redeemed?

1. All parenthetical references to Wroth, *The First Part of the Countess of Montgomery's Urania*, cite the Medieval and Renaissance Texts and Studies (1995) edition, vol. 1, ed. Roberts (Binghamton, NY); all parenthetical references to Wroth, *The Second Part of the Countess of Montgomery's Urania* cite the Renaissance English Text Society/Arizona Center for Medieval and Renaissance Studies (1999) edition, ed. Roberts, Gossett, and Mueller.

2. Lady Mary Wroth's gender cannot be ignored in relationship to the romance tradition. Hutson, *The Usurer's Daughter*, argues that romance narratives were less hospitable to female writers than previously supposed because much early modern romance aimed at a redefinition of masculinity. Although she regrettably does not discuss Wroth's *Urania*, other critics have made much of Wroth's intervention within such a male-dominated genre: Quilligan, *Incest and Agency*, 165–212, at 212, argues that Wroth reformulates "transgressive active female desire" and thus halts the traffic in women common within romance fictions. A seminal discussion of Wroth's self-conscious entry into the all-male literary canon is Carrell, "A Pack of Lies"; other notable accounts include Larouche, "Pamphilia across a Crowded Room"; Paul Salzman, "The Strang(e) Constructions"; S. Miller, "Constructing the Female Self"; and Kusonoki, "Female Selfhood and Male Violence."

3. Scholars have read Wroth's work predominately from a gendered perspective. The influential collection edited by Gary F. Waller and Naomi J. Miller illustrates this trend: Miller and Waller, *Reading Mary Wroth*. Other notable essays that exemplify this approach include Andrea, "Pamphilia's Cabinet"; Shaver, "A New Woman of Romance"; and Hackett, "'Yet Tell Me Some Such Fiction.'" More recently, scholars have sought to move away from a narrow definition of gender and feminine texts to gauge Wroth's contributions to a wider range of topics. See Lockey, *Law and Empire*, 187–95. While I acknowledge the centrality of Wroth's gender to a discussion of romance, I reject an implicit binary that sees her inter-

vention primarily within a gendered realm. Instead, I posit that her figuring of women readers serves as proxy for all romance readers, male or female.

4. Spenser, *The Faerie Queene*, 714.

5. While fountains and other water sources were particular favorites of romance, their densely symbolic nature can be seen in a variety of early modern stories. For their changing implications post-Reformation, see Lees-Jeffries, "From the Fountain to the Well"; expanded in Lees-Jeffries, *England's Helicon*.

6. H. Cooper, *Romance in Time*, 148.

7. Jennifer Lee Carrell has argued that "the closest thing to a Renaissance woman's treatise about women reading romances is Wroth's *Urania*." See Carrell, "A Pack of Lies," 80. Zurcher, "Ethics and the Politic Agent," esp. 83–96, sees the *Urania* as a coterie fiction that fosters a three-way identity among author, reader, and character. See also Hackett, "'Yet Tell Me Some Such Fiction'"; and Lamb, "Women Readers in Mary Wroth's *Urania*."

8. Salzman, *English Prose Fiction*, 142.

9. The connotations of "seduction," according to the *Oxford English Dictionary*, include leading a person "to err in conduct or belief"; creating a desire where there originally was none; an allurement "that leads to error." To "seduce" can imply "to draw away from the right or intended course of action to or into a wrong one; to tempt, entice, or beguile to do something wrong, foolish, or unintended." "Seduction" is most often a gender-specific term, as it is the "action of inducing a woman to surrender her chastity."

10. Burton, *The Anatomy of Melancholy*, 3.109.

11. Ibid.

12. Salter, *Mirrhor of Modestie*. B3^{r}.

13. Ibid.

14. H. Smith, "'More Swete Unto the Eare,'" 14. For the ways that early modern physiologists understood reading, see Craik, *Reading Sensations*; Schoenfeldt, "Reading Bodies"; and Johns, *The Nature of the Book*, esp. chapter 6.

15. Saltonstall, *Picturae Loquentes*, E6^{v}. For a larger discussion about class hierarchy and romance reading habits, see Newcomb, *Reading Popular Romance*, esp. 1–20.

16. Antissia has excited much comment. Mary Ellen Lamb's argument that the text makes her a "kind of lightning rod" to preempt and absorb criticisms of a female author—even as she reflects Wroth's own anxieties—remains a critical touchstone. Lamb, *Gender and Authorship*, esp. 162, 168. Other influential accounts include Kinney, "'Beleeve This Butt a Fiction,'" esp. 242–45, which reads her as a foil to Pamphilia who shows the dangers, not the consolations, of female art; N. Miller, *Changing the Subject*, 174–78, argues that Antissia represents a woman as written by masculine desire.

17. R. Baxter, *A Christian Directory*, 480. Baxter warns especially against reading romances: "But take heed of the poison of the Writings of false Teachers, which would corrupt your understandings: and of vain Romances . . . and false stories, which may bewitch your fantasies, and corrupt your hearts" (60). Baxter, although writing later than Wroth, shows a continuous discourse *ad feminam*. His sentiments echo those expressed earlier, as in Stellato, *The Zodiake of Life*, 22, which states, "So women . . . doe covet most always: Because they lacke both strength and force in minde & have no stayes."

18. Overbury, *Sir Thomas Ouerburie his wife with new elegies*, G8^{r}.

19. J. Fletcher, *The Wild Goose Chase*, act 1, scene 1, B2^r.

20. Ibid., act 4, scene 3, M2^v.

21. R. Baxter, *A Christian Directory*, 480.

22. T. Cooper, *The Mysterie of the Holy Government*, Bv, B2^r.

23. Sidney, *The Defence of Poesy*, E2^{r-v}.

24. T. Wright, *The Passions of the Minde in Generall*.

25. Ibid., 174.

26. J. Miller, "The Passion Signified," esp. 12, discusses how many rhetorical treatises argued that passion was imprinted in a manner similar to what Wright here describes. See also Vickers, "'The Power of Persuasion,'" esp. 136. Vickers argues that between 1540 and 1640 there was an increasing "stress on persuasion via the passions."

27. Calahorra, *Mirrour of Princely Deedes and Knighthood*, A3^{r-v}. On Margaret Tyler's translation, see Krontiris, "Breaking the Barriers"; and Krontiris, *Oppositional Voices*.

28. The diminishment I trace in Antissia's water cure appears to mimic the larger structural deflation of wonder more generally. See Lamb, "Topicality and the Interrogation of Wonder."

29. See n. 5 on the symbolism of fountains after the Reformation.

30. The pervasive, ongoing influence of this medieval hero's legend throughout the Renaissance is traced in A. King, "*Sir Bevis of Hampton*."

31. Urania's extraordinary storytelling opportunities that reconceptualize the traditional female voice are explored by Eckerle, "Urania's Example"; and Cavanagh, "Romancing the Epic."

32. N. Miller, *Changing the Subject*, 55, notes that Wroth's protagonist is no absent ideal and begins the text not by mourning for a man (as Claius and Strephon mourn over their lost Urania) but in search of her own female identity.

33. Hooker, *Works* 1:150. See also 1:323.

34. Shuger, *Habits of Thought*, 27.

35. Tilmouth, *Passion's Triumph over Reason*, esp. 1–36.

36. Strier, "Against the Rule of Reason," 32.

37. For more on the question of interpretation and religious education, see Charlton, *Women, Religion, and Education*, esp. 77–125; and Clarke, *The Politics of Early Modern Women's Writing*, esp. chapter 2, 32–38.

38. Snook, *Women, Reading, and the Cultural Politics*, 25–27.

39. Markham, *The English Housewife*, B^v, qtd. in Peters, *Patterns of Piety*, 324.

40. Brathwaite, *Times treasury, or, Academy*, Tt^v.

41. Clarke, *The Politics of Early Modern Women's Writing*. See also Beilin, *Redeeming Eve*, which discusses how women responded to such misogynist attacks, from Jane Anger in 1589 to Esther Sowernam in 1617. Women's changing religious roles following the Reformation is discussed in Peters, *Patterns of Piety*.

42. Fisken, "Mary Sidney's *Psalmes*," 167. Mary Sidney, while writing within an acceptable genre, attempted more than a mere decorous translation of the Psalms: as Margaret Hannay has argued, she presented them as part of a political gesture to urge Queen Elizabeth to become more actively engaged in Protestant politics abroad. See Hannay, "'Doo What Men May Sing.'"

43. On the relationship between the sacred and secular in early modern women's writing that figures in Wroth's poetry, see Bennett, *Women Writing of Divinest Things*.

44. When Edward Denny attacked Wroth for publishing the first volume of *Urania*, he noted that her "ill spent years of so vain a book" would have been better spent "writing as large a volume of heavenly lays and holy love" and advised that she "follow the example of your virtuous and learned aunt," the Countess of Pembroke; as reproduced in Roberts, "The Life of Lady Mary Wroth," 34.

45. Ariosto, *Orlando Furioso in English*, D3^r.

46. Roberts, *The First Part of Urania*, 733n141.42.

47. The tale explores various asymmetrical love relationships. One central narrative tells of the love triangle involving the shepherdess Diana and her two shepherd suitors, Syrenus and Sylvanus. Diana scorns Sylvanus but loves Syrenus; however, when he is called out of the kingdom, she marries another, Delius. When Syrenus returns, he finds himself in the position of Sylvanus—an unrequited lover.

48. Montemayor, *Diana*, 160. Josephine Roberts notes that Wroth likely had Montemayor's romance in mind when she conceived of Melissea. She records how in the Newberry manuscript, her source is inadvertently revealed when she writes "Felicia" instead of "Melissea" and has to cancel it and insert the correct name above. See Roberts's introduction in Wroth, *The First Part of Urania*, xxxvi.

49. Montemayor, *Diana*, 160.

50. *Oxford English Dictionary*, s.v. "cruet."

51. Montemayor, *Diana*, 187.

52. Ibid.

53. Ibid., 220.

54. Edward Denny's poem written to Wroth that objects to her publication of *Urania* accusing it of being full of slander and "lascivious tales" is reproduced in Roberts, "The Life of Lady Mary Wroth," 32–33.

55. For Wroth's identification with Pamphilia, see, for instance, Hackett *Women and Romance Fiction*, 143, which views such identification as "empowering"; others, such as Sanchez, "The Politics of Masochism," view it as negative. Critics who wish to distance Pamphilia from Wroth include Luckyj, "The Politics of Genre," and Clarke, *The Politics of Early Modern Women's Writing*, esp. 216–17. Most concur with Lamb, *Gender and Authorship*, 142, which notes that regardless of the author-character link, "Wroth's romance heroizes women who love."

56. The *Urania*'s portrayal of Pamphilia's constancy remains a critical locus. Notable studies include Beilin, "'The Onely Perfect Vertue'"; Beilin, *Redeeming Eve*, 202–43; Lamb, *Gender and Authorship*, 142–93; Lewalski, *Writing Women in Jacobean England*, 243–307; N. Miller, *Changing the Subject*, 58; and Quilligan, "The Constant Subject."

57. *Oxford English Dictionary*, s.v. "idol."

58. J. King, *Lectures Upon Jonas* (Oxford: Joseph Barnes, 1597), Z2^r. His argument, unsurprisingly, promotes the reading of scripture.

59. Kinney, "'Beleeve This Butt a Fiction.'" For an opposing view, see Lewalski, *Writing Women in Jacobean England*, 296, which argues that Pamphilia ceases to write because the female claim to the status of a poet has already been made and that Pamphilia moves

beyond private expression to a more public role of caring for her nation and providing poems and songs for many voices at different court occasions.

60. Edward Denny, qtd. in Roberts, "The Life of Lady Mary Wroth," 32.

61. Lamb, "Topicality and the Interrogation of Wonder," sees an increased unraveling in part II's presentation of wonder.

62. The suggestion that Wroth purposely withheld her text from printed circulation in order to circulate it as a private text, designed to be read by "a self-selecting readership," is argued by Clarke, *The Politics of Early Modern Women's Writing*, 240. R. Smith, "Lady Mary Wroth's 'Pamphilia to Amphilanthus,'" reads the withdrawal from print as a political move signaling distance from the Jacobean court politics. Salzman, *Reading Early Modern Women's Writing*, 60–89, discusses the complexity surrounding Wroth's constraint in never publishing the continuation of *Urania*.

63. Wroth scholarship frequently focuses on the close relationship between *Urania* and Wroth's life. Josephine Roberts's introduction to part I illustrates how closely many narrative incidents match historical events; see Wroth, *The First Part of Urania*, xxxix–ciii. Carrell, "A Pack of Lies," offers one of the most nuanced accounts when she argues that in *Urania* one finds tales that both reflect and distort reality. See, in addition, Lamb, "The Biopolitics of Romance"; Luckyj, "The Politics of Genre," which summarizes the critical debate to argue Wroth validates autobiography even as "she turns them into art" (54); and Quilligan, "Lady Mary Wroth: Female Authority." A seminal book-length study is Waller, *The Sidney Family Romance*.

64. Rosenfeld, "Wroth's Clause," reads this "dangling" conclusion as indicative of Wroth's stylistic habit, an exercise in epistemology that not only prolongs an ending but that also queries the boundaries of what lies within and without.

65. Hall, "'Something More Exactly Related,'" explores Wroth's own questions and convictions regarding the religio-political debates of Jacobean England. Specifically, she evaluates the tenets of Protestant resistance and monarchomachist intervention that *Urania* appears to privilege. See also Andrea, *Women and Islam*, chapter 2.

66. Clarke makes a point similar to mine when she argues for the political context of women reading romances in her discussion of Barclay's *Argenis* and Wroth's *Urania*. See Clarke, *The Politics of Early Modern Women's Writing*, esp. 241. Clarke's point, however, serves to locate Wroth's writing in a political rather than religious or literary context.

CODA: *Exceptional Romance*

1. I draw here from theories of microhistory that show how exemplary instances can offer richer insight into wider social paradigms, especially Levi, "On Microhistory"; and Ginzburg and Poni, "The Name and the Game."

2. Ariosto, *Orlando Furioso in English*, L^r.

3. Kahn, "Reinventing Romance," 630, argues that many royalist prose romances of the 1650s render a political crisis as a "crisis of genre." While Kahn's argument does not address the religious dimension, it is notable that later Catholic interests would exploit the romance along religiously divided lines. See Amelia Zurcher, *Seventeenth-Century English*

Romance, for further discussion of romance's complex place within political, theological, and moral philosophies.

4. Bunyan's use of the romance mode has prompted critics to raise parallel questions to mine; see, for example, Davies, "The Radical Reformation of Romance."

5. This phrase occurs three times in Spenser, *The Faerie Queene,* 2.2.10, 2.10.46, and 3.3.59.

Bibliography

PRIMARY TEXTS

Andrewes, Lancelot. *Of Episcopasy Three Epistles of Peter Moulin . . . Answered By . . . Lancelot Andrews*. London, 1647.

Ariosto, Ludovico. *Orlando Furioso in English*. Translated by John Harington. London, 1591.

Ascham, Roger. *The Schoolmaster*. Edited by Lawrence V. Ryan. Ithaca, NY: Cornell University Press, 1967.

———. *Toxophilus*. London, 1545.

Bale, John. *The Pageant of Popes*. London, 1574.

Barlow, William. *A Defence of the Articles of the Protestants Religion*. London, 1601.

Bateman, Stephen. *Travyled Pylgryme*. London, 1569.

Baxter, Nathaniel, trans. *The Lectures or Daily Sermons, of That Reverend Diuine, D. Iohn Caluine*. London, 1578.

Baxter, Richard. *A Christian Directory, or, a Summe of Practical Theology*. London, 1673.

Benson, George. *A Sermon Preached at Paules Crosse*. London, 1609.

Blois, Peter of. *De confessione sacramentali*. In *Patrologiae cursus completus*, vol. 207, *Series Latinus*, edited by J. P. Migne. Paris, 1844–1906.

Brathwaite, Richard. *Times treasury, or, Academy for gentry laying downe excellent grounds*. London: printed for Nath. Brooke, 1652.

Burton, Robert. *The Anatomy of Melancholy*. Edited by William H. Gass. New York: New York Review of Books, 2001.

Butler, Alban. *The Lives of the Saints*. 12 vols. London: Burns, Oates and Washbourne, 1931–42.

Calahorra, Ortuñez de. *Mirrour of Princely Deedes and Knighthood*. Translated by Margaret Tyler. London, 1578.

Camden, William. *Remains Concerning Britain*. Edited by R. D. Dunn. Toronto: University of Toronto Press, 1984.

Caxton, William, trans. *The Golden Legend or Lives of the Saints*. compiled by Jacobus de Voragine. Genoa, 1275. Fordham University Center for Medieval Studies, Internet Medieval Sourcebook, www.fordham.edu/halsall/basis/goldenlegend/, based on Temple Classics edition (1900, reprint 1923, 1931), edited by F. S. Ellis.

Cervantes, Miguel de. *The History of the Valorous Knight-Errant, Don-Quixote of the Mancha*. Translated by Thomas Shelton. London, 1612.

Chambers, Robert. *Palestina*. London, 1600.

Church of England. *Thirty-Nine Articles*. London, 1564.

Cooper, Thomas. *The Mysterie of the Holy Government of Our Affections*. London: printed by Bernard Alsop, 1620.

Crosse, Henry. *Vertues Common-Vvealth: Or the High-Way to Honour*. London: printed by Thomas Creede for Iohn Newbery, 1603.

Dante. *The Inferno of Dante*. Translated by Robert Pinsky. New York: Noonday, 1994.

Daus, John. *Bullinger's Hundred Sermons Upon the Apocalips*. London, 1573.

Dekker, Thomas. *The Whore of Babylon*. Vol. 2 of *The Dramatic Works of Thomas Dekker*. Edited by Fredson Bowers. Cambridge: Cambridge University Press, 1955.

Dent, Arthur. *Plaine Mans Path-way to Heaven*. London, 1605.

Dering, Edward. *A Briefe and Necessarie Catachisme or Instrucion, Verie Needefull to Bee Knowne of All Housholders*. London, 1575.

———. *A Sparing Restraint of Many Lavishe Untruthes, Which M. Doctor Harding Dothe Challenge*. London, 1568.

Elyot, Thomas. *The Boke Named the Governour*. London, 1531.

Fletcher, Giles. *Of the Russe Common Wealth*. London, 1591.

Fletcher, John. *The Wild Goose Chase*. London: printed for Humpherey Moseley, 1652.

Ford, Emanuel. *Parismenos: The Second Part of the Most Famous, Delectable and Pleasant Historie of Parismus and the Adventurous Travels and Noble Chivalrie of Parismenos*. London, 1599.

———. *Parismus the Renowned Prince of Bohemia*. London, 1598.

Foxe, John. *Acts and Monuments.... The Variorum Edition*. Online version 1.1. Sheffield, UK: Humanities Research Institute, 2006. www.hrionline.ac.uk/johnfoxe/.

The Geneva Bible, a Facsimile of the 1560 Edition. Edited by Lloyd Eason and William Whittingham Berry. Madison: University of Wisconsin Press, 1969.

Gifford, William, ed. *The Works of Ben Jonson*. Boston: Phillips, Sampson, 1857.

Gratarolo, Guglielmo. *The Castel of Memorie: Wherein Is Conteyned the Restoring, Augmenting, and Conseruing of the Memorye and Remembraunce, Englished by Willyam Fulvvod*. Translated by William Fulwood. Londo[n]: printed by Rouland Hall, 1562.

Greville, Fulke. *The Life of the Renowned Sr Philip Sidney*. London, 1651.

Hakewill, George. *Apologie of the Power and Providence of God*. London, 1627.

Harington, John. *A Tract on the Succession to the Crown*. Edited by Clements R. Markham. London: J. B. Nichols and Sons, 1880.

Harvey, John. *A Discursive Probleme Concerninge Prophesies*. London, 1588.

Heisterbach, Caesarius of. *Dialogus Miraculorum*. Vol. 1. Edited by Joseph Strange. London: George Routledge and Sons, 1921.

Heliodorus. *An Aethiopian Historie, Written in Greeke by Heliodorus, No Lesse Wittie Then Pleasant: Englished by Thomas Vnderdowne*. London, 1577.

Holinshed, Raphael. *Chronicles of England, Scotland, and Ireland*. 3 vols. London, 1587.

Hooker, Richard. *The Works of That Learned and Judicious Divine, Mr. Richard Hooker: With an Account of His Life and Death*. Vol. 3. Edited by Rev. John Keble. Oxford: Oxford University Press, 1836.

The hystory of the two valyaunte brethren Valentyne and Orson sonnes unto the Emperor of Grece. London: William Copland, 1555.

Johnson, Richard. *The Most Famous History of the Seven Champions of Christendom.* London: Cuthbert Burbie, 1596.

———. *The Seven Champions of Christendom.* Edited by Jennifer Fellows. Burlington, VT: Ashgate, 2003.

Jonson, Ben. *The Works of Ben Jonson.* London, 1692.

———. *The Works of Ben Jonson.* Edited by William Gifford. Boston: Phillips, Sampson, 1857.

King, John. *Lectures Upon Jonas.* Oxford: Joseph Barnes, 1597.

Lane, John. "Corrected Historie of Guy Earle of Warwick." 1621. In British Library, Harley Manuscripts, MS 5243.

Malory, Thomas. *Caxton's Malory.* Edited by James W. Spisak et al. Berkeley: University of California Press, 1983.

———. *The story of the moste noble and worthy kynge Arthur, the whiche was the fyrst of the worthyes chrysten, and also of his noble and valyaunt knyghtes of the rounde table.* London, 1557.

Markham, Gervase. *The English Housewife.* London, 1625.

Mason, James. *The Anatomie of Sorcerie Wherein the Wicked Impietie of Charmers Inchanters, and Such Like, Is Discovered and Confuted.* London, 1612.

Meres, Francis. *Palladis Tamia.* London: printed by P. Short, for Cuthbert Burbie, 1598.

The Middle English "Mirror": An Edition Based on Bodleian Library, MS Holkham Misc. 40. Edited by Kathleen Marie Blumreich. Tempe: Arizona Center for Medieval and Renaissance Studies, 2002.

Milton, John. *Complete Poems and Major Prose.* Edited by Merritt Y. Hughes. Upper Saddle River, NJ: Prentice Hall, 1957.

Mirour for Magistrates. London: Thomas Marshe, 1575.

Moffet, Thomas. *Nobilis, or, A view of the life and death of a Sidney.* San Marino, CA: Huntington Library, 1940.

Montemayor, Jorge de. *Diana.* In *A Critical Edition of Yong's Translation of George of Montemayor's "Diana" and Gil Polo's "Enamoured Diana,"* edited by Judith M. Kennedy, 1–242. Oxford: Clarendon, 1968.

More, Thomas. *The Co[n]futacyon of Tyndales Answere Made by Syr Thomas More Knyght.* London, 1532.

Munday, Anthony, trans. *The Third and Last Part of Palmerin of England.* London, 1602.

Nashe, Thomas. *The Anatomie of Absurditie.* London: Charlewood for Thomas Hacket, 1589.

———. *Pierce Penilesse His Supplication to the Divell.* London, 1592.

Overbury, Thomas. *Sir Thomas Ouerburie his wife with new elegies vpon his (now knowne) vntimely death: whereunto are annexed, new newes and characters.* London : printed by Edward Griffin for Laurence L'isle, 1616.

Perkins, William. *A Discourse of the Damned Art of Witchcraft.* London, 1610.

Piramus, Denis. *La Vie Seint Edmund Le Rei: An Anglo-Norman Poem of the Twelfth Century.* Edited by Florence Leftwich Ravenel. Philadelphia: John C. Winston, 1906.

Pollard, Alfred W., ed. *Records of the English Bible: The Documents Relating to the Translation and Publication of the Bible in English, 1525–1611.* London: Oxford University Press, 1911.

Prideaux, Mathias. *An Easy and Compendious Introduction for Reading All Sorts of Histories.* London, 1648.

Puttenham, George. *The Arte of English Poesie.* Edited by Gladys Doidge Willcock and Alice Walker. Cambridge: Cambridge University Press, 1970.

A Record of Ancient Histories, Entitled in Latine: Gesta Romanorum. London: printed by Richard Bishop, 1640.

A Reply with the Occasion Thereof, to a Late Rayling, Lying Reprochful and Blasphemous Libel, of the Papists. London, 1579.

Rievaulx, Ailred of. *The Mirror of Charity: The Speculum Caritatis of St. Aelred of Rievaulx.* Translated and arranged by Geoffrey Webb and Adrian Walker. London: A. R. Mowbray, 1962.

Rievaulx, Ailred of. *Speculum Caritatis.* In *Patrologiae cursus completus,* edited by J. P. Migne, *Series Latinus,* 195:565. Paris, 1857–1912.

Salter, Thomas. *A Mirrhor Mete for All Mothers, Matrones, and Maidens, Intituled the Mirrhor of Modestie.* London, 1574.

Saltonstall, Wye. *Picturae Loquentes, Or Pictuers Drawne Forth in Characters.* London, 1631.

Sannazaro, Jacopo. *Arcadia, & Piscatorial Eclogues.* Translated by Ralph Nash. Detroit: Wayne State University Press, 1966.

Scot, Reginald. *The Discoverie of Witchcraft.* London, 1584.

Shakespeare, William. *King Henry V.* Arden Shakespeare. Edited by T. W. Craik. London: Arden, 1995.

———. *Othello, the Moor of Venice.* In *The Norton Shakespeare,* edited by Stephen Greenblatt et al., 2100–74. New York: W. W. Norton, 1997.

———. *Pericles.* Edited by Suzanne Gossett. Arden Shakespeare, 3rd ser. London: Arden, 2004.

———. *Shakespeare's Sonnets.* Edited by Stephen Booth. New Haven, CT: Yale University Press, 1977.

———. *The Tragedy of Hamlet, Prince of Denmark.* In *The Norton Shakespeare,* edited by Stephen Greenblatt et al., 1668–1759. New York: W. W. Norton, 2008.

———. *The Winter's Tale.* Edited by J. H. P. Pafford. Arden Shakespeare. London: Routledge, 1963. Reprint, 1994.

Sidney, Philip. *The Countesse of Pembrokes Arcadia.* London, 1590.

———. *The Defence of Poesy.* London, 1595.

———. *The Old Arcadia.* Edited by Katherine Duncan-Jones. Oxford: Oxford University Press, 1985.

South English Legendary. In *The Idea of the Vernacular: An Anthology of Middle English Theory, 1280–1520,* edited by Jocelyn Wogan-Browne et al., 195–99. University Park: Pennsylvania State University Press, 1999.

Spenser, Edmund. *The Faerie Queene.* Edited by A. C. Hamilton, Hiroshi Yamashita, and Toshiyuki Suzuki. London: Longman, 2001.

———. *The Yale Edition of the Shorter Poems of Edmund Spenser.* Edited by William A. Oram et al. New Haven, CT: Yale University Press, 1989.

Stellato, Palingenio. *The Zodiake of Life.* Translated by Barnabie Googe. London, 1576.

Stow, John. *The Chronicles of England, from Brute Unto This Present Yeare.* London: imprinted by Henry Bynneman for Ralphe Newberie, 1580.

Strype, John. *Annals of the Reformation and Establishment of Religion*. Vol. 1.1. Oxford: Clarendon, 1824.

Torshell, Samuel. *The Woman's Glorie*. London, 1645.

The treasurie of Amadis of Fraunce: conteyning eloquente orations, pythie epistles, learned letters, and feruent complayntes, seruing for sundrie purposes. Translated by Thomas Paynell. London: Printed by Henry Bynneman for Thomas Hacket, 1572.

Turner, William. *The Hunting of the Fox and the Wolfe*. London, 1565.

Twine, Laurence. *The Pattern of Painful Adventures*. In *Narrative and Dramatic Sources of Shakespeare*, vol. 6, *Other "Classical" Plays*, edited by Geoffrey Bullough. New York: Columbia University Press, 1966.

Tyndale, William. *An Answere Vnto Sir Thomas Mores Dialoge Made by Willyam Tindale*. London, 1531.

——. *The Pentateuch*. Edited by F. F. Bruce. Carbondale: Southern Illinois University Press, 1967.

Vaughan, William. *Golden Fleece*. London, 1626.

Vicars, John. *Babylons Beautie: Or the Romish-Catholcks Sweet-Heart*. London, 1644.

Vives, Juan Luis. *A Very Fruteful and Plesant Booke Called the Instruction of a Christen Woman*. Translated by Richard Hyrde. London, 1529.

Wager, Lewis. *The Life and Repentaunce of Marie Magdalene*. London, 1566.

Whitgift, John. *Defence of the Answer to the Admonition Against the Reply of Thomas Cartwright*. In vol. 3 of *The Works of John Whitgift*. Edited by John Ayre. Cambridge: Cambridge University Press, 1851.

Whitney, Geffrey. *A Choice of Emblemes*. London, 1586.

Wright, Thomas. *The Passions of the Minde in Generall*. London: printed by Valentine Simmes and Adam Islip for Walter Burre and Thomas Thorpe, 1604.

Wroth, Lady Mary. *The First Part of the Countess of Montgomery's Urania*. Edited by Josephine A. Roberts. Binghamton, NY: Medieval and Renaissance Texts and Studies, 1995.

——. *The Poems of Lady Mary Wroth*. Edited by Josephine A. Roberts. Baton Rouge: Louisiana State University Press, 1983.

——. *The Second Part of the Countess of Montgomery's Urania*. Edited by Josephine A. Roberts, Suzanne Gossett, and Janel Mueller. Tempe, AZ: Renaissance English Text Society / Arizona Center for Medieval and Renaissance Studies, 1999.

SECONDARY TEXTS

Adams, Robert P. "Bold Bawdry and Open Manslaughter: The English New Humanist Attack on Medieval Romance." *Huntington Library Quarterly* 23, no. 1 (1959): 33–48.

Alexander, Gavin. *Writing after Sidney: The Literary Response to Sir Philip Sidney, 1588–1640*. Oxford: Oxford University Press, 2006.

Andersen, Jennifer Lotte, and Elizabeth Sauer, eds. *Books and Readers in Early Modern England: Material Studies*. Philadelphia: University of Pennsylvania Press, 2002.

Anderson, Judith H. "'Myn Auctour': Spenser's Enabling Fiction and Eumnestes' 'Immortall Scrine.'" In *Unfolded Tales: Essays on Renaissance Romance*, edited by George M. Logan and Gordon Teskey, 16–31. Ithaca, NY: Cornell University Press, 1989.

Andrea, Bernadette. "Pamphilia's Cabinet: Gendered Authorship and Empire in Lady Mary Wroth's *Urania*." *English Literary History* 68, no. 2 (2001): 335–58.

———. *Women and Islam in Early Modern English Literature*. Cambridge: Cambridge University Press, 2007.

Aston, Margaret. *England's Iconoclasts*. Oxford: Clarendon; New York: Oxford University Press, 1988.

———. *Faith and Fire: Popular and Unpopular Religion, 1350–1600*. London: Hambledon, 1993.

Badir, Patricia. *The Maudlin Impression: English Literary Images of Mary Magdalene, 1550–1700*. Notre Dame, IN: University of Notre Dame Press, 2009.

Barber, C. L. "'Thou That Beget'st Him That Did Thee Beget': Transformation in *Pericles* and *The Winter's Tale*." *Shakespeare Studies* 22 (1969): 59–67.

Barber, Giles. *Textile and Embroidered Bindings*. Oxford: Oxford University Press, 1971.

Baring, Anne, and Jules Cashford. *The Myth of the Goddess: Evolution of an Image*. London: Viking, 1991.

Beauregard, David N. *Catholic Theology in Shakespeare's Plays*. Newark: University of Delaware Press, 2008.

Beckwith, Sarah. "Shakespeare's Resurrections." In *Shakespeare and the Middle Ages*, edited by Curtis Perry and John Watkins, 45–67. Oxford: Oxford University Press, 2009.

Beilin, Elaine V. "'The Onely Perfect Vertue': Constancy in Mary Wroth's *Pamphilia to Amphilanthus*." *Spenser Studies* 2 (1981): 229–45.

———. *Redeeming Eve: Women Writers of the English Renaissance*. Princeton, NJ: Princeton University Press, 1987.

Bennett, Lyn. *Women Writing of Divinest Things: Rhetoric and the Poetry of Pembroke, Wroth and Lanyer*. Pittsburgh: Duquesne University Press, 2004.

Benson, Sean. *Shakespearean Resurrection: The Art of Almost Raising the Dead*. Pittsburgh: Dusquesne University Press, 2009.

Berger, Harry. *The Allegorical Temper: Vision and Reality in Book II of Spenser's "Faerie Queene"*. New Haven, CT: Yale University Press, 1957.

Berger, Pamela. *The Goddess Obscured: Transformation of the Grain Protectress from Goddess to Saint*. London: Robert Hale, 1988.

Betteridge, Maurice S. "The Bitter Notes: The Geneva Bible and Its Annotations." *Sixteenth Century Journal* 14 (1983): 41–62.

Bhabha, Homi K. *The Location of Culture*. New York: Routledge, 2004. Reprint, 2010.

Bicks, Caroline. "Backsliding at Ephesus: Shakespeare's Diana and the Churching of Women." In *Pericles: Critical Essays*, edited by David Skeele, 205–27. New York: Garland, 2000.

Biester, James. *Lyric Wonder: Rhetoric and Wit in Renaissance English Poetry*. Rhetoric and Society Series. Ithaca, NY: Cornell University Press, 1997.

Bishop, T. G. *Shakespeare and the Theatre of Wonder*. Edited by Stephen Orgel. Cambridge Studies in Renaissance Literature and Culture. Cambridge: Cambridge University Press, 1996.

Bond, Christopher. "Medieval Harrowings of Hell and Spenser's House of Mammon." *English Literary Renaissance* 37, no. 2 (2007): 175–92.

Boro, Joyce. "All for Love: Lord Berners and the Enduring, Evolving Romance." In *The Oxford Handbook to Tudor Literature, 1485-1603*, edited by Mike Pincombe and Cathy Shrank, 87-10. Oxford University Press, 2009.

Borris, Kenneth. *Allegory and Epic in English Renaissance Literature: Heroic Form in Sidney, Spenser, and Milton*. Cambridge: Cambridge University Press, 2000.

Brumbaugh, Barbara. "Cecropia and the Church of Antichrist in Sir Philip Sidney's *New Arcadia*." *SEL: Studies in English Literature, 1500-1900* 38, no. 1 (1998): 19-43.

———. "Edgar's Wolves as 'Romish' Wolves: John Bale, before Sidney and Spenser." *Spenser Studies* 21 (2006): 223-30.

Burrow, Colin. *Epic Romance: Homer to Milton*. Oxford: Clarendon, 1993.

Butler, Martin. "Ben Jonson and Other Catholic Dramatists." Unpublished paper delivered at Representing Politics on the Shakespearean Stage, Huntington Library seminar, September 2009.

Bynum, Caroline Walker. "The Female Body and Religious Practice in the Later Middle Ages." In *Fragments for a History of the Body*, edited by Michel Feher et al., 160-219. New York: Zone Books, 1989.

———. *Metamorphosis and Identity*. Cambridge, MA: Zone Books, 2001.

———. "Wonder." *American Historical Review* 102, no. 1 (1997): 1-26.

Campbell, Lily. "The Christian Muse." *Huntington Library Bulletin* 8 (1935): 29-70.

Carr, Nicholas. *The Shallows: What the Internet Is Doing to Our Brains*. New York: W. W. Norton, 2010.

Carrell, Jennifer Lee. "A Pack of Lies in a Looking Glass: Lady Mary Wroth's *Urania* and the Magic Mirror of Romance." *SEL: Studies in English Literature, 1500-1900* 34, no. 1 (1994): 79-107.

Carruthers, Mary. *The Book of Memory: A Study of Memory in Medieval Culture*. Cambridge: Cambridge University Press, 1990.

Carruthers, Mary, and Jan Ziolkowski, eds. *The Medieval Craft of Memory*. Philadelphia: University of Pennsylvania Press, 2002.

Cavanagh, Sheila T. "Romancing the Epic: Lady Mary Wroth's *Urania* and Literary Traditions." In *Approaches to the Anglo and American Female Epic*, edited by Bernard Schweizer, 19-36. Burlington, VT: Ashgate, 2006.

Cefalu, Paul. *Moral Identity in Early Modern English Literature*. Cambridge: Cambridge University Press, 2004.

Charlton, Kenneth. *Women, Religion, and Education in Early Modern England*. New York: Routledge, 1999.

Cheney, Donald. "Spenser's Undergoing of Ariosto." In *Renaissance Historicisms: Essays in Honor of Arthur F. Kinney*, edited by James M. Dutcher and Anne Lake Prescott, 120-36. Newark: University of Delaware Press, 2008.

Cheney, Patrick. *Spenser's Famous Flight: A Renaissance Idea of a Literary Career*. Toronto: University of Toronto Press, 1993.

Clark, Stuart. *Thinking with Demons: The Idea of Witchcraft in Early Modern Europe*. Oxford: Clarendon, 1997.

Clarke, Danielle. *The Politics of Early Modern Women's Writing*. Longman Medieval and Renaissance Library. New York: Longman, 2001.

Cobb, Christopher J. *The Staging of Romance in Late Shakespeare: Text and Theatrical Technique.* Newark: University of Delaware Press, 2007.

Cockcroft, Robert. *Rhetorical Affect in Early Modern Writing: Renaissance Passions Reconsidered.* New York: Palgrave Macmillan, 2003.

Cohen, Jeffrey Jerome. *Hybridity, Identity, and Monstrosity in Medieval Britain: On Difficult Middles.* The New Middle Ages. New York: Palgrave, 2006.

Cohen, Stephen, ed. *Shakespeare and Historical Formalism.* Burlington, VT: Ashgate, 2007.

Cohen, Walter. Introduction to *Pericles, Prince of Tyre,* by William Shakespeare. In *The Norton Shakespeare,* edited by Stephen Greenblatt et al., 2709–18. New York: W. W. Norton, 1997.

Cohen, Walter. Introduction to *Pericles, Prince of Tyre,* by William Shakespeare. In *The Norton Shakespeare,* edited by Stephen Greenblatt et al., 2723–30. New York: W. W. Norton, 2008.

Colie, Rosalie L. *The Resources of Kind: Genre-Theory in the Renaissance.* Berkeley: University of California Press, 1973.

Collinson, Patrick. *The Birthpangs of Protestant England: Religious and Cultural Change in the Sixteenth and Seventeenth Centuries.* Houndmills, UK: Macmillan, 1988.

———. "From Iconoclasm to Iconophobia: The Cultural Impact of the Second English Reformation." In *The Impact of the English Reformation, 1500–1640,* edited by Peter Marshall, 279–307. New York: St. Martin's, 1997.

———. *Godly People: Essays on English Protestantism and Puritanism.* London: Hambledon, 1983.

Cooper, Helen. "Magic That Does Not Work." *Studies in Medieval and Renaissance Culture* 7 (1976): 131–46.

———. "Romance after 1400." In *The Cambridge History of Medieval English Literature,* edited by David Wallace, 690–719. Cambridge: Cambridge University Press, 1999.

———. *Romance in Time: Transforming Motifs from Geoffrey of Monmouth to the Death of Shakespeare.* New York: Oxford University Press, 2004.

———. "'This Worthy Olde Writer': Pericles and Other Gowers, 1592–1640." In *A Companion to Gower,* edited by Siân Echard, 99–113. Cambridge: D. S. Brewer, 2004.

Craik, Katharine. *Reading Sensations in Early Modern England.* Basingstoke, UK: Palgrave Macmillan, 2007.

Crane, Ronald S. *The Vogue of Medieval Chivalric Romance during the English Renaissance.* Menasha, WI: George Banta, 1919.

Crane, Susan. *Insular Romance: Politics, Faith, and Culture in Anglo-Norman and Middle English Literature.* Berkeley: University of California Press, 1986.

Crawford, Julie. *Marvelous Protestantism: Monstrous Births in Post-Reformation England.* Baltimore: Johns Hopkins University Press, 2005.

Cummings, Brian. "Iconoclasm and Bibliophobia in the English Reformations, 1521–1558." In *Images, Idolatry and Iconoclasm in Late Medieval England,* edited by James Simpson Jeremy Dimmock, and Nicolette Zeeman, 185–200. Oxford: Oxford University Press, 2002.

———. *The Literary Culture of the Reformation: Grammar and Grace.* Oxford: Oxford University Press, 2002.

Darnton, Robert. "First Steps toward a History of Reading." *Australian Journal of French Studies* 23, no. 1 (1986): 5–30.

Daston, Lorraine, and Katharine Park. *Wonders and the Order of Nature, 1150–1750*. New York: Zone Books, 1998.

Davenport, Cyril. *English Embroidered Bookbindings*. London: Kegan Paul, Trench, Trubner, 1899.

Davies, Michael. "'Stout & Valiant Champions for God': The Radical Reformation of Romance in *The Pilgrim's Progress*." In *John Bunyan: Reading Dissenting Writing*, edited by N. H. Keeble, 103–32. Bern, Switzerland: Peter Lang, 2002.

Davis, Alex. *Chivalry and Romance in the English Renaissance*. Cambridge: D. S. Brewer, 2003.

Davis, Walter R. *Sidney's Arcadia. A Map of Arcadia: Sidney's Romance in Its Tradition*. New Haven, CT: Yale University Press, 1965.

Dean, Christopher. *Arthur of England: English Attitudes to King Arthur and the Knights of the Round Table in the Middle Ages and the Renaissance*. Toronto: University of Toronto Press, 1987.

Dean, Paul. "Pericles' Pilgrimage." *Essays in Criticism* 50, no. 2 (2000): 125–144.

Diehl, Huston. *Staging Reform, Reforming the Stage: Protestantism and Popular Theater in Early Modern England*. Ithaca, NY: Cornell University Press, 1997.

Dobranski, Stephen B. *Readers and Authorship in Early Modern England*. Cambridge: Cambridge University Press, 2005.

Dolan, Frances E. *Whores of Babylon: Catholicism, Gender, and Seventeenth-Century Print Culture*. Ithaca, NY: Cornell University Press, 1999.

Dolven, Jeffrey. *Scenes of Instruction in Renaissance Romance*. Chicago: University of Chicago Press, 2007.

Doody, Margaret Anne. *The True Story of the Novel*. New Brunswick, NJ: Rutgers University Press, 1996.

Douglas, Mary. *Purity and Danger: An Analysis of Pollution and Taboo*. New York: Praeger, 1966.

Duffy, Eamon. *The Stripping of the Altars: Traditional Religion in England, c.1400–c.1580*. New Haven, CT: Yale University Press, 1992.

Duncan-Jones, Katherine. "Sidney's *Urania*." *Review of English Studies*, n.s., 17 (1966): 123–32.

Dynmkowski, Christine. "'Ancient [and Modern] Gower': Presenting Shakespeare's *Pericles*." In *The Narrator, the Expositor, and the Prompter in European Medieval Theatre*, edited by Philip Butterworth, 235–64. Turnhout, Belgium: Brepols, 2007.

Eckerle, Julie A. "Urania's Example: The Female Storyteller in Early Modern English Romance." In *Oral Traditions and Gender in Early Modern Literary Texts*, edited by Mary Ellen Lamb and Karen Brown, 25–39. Aldershot, UK: Ashgate, 2008.

Eisenberg, Daniel. *Romances of Chivalry in the Spanish Golden Age*. Newark, DE: Juan de la Cuesta, 1982.

Escobedo, Andrew. *Nationalism and Historical Loss: Foxe, Dee, Spenser, Milton*. Ithaca, NY: Cornell University Press, 2004.

Everson, J. E. *The Italian Romance Epic in the Age of Humanism: The Matter of Italy and the World of Rome*. New York: Oxford University Press, 2001.

Felperin, Howard. *Shakespearean Romance*. Princeton, NJ: Princeton University Press, 1972.

Fewster, Carol. *Traditionality and Genre in Middle English Romance*. Wolfeboro, NH: D. S. Brewer, 1987.

Fisken, Beth Wynne. "Mary Sidney's *Psalmes*: Education and Wisdom." In *Silent but for the Word: Tudor Women as Patrons, Translators, and Writers of Religious Works*, edited by Margaret Hannay, 166–83. Kent, OH: Kent State University Press, 1985.

Fowler, Alastair. "Emblems of Temperance in *The Faerie Queene*, Book II." *Review of English Studies* 11 (1960): 143–9.

———. *Kinds of Literature: An Introduction to the Theory of Genres and Modes*. Cambridge, MA: Harvard University Press, 1982.

———. "Spenser's Names." In *Unfolded Tales: Essays on Renaissance Romance*, edited by George M. Logan and Gordon Teskey, 32–48. Ithaca, NY: Cornell University Press, 1989.

Friesen, Ryan Curtis. *Supernatural Fiction in Early Modern Drama and Culture*. Portland: Sussex Academic Press, 2010.

Frye, Northrop. *Anatomy of Criticism: Four Essays*. Princeton, NJ: Princeton University Press, 1957. Reprint, New York: Atheneum, 1968.

———. *The Secular Scripture: A Study of the Structure of Romance*. Cambridge, MA: Harvard University Press, 1976.

Fuchs, Barbara. *Romance*. New York: Routledge, 2004.

Fumaroli, Marc. "Jacques Amyot and the Clerical Polemic against the Chivalric Novel." *Renaissance Quarterly* 38 (1985): 22–40.

Furrow, Melissa. *Expectations of Romance: The Reception of a Genre in Medieval England*. Cambridge: D. S. Brewer, 2009.

Garber, Marjorie. "The Healer in Shakespeare." In *Medicine and Literature*, edited by Enid Rhodes Peschel, 103–9. New York: Neale Watson Academic Publications, 1980.

Gennep, Arnold Van. *The Rites of Passage*. Chicago: University of Chicago Press, 1960.

Gesner, Carol. *Shakespeare and the Greek Romance: A Study of Origins*. Lexington: University Press of Kentucky, 1970.

Gilman, Ernest B. *Iconoclasm and Poetry in the English Reformation: Down Went Dagon*. Chicago: University of Chicago Press, 1986.

Ginzburg, Carlo, and Carlo Poni. "The Name and the Game: Unequal Exchange and the Historigraphic Marketplace." In *Microhistory and the Lost Peoples of Europe*, edited by Edward Muir and Guido Ruggiero. Baltimore: Johns Hopkins University Press, 1991.

Godman, Peter. *The Saint as Censor: Robert Bellarmine between Inquisition and Index*. Leiden, Netherlands: Brill, 2000.

Goldman, Marcus Selden. "Sidney and Harington as Opponents of Superstition." *Journal of English and Germanic Philology* 54, no. 4 (1955): 526–48.

Gossett, Suzanne, ed. *Pericles*. By William Shakespeare. Arden Shakespeare, 3rd ser. London: Arden, 2004.

Gray, Erik. Introduction to *The Faerie, Queene Book Two*, by Edmund Spenser, xi–xxvii. Edited by Erik Gray. Indianapolis: Hackett, 2006.

Greenblatt, Stephen. *Marvelous Possessions: The Wonder of the New World*. Chicago: University of Chicago Press, 1991.

———. *Renaissance Self-Fashioning: From More to Shakespeare*. Chicago: University of Chicago Press, 1980.

Greenblatt, Stephen, et al., eds. *The Norton Shakespeare*. New York: W. W. Norton, 2008.

Greene, Thomas. *The Descent from Heaven: A Study in Epic Continuity*. New Haven, CT: Yale University Press, 1963.

Greenlaw, Edwin. "The Captivity Episode in Sidney's *Arcadia*." In *The Manly Anniversary Studies in Language and Literature*, 54–63. Chicago: University of Chicago Press, 1923.

Gregory, Tobias. *From Many Gods to One: Divine Action in Renaissance Epic*. Chicago: University of Chicago Press, 2006.

Hackel, Heidi Brayman. *Reading Material in Early Modern England: Print, Gender, and Literacy*. Cambridge: Cambridge University Press, 2005.

Hackett, Helen. *Women and Romance Fiction in the English Renaissance*. Cambridge: Cambridge University Press, 2000.

———. "'Yet Tell Me Some Such Fiction': Lady Mary Wroth's *Urania* and the 'Femininity' of Romance." In *Women, Texts, and Histories, 1575–1760*, edited by Clare Brant and Diane Purkiss, 39–68. London: Routledge, 1992.

Hägg, Thomas. *The Novel in Antiquity*. Berkeley: University of California Press, 1983.

Haigh, Christopher. *English Reformations: Religion, Politics, and Society under the Tudors*. Oxford: Oxford University Press, 1993.

Hall, Jennifer Wallace. "'Something More Exactly Related Then a Fixion': Lady Mary Sidney Wroth's 'Urania' and Jacobean Religio-Political Controversy." PhD diss., University of Tennessee, 2001.

Halliwell, James Orchard, ed. *The Thornton Romances; the Early English Metrical Romances of Perceval, Isumbras, Eglamour, and Degrevant*. . . . London: Camden Society, 1844.

Hamilton, A. C., ed. *The Faerie Queene*. By Edmund Spenser. New York: Longman, 1977.

Hamilton, Donna B. *Anthony Munday and the Catholics, 1560–1633*. Aldershot, UK: Ashgate, 2005.

Hamilton, Edith. *Mythology: Timeless Tales of Gods and Heroes*. New York: Penguin, 1942. Reprint, New York: Mentor, 1969.

Hankins, John Erskine. *Source and Meaning in Spenser's Allegory: A Study of "The Faerie Queene."* Oxford: Clarendon, 1971.

Hannay, Margaret. "'Doo What Men May Sing': Mary Sidney and the Tradition of Admonitory Dedication." In *Silent but for the Word: Tudor Women as Patrons, Translators, and Writers of Religious Works*, edited by Margaret Hannay, 149–65. Kent, OH: Kent State University Press, 1985.

Happé, Peter. "The Protestant Adaptation of the Saint Play." In *The Saint Play in Medieval Europe*, edited by Clifford Davidson, 205–40. Kalamazoo, MI: Medieval Institute, 1986.

Harper, Carrie Anna. *The Sources of the British Chronicle History in Spenser's "Faerie Queen."* Bryn Mawr, PA: Bryn Mawr College, 1910.

Hart, F. Elizabeth. "Cerimon's 'Rough' Music in *Pericles*, 3.2." *Shakespeare Quarterly* 51 (2000): 313–31.

———. "'Great Is Diana' of Shakespeare's Ephesus." *SEL: Studies in English Literature, 1500–1900* 43, no. 2 (2003): 347–74.

Harvey, E. Ruth. *The Inward Wits: Psychological Theory in the Middle Ages and the Renaissance*. London: Warburg Institute, 1975.

Hathaway, Baxter. *Marvels and Commonplaces: Renaissance Literary Criticism*. New York: Random House, 1968.

Heal, Felicity. "Appropriating History: Catholic and Protestant Polemics and the National Past." *Huntington Library Quarterly* 68, nos. 1 and 2 (2005): 109–32.

Helms, Lorraine. "The Saint in the Brothel; or, Eloquence Rewarded." *Shakespeare Quarterly* 41, no. 3 (1990): 319–32.

Heng, Geraldine. *Empire of Magic: Medieval Romance and the Politics of Cultural Fantasy*. New York: Columbia University Press, 2003.

Heninger, S. K., Jr. "The Typographical Layout of Spenser's *Shepheardes Calendar*." In *The Word and Visual Imagination*, edited by Karl Joseph Höltgen et al., 33–71. Erlangen, Germany: Universitätsbibliothek Erlangen-Nürnberg, 1988.

Hillman, Richard. "Shakespeare's Gower and Gower's Shakespeare: The Larger Debt of *Pericles*." *Shakespeare Quarterly* 36, no. 4 (1985): 427–37.

Hoeniger, F. D., ed. *Pericles*. By William Shakespeare. Arden Shakespeare. Walten-on-Thames, UK: Methuen, 1963.

Hoopes, Robert. *Right Reason in the English Renaissance*. Cambridge, MA: Harvard University Press, 1962.

Hopkins, Andrea. *The Sinful Knights: A Study of Middle English Penitential Romance*. Oxford: Oxford University Press, 1990.

Howard, Jean. *Theater of a City: Social Change and Generic Innovation on the Early Modern Stage*. Philadelphia: University of Pennsylvania Press, 2006.

Hume, Anthea. *Edmund Spenser: Protestant Poet*. Cambridge: Cambridge University Press, 1984.

Hunt, Maurice. "Shakespeare's *Pericles* and the *Acts of the Apostles*." In *Selected Comedies and Late Romances of Shakespeare from a Christian Perspective*, edited by E. Beatrice Batson, 132–49. Lewiston, NY: Edwin Mellen, 2002.

Hunter, Robert Grams. *Shakespeare and the Comedy of Forgiveness*. New York: Columbia University Press, 1965.

Hutson, Lorna. "Fortunate Travelers: Reading for Plot in Sixteenth-Century England." *Representations* 41 (1993): 83–103.

———. *The Usurer's Daughter: Male Friendship and Fictions of Women in Sixteenth-Century England*. New York: Routledge, 1994.

Ife, B. W. *Reading and Fiction in Golden-Age Spain: A Platonist Critique and Some Picaresque Replies*. New York: Cambridge University Press, 1985.

Ingham, Patricia Clare. *Sovereign Fantasies: Arthurian Romance and the Making of Britain*. Philadelphia: University of Pennsylvania Press, 2001.

Iser, Wolfgang. *The Act of Reading: A Theory of Aesthetic Response*. Baltimore: John Hopkins University Press, 1978.

———. *The Implied Reader: Patterns of Communication in Prose Fiction from Bunyan to Beckett*. Baltimore: Johns Hopkins University Press, 1974.

Jameson, Fredric. "Magical Narratives: Romance as Genre." *New Literary History* 7, no. 1 (1975): 129–63.

Jardine, Lisa, and Anthony Grafton. "'Studied for Action': How Gabriel Harvey Read His Livy." *Past and Present* 129 (1990): 30–78.

Jauss, Hans Robert. *Toward an Aesthetic of Reception*. Translated by Timothy Bahti. Minneapolis: University of Minnesota Press, 1982.

Javitch, Daniel. *Proclaiming a Classic: The Canonization of Orlando Furioso.* Princeton, NJ: Princeton University Press, 1991.

Johns, Adrian. *The Nature of the Book: Print and Knowledge in the Making.* Chicago: University of Chicago Press, 1998.

Jones, Norman. *The English Reformation: Religion and Cultural Adaptation.* Malden, MA: Blackwell, 2002.

Kaeuper, Richard. *Holy Warrior: The Religious Ideology of Chivalry.* Philadelphia: University of Pennsylvania Press, 2009.

Kahn, Victoria. "Reinventing Romance; or, the Surprising Effects of Sympathy." In *Renaissance Quarterly* 55, no. 2 (2002): 625–61.

Kaske, Carol. *Spenser and Biblical Poetics.* Ithaca, NY: Cornell University Press, 1999.

Kearney, James. *The Incarnate Text: Imagining the Book in Reformation England.* Philadelphia: University of Pennsylvania Press, 2009.

Keenan, Siobhan. *Travelling Players in Shakespeare's England.* New York: Palgrave Macmillan, 2002.

Kermode, Frank. *Shakespeare, Spenser, Donne: Renaissance Essays.* London: Routledge, 1971.

Kilroy, Gerard. "Advertising the Reader: Sir John Harington's 'Directions in the Margent.'" *English Literary Renaissance* 44.1 (2011): 64–110.

King, Andrew. *"The Faerie Queene" and Middle English Romance: The Matter of Just Memory.* Oxford English Monographs. Oxford: Clarendon, 2000.

———. "Lines of Authority: The Genealogical Theme in *The Faerie Queene.*" *Spenser Studies* 18 (2003): 59–77.

———. "Sidney and Spenser." In *Romance from Classical to Contemporary,* edited by Corinne Saunders, 140–59. Malden, MA: Blackwell, 2004.

———. "*Sir Bevis of Hampton*: Renaissance Influence and Reception." In *"Sir Bevis of Hampton" in Literary Tradition,* edited by Jennifer Fellows and Ivana Djordjević, 176–91. Cambridge: D. S. Brewer, 2008.

———. "'Well Grounded, Finely Framed, and Strongly Trussed up Together': The 'Medieval' Structure of *The Faerie Queene.*" *Review of English Studies* 52, no. 205 (2001): 22–58.

King, John N. *English Reformation Literature: The Tudor Origins of the Protestant Tradition.* Princeton, NJ: Princeton University Press, 1982.

———. "The Godly Woman in Elizabethan Iconography." *Renaissance Quarterly* 38, no. 1 (1985): 41–84.

———. *Spenser's Poetry and the Reformation Tradition.* Princeton, NJ: Princeton University Press, 1990.

Kingsley-Smith, Jane. "Cupid, Idolatry, and Iconoclasm in Sidney's *Arcadia.*" *SEL: Studies in English Literature, 1500–1900* 48, no. 1 (2008): 65–91.

Kinney, Clare R. "'Beleeve This Butt a Fiction': Female Authorship, Narrative Undoing, and the Limits of Romance in *The Second Part of the Countess of Montgomery's Urania.*" *Spenser Studies* 17, (2003): 239–50.

———. "On the Margins of Romance, at the Heart of the Matter: Revisionary Fabulation in Sidney's *New Arcadia.*" *Journal of Narrative Technique* 21, no. 2 (1991): 143–52.

Kintgen, Eugene. *Reading in Tudor England.* Pittsburgh Series in Composition, Literacy, and Culture. Pittsburgh: University of Pittsburgh Press, 1996.

Knighton, C. S., and Richard Mortimer, eds. *Westminster Abbey Reformed: 1540–1640*. Burlington, VT: Ashgate, 2003.

Krontiris, Tina. "Breaking the Barriers of Genre and Gender: Margaret Tyler's Translation of *The Mirrour of Knighthood*." *English Literary Renaissance* 18, no. 1 (1988): 19–39.

———. *Oppositional Voices: Women as Writers and Translators of Literature in the English Renaissance*. New York: Routledge, 1992.

Kuin, Roger. "Querre-Muhau: Sir Philip Sidney and the New World." *Renaissance Quarterly* 51, no. 2 (1998): 549–85.

———. "Sir Philip Sidney's Model of the Statesman." *Reformation* 4 (1999): 93–117.

Kusonoki, Akiko. "Female Selfhood and Male Violence in English Renaissance Drama: A View from Mary Wroth's *Urania*." In *Women, Violence, and English Literature: Essays Honoring Paul Jorgensen*, edited by Linda Woodbridge and Sharon Beehler, 125–48. Tempe, AZ: Medieval and Renaissance Texts and Studies, 2003.

Lamb, Mary Ellen. "The Biopolitics of Romance in Mary Wroth's *The Countess of Montgomery's Urania*." *English Literary Renaissance* 31, no. 1 (2001): 107–30.

———. *Gender and Authorship in the Sidney Circle*. Madison: University of Wisconsin Press, 1990.

———. "Topicality and the Interrogation of Wonder in Mary Wroth's *Second Part of the Countess of Montgomery's Urania*." In *Renaissance Historicisms: Essays in Honor of Arthur F. Kinney*, edited by James Dutcher and Anne Lake Prescott, 247–58. Newark: University of Delaware Press, 2008.

———. "Women Readers in Mary Wroth's *Urania*." In *Reading Mary Wroth: Representing Alternatives in Early Modern England*, edited by Naomi J. Miller and Gary Waller, 210–27. Knoxville: University of Tennessee Press, 1991.

Lamb, Mary Ellen, and Valerie Wayne, eds. *Staging Early Modern Romance: Prose Fiction, Dramatic Romance, and Shakespeare*. New York: Routledge, 2009.

Larouche, Rebecca. "Pamphilia across a Crowded Room: Mary Wroth's Entry into Literary History." *Genre* 30 (1997): 267–88.

Lee, Judith. "The English Ariosto: The Elizabethan Poet and the Marvelous." *Studies in Philology* 80, no. 3 (1983): 277–99.

Lees-Jeffries, Hester. *England's Helicon: Fountains in Early Modern Literature and Culture*. Oxford: Oxford University Press, 2007.

———. "From the Fountain to the Well: Redcrosse Learns to Read." *Studies in Philology* 100, no. 2 (2003): 135–76.

Legge, M. Dominica. "Anglo-Norman Hagiography and the Romances." *Medievalia et Humanistica: Studies in Medieval and Renaissance Culture*, n.s., 6 (1975): 41–49.

Levao, Ronald. *Renaissance Minds and Their Fictions*. Berkeley: University of California Press, 1985.

Levi, Giovanni. "On Microhistory." In *New Perspectives on Historical Writing*, edited by Peter Burke, 97–119. Cambridge: Polity, 1991.

Lewalski, Barbara Kiefer. *Writing Women in Jacobean England*. Cambridge, MA: Harvard University Press, 1993.

Lewis, C. S. *English Literature in the Sixteenth Century Excluding Drama*. Oxford: Clarendon, 1954.

Lockey, Brian C. *Law and Empire in English Renaissance Literature.* Cambridge: Cambridge University Press, 2006.

Luborsky, Ruth Samson, and Elizabeth Morley Ingram. *A Guide to English Illustrated Books, 1536–1603.* 2 vols. Tempe, AZ: Medieval and Renaissance Texts and Studies, 1998.

Luckyj, Christina. "The Politics of Genre in Early Women's Writing: The Case of Lady Mary Wroth." *English Studies in Canada* 27, no. 3 (2001): 253–82.

Lupton, Julia. *Afterlives of the Saints: Hagiography, Typology, and Renaissance Literature.* Stanford, CA: Stanford University Press, 1996.

MacCaffrey, Isabel. *Spenser's Allegory: The Anatomy of Imagination.* Princeton, NJ: Princeton University Press, 1976.

Mallette, Richard. *Spenser and the Discourses of Reformation England.* Lincoln: University of Nebraska Press, 1997.

Marotti, Arthur F. *Religious Ideology and Cultural Fantasy: Catholic and Anti-Catholic Discourses in Early Modern England.* Notre Dame, IN: University of Notre Dame Press, 2005.

Marshall, Peter. "(Re)Defining the English Reformation." *Journal of British Studies* 48 (2009): 564–86.

Maxwell, J. C. Introduction to *Pericles, Prince of Tyre,* by William Shakespeare, ix–xxix. Edited by J. C. Maxwell. Cambridge: Cambridge University Press, 1956.

Mayer, Jean-Christophe. *Shakespeare's Hybrid Faith: History, Religion, and the Stage.* New York: Palgrave Macmillan, 2006.

McCabe, Richard A. *The Pillars of Eternity: Time and Providence in "The Faerie Queene."* Dublin Studies in Medieval and Renaissance Literature. Dublin: Irish Academic Press, 1989.

McCarthy, Penny. "E.K. Was Only the Postman." *Notes and Queries,* n.s., 47, no. 1 (2000): 28–31.

McJannet, Linda. "Genre and Geography: The Eastern Mediterranean in *Pericles* and the *Comedy of Errors.*" In *Playing the Globe: Genre and Geography in English Renaissance Drama,* edited by John Gillies and Virginia Mason Vaughan, 86–106. Madison, NJ: Fairleigh Dickinson University Press, 1998.

McMullan, Gordon, and David Matthews, eds. *Reading the Medieval in Early Modern England.* Cambridge: Cambridge University Press, 2007.

McMurphy, Susannah Jane. *Spenser's Use of Ariosto for Allegory.* Seattle: University of Washington Press, 1924.

Mentz, Steve. *Romance for Sale in Early Modern England.* Aldershot, UK: Ashgate, 2006.

Miller, Jacqueline T. "The Passion Signified: Imitation and the Construction of Emotions in Sidney and Wroth." *Criticism* 43, no. 4 (2001): 407–21.

Miller, Naomi J. *Changing the Subject : Mary Wroth and Figurations of Gender in Early Modern England.* Studies in the English Renaissance. Lexington: University Press of Kentucky, 1996.

Miller, Naomi J., and Gary F. Waller. *Reading Mary Wroth: Representing Alternatives in Early Modern England.* Knoxville: University of Tennessee Press, 1991.

Miller, Shannon. "Constructing the Female Self: Architectural Structures in Mary Wroth's *Urania.*" In *Renaissance Culture and the Everyday,* edited by Patricia Fumerton and Simon Hunt, 139–61. Philadelphia: University of Pennsylvania Press, 1999.

Millican, Charles Bowie. *Spenser and the Table Round: A Study in the Contemporaneous Back-*

ground for Spenser's Use of the Arthurian Legend. Cambridge, MA: Harvard University Press, 1932.

Mills, Jerry Leath. "Spenser and the Numbers of History: A Note on the British and Elfin Chronicles in *The Faerie Queene*." *Philological Quarterly* 55, no. 2 (1976): 281–87.

Miola, Robert S. *Shakespeare and Classical Comedy: The Influence of Plautus and Terence*. Oxford: Oxford University Press, 1994.

Moore, Helen. "Romance." In *A New Companion to English Renaissance Literature and Culture*, edited by Michael Hattaway, 238–48. Oxford: Wiley-Blackwell, 2010.

Moretti, Franco. *Graphs, Maps, and Trees: Abstract Models for a Literary History*. London: Verso, 2005.

Morgan, Gerald. "The Idea of Temperance in the Second Book of *The Faerie Queene*." *Review of English Studies* 37, no. 145 (1986): 11–39.

Mulready, Cyrus. "'Asia of the One Side, and Afric of the Other': Sidney's Unities and the Staging of Romance." In *Staging Early Modern Romance: Prose Fiction, Dramatic Romance, and Shakespeare*, edited by Mary Ellen Lamb and Valerie Wayne, 47–71. New York: Routledge, 2009.

Murray, Molly. *The Poetics of Conversion in Early Modern English Literature: Verse and Change from Donne to Dryden*. Cambridge: Cambridge University Press, 2009.

Nelson, T. G. A. "Sir John Harington and the Renaissance Debate over Allegory." *Studies in Philology* 82, no. 3 (1985): 359–79.

Newcomb, Lori Humphrey. *Reading Popular Romance in Early Modern England*. New York: Columbia University Press, 2002.

———. "The Sources of Romance, the Generation of Story, and the Patterns of the Pericles Tales." In *Staging Early Modern Romance*, edited by Mary Ellen Lamb and Valerie Wayne, 21–46. New York: Routledge, 2009.

Nohrnberg, James. *The Analogy of "The Faerie Queene."* Princeton, NJ: Princeton University Press, 1976.

O'Connell, Michael. "Continuities between 'Medieval' and 'Early Modern' Drama." In *A New Companion to English Renaissance Literature and Culture*, edited by Michael Hattaway, 60–69. Oxford: Wiley-Blackwell, 2010.

———. "History and the Poet's Golden World: The Epic Catalogues in *The Faerie Queene*." *English Literary Renaissance* 4, no. 2 (1974): 241–67.

———. *The Idolatrous Eye: Iconoclasm and Theater in Early-Modern England*. New York: Oxford University Press, 2000.

———. *Mirror and Veil: The Historical Dimension of Spenser's "Faerie Queene."* Chapel Hill: University of North Carolina Press, 1977.

Oesterlen, Eve-Marie. "Why Bodies Matter in Mouldy Tales: Material (Re)Turns in *Pericles, Prince of Tyre*." *Upstart Crow* 24 (2004): 36–45.

O'Malley, John. *Trent and All That: Renaming Catholicism in the Early Modern Era*. Cambridge, MA: Harvard University Press, 2000.

Ord, Melanie. "Classical and Contemporary Italy in Roger Ascham's *The Scholemaster* (1570)." *Renaissance Studies* 16, no. 2 (2002): 202–16.

Owst, G. R. *Literature and Pulpit in Medieval England*. Cambridge: Cambridge University Press, 1933.

Oxford English Dictionary, 2nd ed. www.oed.com/.

Parish, Helen. *Monks, Miracles and Magic: Reformation Representations of the Medieval Church.* New York: Routledge, 2005.

Parker, Patricia A. *Inescapable Romance: Studies in the Poetics of a Mode.* Princeton, NJ: Princeton University Press, 1979.

Paster, Gail Kern. *The Body Embarrassed: Drama and the Disciplines of Shame in Early Modern England.* Ithaca, NY: Cornell University Press, 1993.

———. *Humoring the Body: Emotions and the Shakespearean Stage.* Chicago: University of Chicago Press, 2004.

Paster, Gail Kern, Katherine Rowe, and Mary Floyd-Wilson, eds. *Reading the Early Modern Passions: Essays in the Cultural History of Emotion.* Philadelphia: University of Pennsylvania Press, 2004.

Patchell, Mary Frances Corinne. *The Palmerin Romances in Elizabethan Prose Fiction.* New York: Columbia University Press, 1947.

Patterson, Annabel M. "'Under . . . Pretty Tales': Intention in Sidney's *Arcadia.*" *Studies in the Literary Imagination* 15, no. 1 (1982): 5–21.

Patterson, Mary Hampson. *Domesticating the Reformation: Protestant Best Sellers, Private Devotion, and the Revolution of English Piety.* Madison, NJ: Fairleigh Dickinson University Press, 2007.

Pearsall, Derek. "John Capgrave's *Life of St. Katherine* and Popular Romance Style." *Medievalia et Humanistica: Studies in Medieval and Renaissance Culture*, n.s., 6 (1975): 121–37.

Pendergast, John. *Religion, Allegory, and Literacy in Early Modern England, 1560–1640.* Burlington VT: Ashgate, 2006.

Peters, Christine. *Patterns of Piety: Women, Gender, and Religion in Late Medieval and Reformation England.* Cambridge: Cambridge University Press, 2003.

Phillips, John. *The Reformation of Images: Destruction of Art in England, 1535–1660.* Berkeley: University of California Press, 1973.

Platt, Peter G. *Reason Diminished: Shakespeare and the Marvelous.* Lincoln: University of Nebraska Press, 1997.

Prescott, Anne Lake. *French Poets and the English Renaissance: Studies in Fame and Transformation.* New Haven, CT: Yale University Press, 1978.

———. *Imagining Rabelais in Renaissance England.* New Haven, CT: Yale University Press, 1998.

———. "The Reception of Du Bartas in England." *Studies in the Renaissance* 15 (1968): 144–73.

———. "Spenser's Chivalric Restoration: From Bateman's *Travayled Pylgryme* to the Redcrosse Knight." *Studies in Philology* 86 (1989): 166–97.

———. "Tracing Astrophil's 'Coltish Gyres': Sidney and the Horses of Desire." *Renaissance Papers* (2005): 25–42.

Quilligan, Maureen. "The Constant Subject: Instability and Authority in Wroth's *Urania* Poems." In *Soliciting Interpretation: Literary Theory and Seventeenth-Century English Poetry*, edited by Elizabeth D. Harvey and Katharine Eisaman Maus, 307–35. Chicago: University of Chicago Press, 1990.

———. *Incest and Agency in Elizabeth's England.* Philadelphia: University of Pennsylvania Press, 2005.

———. "Lady Mary Wroth: Female Authority and the Family Romance." In *Unfolded Tales: Essays on Renaissance Romance*, edited by George M. Logan and Gordon Teskey, 257–80. Ithaca, NY: Cornell University Press, 1989.

Quint, David. "The Boat of Romance and Renaissance Epic." In *Romance: Generic Transformation from Chretien De Troyes to Cervantes*, edited by Kevin Brownlee and Marina Scordilis Brownlee, 178–201. Hanover, NH: University Press of New England, 1985.

———. *Epic and Empire: Politics and Generic Form from Virgil to Milton*. Princeton, NJ: Princeton University Press, 1993.

Raber, Karen L., and Treva J. Tucker, eds. *The Culture of the Horse: Discipline, Status and Identity in the Early Modern World*. New York: Palgrave 2005.

Raitiere, Martin N. *Faire Bitts: Sir Philip Sidney and Renaissance Political Theory*. Pittsburgh: Duquesne University Press, 1984.

Ramsey, W. M. "The Worship of the Virgin Mary at Ephesus." *Expositor*, 6th ser., 12 (1905): 81–98.

Rasmussen, Mark David, ed. *Renaissance Literature and Its Formal Engagements*. New York: Palgrave, 2002.

Rathborne, Isabel E. *The Meaning of Spenser's Fairyland*. New York: Columbia University Press, 1937.

Reid, Robert. "Alma's Castle and the Symbolization of Reason in *The Faerie Queene*." *Journal of English and Germanic Philology* 80 (1981): 512–27.

Relihan, Constance C. "Liminal Geography: *Pericles* and the Politics of Place." *Philological Quarterly* 71, no. 3 (1992): 281–99.

Rhodes, Neil, and Jonathan Sawday. "Paper Worlds: Imagining the Renaissance Computer." In *The Renaissance Computer: Knowledge Technology in the First Age of Print*, edited by Neil Rhodes and Jonathan Sawday, 1–17. New York: Routledge, 2000.

Richards, Jennifer, and Fred Schurink. "The Textuality and Materiality of Reading in Early Modern England." *Huntington Library Quarterly* 73, no. 3 (2010): 345–61.

Richmond, Velma Bourgeois. *The Legend of Guy of Warwick*. New York: Garland, 1996.

———. *Shakespeare, Catholicism, and Romance*. New York: Continuum, 2000.

Ringler, W. A., ed. *Sidney's Poems*. Oxford: Oxford University Press, 1962.

Rist, Thomas. *Shakespeare's Romances and the Politics of Counter-Reformation*. Vol. 3. Lewiston, NY: Edwin Mellen, 1999.

Roberts, Josephine A., ed. *The First Part of the Countess of Montgomery's Urania*. By Lady Mary Wroth. Binghamton, NY: Medieval and Renaissance Texts and Studies, 1995.

———. "The Life of Lady Mary Wroth." In *The Poems of Lady Mary Wroth*, by Lady Mary Wroth, edited by Josephine A. Roberts, 3–40. Baton Rouge: Louisiana State University Press, 1983.

Roberts, Sasha. Unpublished paper delivered at the Shakespeare Association of America Conference, 2004.

Robinson, Benedict S. *Islam and Early Modern English Literature: The Politics of Romance from Spenser to Milton*. New York: Palgrave Macmillan, 2007.

Rosenfeld, Colleen Ruth. "Wroth's Clause." *English Literary History* 76, no. 4 (2009): 1049–71.

Ross, Trevor Thornton. *The Making of the English Literary Canon: From the Middle Ages to the Late Eighteenth Century*. Montreal: McGill-Queen's University Press, 1998.

Rossi, Joan Warchol. "Britons moniments: Spenser's Definition of Temperance in History." *English Literary Renaissance* 15 (1985): 42–58.

Rustici, Craig. *The Afterlife of Pope Joan: Deploying the Popess Legend in Early Modern England.* Ann Arbor: University of Michigan Press, 2006.

Salzman, Paul. *English Prose Fiction, 1558–1700: A Critical History.* Oxford: Clarendon, 1985.

———. *Reading Early Modern Women's Writing.* Oxford: Oxford University Press, 2006.

———. "The Strang(e) Constructions of Mary Wroth's *Urania*: Arcadian Romance and the Public Realm." In *English Renaissance Prose: History, Language, and Politics,* edited by Neil Rhodes, 109–24. Tempe, AZ: Medieval and Renaissance Texts and Studies, 1997.

Samson, Alexander. "A Bibliography of Spanish-English Translations 1500–1640." Early Modern Spain website. www.ems.kcl.ac.uk/apps/persons/index.html.

Sanchez, Melissa. "The Politics of Masochism in Mary Wroth's *Urania*." *English Literary History* 74 (2007): 449–78.

Saunders, Corinne. *Magic and the Supernatural in Medieval English Romance.* Cambridge: D. S. Brewer, 2010.

Scherb, Victor. "Assimilating Giants: The Appropriation of Gog and Magog in Medieval and Early Modern England." *Journal of Medieval and Early Modern Studies* 32, no. 1 (2002): 59–84.

Schleiner, Louise. "Spenser's 'E.K.' as Edmund Kent (Kenned/of Kent: Kyth [Couth]), Kissed, and Kunning-Conning." *English Literary Renaissance* 20, no. 3 (1990): 374–407.

Schneider, Regina. *Sidney's (Re)Writing of the "Arcadia."* New York: AMS, 2008.

Schoenfeldt, Michael. *Bodies and Selves in Early Modern England: Physiology and Inwardness in Spenser, Shakespeare, Herbert, and Milton.* New York: Cambridge University Press, 1999.

———. "Reading Bodies." In *Reading, Society, and Politics in Early Modern England,* edited by Kevin Sharpe and Stephen Zwicker, 215–43. Cambridge: Cambridge University Press, 2003.

Scott-Warren, Jason. *Sir John Harington and the Book as Gift.* Oxford: Oxford University Press, 2001.

Scribner, Robert W. *For the Sake of Simple Folk: Popular Propaganda for the German Reformation.* Oxford: Oxford University Press, 1994.

Shagan, Ethan, ed. *Catholics and the "Protestant Nation": Religious Politics and Identity in Early Modern England.* Manchester: Manchester University Press, 2005.

———. *Popular Politics and the English Reformation.* Cambridge: Cambridge University Press, 2003.

Shaver, Ann. "A New Woman of Romance." *Modern Language Studies* 21 (1991): 63–71.

Shell, Alison. *Catholicism, Controversy, and the English Literary Imagination, 1558–1660.* Cambridge: Cambridge University Press, 1999.

Sherman, William H. *John Dee: The Politics of Reading and Writing in the English Renaissance.* Amherst: University of Massachusetts Press, 1995.

———. *Used Books: Marking Readers in Renaissance England.* Philadelphia: University of Pennsylvania Press, 2008.

Shuger, Debora K. *Habits of Thought in the English Renaissance: Religion, Politics, and the Dominant Culture.* Berkeley: University of California Press, 1990.

Silberman, Lauren. "*The Faerie Queene*, Book II, and the Limitations of Temperance." *Modern Language Studies* 17, no. 4 (1987): 9–22.

Simpson, James. *1350–1547: Reform and Cultural Revolution*. The Oxford English Literary History, vol. 2. Oxford: Oxford University Press, 2002.

Sinfield, Alan. *Literature of Protestant England, 1560–1660*. Totowa, NJ: Barnes and Noble Books, 1983.

———. "Protestantism: Questions of Subjectivity and Control." In *Faultlines: Cultural Materialism and the Politics of Dissident Reading*, 143–80. Berkeley: University of California Press, 1992.

Siraisi, Nancy G. *Medieval & Early Renaissance Medicine: An Introduction to Knowledge and Practice*. Chicago: University of Chicago Press, 1990.

Sirluck, Ernest. "*The Faerie Queene*, Book II, and the Nicomachean Ethics." *Modern Philology* 49 (1951): 73–100.

Skretkowicz, Victor. *European Erotic Romance: Philhellene Protestantism, Renaissance Translation and English Literary Politics*. Manchester: Manchester University Press, 2009.

Slights, William W. E. *Managing Readers: Printed Marginalia in English Renaissance Books*. Ann Arbor: University of Michigan Press, 2001.

Smith, Helen. "'More Swete Unto the Eare / Than Holsome for Ye Mynde': Embodying Early Modern Women's Reading." *Huntington Library Quarterly* 73, no. 3 (2010): 413–32.

Smith, Rosalind. "Lady Mary Wroth's 'Pamphilia to Amphilanthus': The Politics of Withdrawal." *English Literary Renaissance* 30, no. 3 (2000): 408–31.

Snook, Edith. *Women, Reading, and the Cultural Politics of Early Modern England*. Burlington, VT: Ashgate, 2005.

Snyder, Susan. "Guyon the Wrestler." *Renaissance News* 14, no. 4 (1961): 249–52.

Speed, Diane. "The Construction of the Nation in Medieval English Romance." In *Readings in Medieval English Romance*, edited by Carol M. Meale, 135–58. Cambridge: D. S. Brewer, 1994.

Spevak, John A. "Sir John Harington's Theoretical and Practical Criticism: The Sources and Originality of His Apparatus to the *Orlando Furioso*." PhD diss., University of Chicago, 1978.

Spitzer, Leo. *Classical and Christian Ideas of World Harmony: Prolegomena to an Interpretation of the Word "Stimmung."* New York: Cosmopolitan Science and Art Service, 1944.

Stanivukovic, Goran. "English Renaissance Romances as Conduct Books for Young Men." In *Early Modern Prose Fiction: The Cultural Politics of Reading*, edited by Naomi Conn Liebler, 60–78. New York: Routledge, 2007.

Stephens, Walter. "Incredible Sex: Witches, Demons, and Giants in the Early Modern Imagination." In *Monsters in the Italian Literary Imagination*, edited by Keala Jewell, 153–76. Detroit: Wayne State University Press, 2001.

Stewart, Alan, and Garrett A. Sullivan. "'Worme-Eaten, and Full of Canker Holes': Materializing Memory in *The Faerie Queene* and *Lingua*." *Spenser Studies* 17 (2003): 215–38.

Stillman, Robert. *Philip Sidney and the Poetics of Renaissance Cosmopolitanism*. Burlington, VT: Ashgate, 2008.

Strauss, Paul. "Allegory and the Bower of Bliss." *Ben Jonson Journal* 2 (1995): 59–71.

Strier, Richard. "Against the Rule of Reason: Praise of Passion from Petrarch to Luther to Shakespeare to Herbert." In *Reading the Early Modern Passions: Essays in the Cultural*

History of Emotion, edited by Katherine Rowe, Gail Kern Paster, and Mary Floyd-Wilson, 23–42. Philadelphia: University of Pennsylvania Press, 2004.

Strohm, Paul. "The Origin and Meaning of Middle English Romaunce." In *Genre* 10, no. 1 (1977): 1–29.

Sullivan, Ceri. *Dismembered Rhetoric: English Recusant Writing, 1580 to 1603*. London: Associated University Presses, 1995.

Sullivan, Garret A. *Memory and Forgetting in English Renaissance Drama: Shakespeare, Marlowe, Webster*. Cambridge: Cambridge University Press, 2005.

Summers, David A. *Spenser's Arthur: The British Arthurian Tradition and "The Faerie Queene."* Lanham, MD: University Press of America, 1997.

Summit, Jennifer. *Memory's Library: Medieval Books in Early Modern England*. Chicago: University of Chicago Press, 2008.

———. "Monuments and Ruins: Spenser and the Problem of the English Library." *English Literary History* 70 (2003): 1–34.

Suttie, Paul. "Moral Ambivalence in the Legend of Temperance." *Spenser Studies* 19 (2004): 125–33.

Syford, Constance Miriam. "The Direct Source of the Pamela-Cecropia Episode in the Arcadia." *PMLA: Publications of the Modern Language Association of America* 49, no. 2 (1934): 472–89.

Thomas, Henry. *Spanish and Portuguese Romances of Chivalry*. New York: Kraus Reprint, 1969.

Thomas, Keith. "Art and Iconoclasm in Early Modern England." In *Religious Politics in Post-Reformation England*, edited by Kenneth Fincham and Peter Lake, 16–40. Suffolk, UK: Boydell, 2006.

———. *Religion and the Decline of Magic*. Oxford: Oxford University Press, 1971.

Tilmouth, Christopher. *Passion's Triumph over Reason: A History of the Moral Imagination from Spenser to Rochester*. Oxford: Oxford University Press, 2007.

Townsend, Rich. *Harington and Ariosto: A Study in Elizabethan Verse Translation*. New Haven, CT: Yale University Press, 1940.

Turner, Victor. *The Ritual Process: Structure and Anti-Structure*. Chicago: Aldine, 1969.

Urban, Misty. *Monstrous Women in Middle English Romance: Representations of Mysterious Female Power*. Lewiston, NY: Edwin Mellen, 2010.

Vaught, Jennifer. *Masculinity and Emotion in Early Modern English Literature*. Burlington, VT: Ashgate, 2008.

Vickers, Brian. "Leisure and Idleness in the Renaissance: The Ambivalence of Otium." *Renaissance Studies* 4, nos. 1 and 2 (1990): 1–37; 107–54.

———. "'The Power of Persuasion': Images of the Orator, Elyot to Shakespeare." In *Renaissance Eloquence: Studies in the Theory and Practice of Renaissance Rhetoric*, edited by James J. Murphy, 411–35. Berkeley: University of California Press, 1983.

Waldman, Louis. "Spenser's Pseudonym 'E. K.' and Humanist Self-Naming." *Spenser Studies* 9 (1991): 21–31.

Waller, Gary F. *The Sidney Family Romance: Mary Wroth, William Herbert, and the Early Modern Construction of Gender*. Detroit: Wayne State University Press, 1993.

Walsham, Alexandra. *Providence in Early Modern England*. New York: Oxford University Press, 1999.

Warner, Marina. *Alone of All Her Sex: The Myth and the Cult of the Virgin Mary*. London: Weidenfeld and Nicolson, 1976.

Watkins, John. *The Specter of Dido: Spenser and Virgilian Epic*. New Haven, CT: Yale University Press, 1995.

Watson, Elizabeth Porges. "Folklore in Arcadia: Mopsa's 'Tale of the Old Cut' Re-Cut and Set." *Sidney Journal* 16, no. 2 (1998): 3–15.

Wayne, Valerie. "Some Sad Sentence: Vives' *Instruction of a Christian Woman*." In *Silent but for the Word: Tudor Women as Patrons, Translators, and Writers of Religious Works*, edited by Margaret Patterson Hannay, 15–29. Kent, OH: Kent State University Press, 1985.

Weinberg, Bernard. *A History of Literary Criticism in the Italian Renaissance*. Vol. 2. Chicago: University of Chicago Press, 1961.

Weiner, Andrew D. "Sidney, Protestantism, and Literary Critics: Reflections on Some Recent Criticism of *The Defense of Poetry*." In *Sir Philip Sidney's Achievements*, edited by M. J. B. Allen et al., 117–26. New York: AMS, 1990.

———. *Sir Philip Sidney and the Poetics of Protestantism*. Minneapolis: University of Minnesota Press, 1978.

Whetter, K. S. *Understanding Genre and Medieval Romance*. Burlington, VT: Ashgate, 2008.

White, Helen Constance. *Tudor Books of Saints and Martyrs*. Madison: University of Wisconsin Press, 1963.

Williams, Deanne. "Papa Don't Preach: The Power of Prolixity in *Pericles*." *University of Toronto Quarterly* 71, no. 2 (2002): 595–622.

Wilson, Richard. "Jesuit Drama in Early Modern England." In *Theatre and Religion: Lancastrian Shakespeare*, edited by Alison Finlay, Richard Dutton, and Richard Wilson, 71–86. Manchester: Manchester University Press, 2003.

Wilson-Okamura, David Scott. "Errors about Ovid and Romance." *Spenser Studies* 23 (2008): 215–34.

Winstead, Karen A. *Virgin Martyrs: Legends of Sainthood in Late Medieval England*. Ithaca, NY: Cornell University Press, 1997.

Wofford, Susanne. *The Choice of Achilles: The Ideology of Figure in the Epic*. Stanford, CA: Stanford University Press, 1992.

Wogan-Browne, Jocelyn. "'Bet . . . To . . . Rede on Holy Seyntes Lyves . . .': Romance and Hagiography Again." In *Readings in Medieval English Romance*, edited by Carol M. Meale, 83–97. Cambridge: D. S. Brewer, 1994.

Wolff, Samuel Lee. *The Greek Romances in Elizabethan Prose Fiction*. New York: Burt Franklin, 1912.

Womack, Peter. "Shakespeare and the Sea of Stories." *Journal of Medieval and Early Modern Studies* 29, no. 1 (1999): 169–87.

Woolf, D. R. *Reading History in Early Modern England*. Cambridge: Cambridge University Press, 2000.

Worden, Blair. *The Sound of Virtue: Philip Sidney's Arcadia and Elizabethan Politics*. New Haven, CT: Yale University Press, 1996.

Wright, Louis B. *Middle-Class Culture in Elizabethan England*. Ithaca, NY: Cornell University Press, 1958.

Yates, Frances Amelia. *The Art of Memory*. Chicago: University of Chicago Press, 1966.

Yates, Julian. *Error, Misuse, Failure: Object Lessons from the English Renaissance*. Minneapolis: University of Minnesota Press, 2003.

Young, Robert J. C. *Colonial Desire: Hybridity in Theory, Culture, and Race*. New York: Routledge, 1995.

Zurcher, Amelia. "Ethics and the Politic Agent of Early Seventeenth-Century Prose Romance." *English Literary Renaissance* 35 (2005): 73–101.

———. *Seventeenth-Century English Romance: Allegory, Ethics, and Politics*. New York: Palgrave Macmillan, 2007.

Index